PRAISE FOR THE

'Current global disruption and the pace of change have everyone questioning the type of future that our children face. In their book *Future-proof Your Child for the 2020s and Beyond*, Nikki and Graeme provide a framework for parenting that penetrates the negative forecasts, presents possibility, and also helps parents to guide their children into being fully human and skilled to thrive in any future.'
Deanne King, Head of School, St Mary's School, Waverley, Johannesburg

'Far too many books about the future are alarmist or naive. Nikki Bush and Graeme Codrington avoid either extreme. As leading global experts on parenting and future trends, they offer us a book that is immensely inspiring, practical, and something anyone working with Gen Z and Millennials needs to read.'
David Livermore, PhD, Thought Leader on Cultural Intelligence and Global Leadership

'This book should be the treasure that every household keeps. It gives adults ideas on how to start endless conversations with fellow parents and children. It reminds us to accept change and to adapt. It is a book that can be used by parents and professionals from any background who are raising children for the future and need to be skilful, creative and critical thinkers.'
Mike Thobejane, Headmaster, Iphutheng Primary School, Alexandra

'Building on the success of their first edition, Nikki and Graeme's new book offers real and fascinating insights into the dynamically changing world we and our children will inhabit over the next 10 years. As an educator, I appreciate the sensible advice given to parents on schools and schooling. As a parent, I value the heads-up on what's coming our way. The book is written for the ultimate benefit of our children, and that is its great strength.'
Brendan Grant, Headmaster, South African College High School (SACS), Cape Town

'If you are anxious about your child's future … this is the book for you. The answers are all here. The best parenting book I have read in a long time. Nikki and Graeme's world-class insights have been put to great use.'
Phemelo Motene, Broadcaster and Media Consultant

'It's remarkable how much time and energy we invest in learning to be relevant in the workplace and the comparatively small investment that most of us make to prepare for parenthood. Whilst values may endure, the spaces and places we need to create for our children to learn to thrive in a changing world have shifted dramatically. Nikki and Graeme's updated version of their bestselling book provides an invaluable perspective into the roles we need to play, not just as parents to our own children, but as guardians tasked to ensure the well-being of future generations.'
Prof. Nicola Kleyn, Dean, Gordon Institute of Business Science, University of Pretoria

'This book articulates the realities of a new world order – politically, socially and economically – while providing a compass for courageous conversations and a map for just that! It is a must-have in every home and for every educator.'
Kubeshini Govender, Chief Education Specialist and Innovator, Special Projects, Western Cape Education Department

'It is never too early to begin thinking about our children and grandchildren's future careers and the studies that will prepare them for it. *Future-proof Your Child for the 2020s and Beyond* is the guidebook you need to help you prepare your children for the future right from the start. The authors provide valuable insights based on research, their work with young people, in schools and in the business world, and from their own experiences as parents.'
Prof. Loyiso Nongxa, former Vice-Chancellor and Principal and Emeritus Professor, School of Mathematics, University of the Witwatersrand

'Brilliant. I read this book and immediately bought loads of them to give to my friends who are parents. It's the book I'd been searching for. A must-read for every parent. It will change your children's lives.'
      Andy Bounds, Bestselling Author of *Top Dog: Impress and influence everyone you meet*, **and creator of www.andyboundsonline.com**

'Two global citizens out of Africa have built a book of worldwide relevance to parents, educators and leaders. As a parent of two children of 13 and 15, I found every page resonates and gently provokes. Helpful, relevant, readable and compassionate, a book for life and living with.'
      Jon Foster-Pedley, Dean and Director, Henley Business School, Africa

'As a parent, I'm okay with being uncool and out of date – but I'm *not* okay with being uninformed and out of touch! Which is why I'm so stoked about Nikki and Graeme's updated antidote to ignorance. You're holding in your hands a parental prescription for future preparedness that you probably didn't know you needed – so hold tight, hold on, and finish the whole course – because no one is immune to what tomorrow might bring.'
      Dr Michael Mol, TV Presenter and Producer, Founding Director of Hello Doctor

'This is a book that parents and educators have been waiting and hoping for! Bush and Codrington have skilfully blended their personal experiences of parenting and raising young people with their expertise around change and future worlds into a practical and sensible read. Links to online resources and video inserts further extend the conversation as to how to raise children and navigate the landscape of a disruptive world. This book is mandatory reading for anyone raising or working with young people in today's complex world.'   **Dr Sally James, Head of St Stithians Girls' College**

'Nikki and Graeme have taken the fear and confusion out of the future. Their updated book, *Future-proof your Child for the 2020s and Beyond*, is an indispensable guidebook that makes the future a place of wonder and adventure.'
      Andile Mazwai, Governor, National Stokvels Association of South Africa

To Dean, Alexandra and Zylla

FUTURE-PROOF

YOUR CHILD FOR THE 2020s AND BEYOND

*Be the door to the future.
Be your best x-factor for success.*

Nikki Bush

FUTURE-PROOF

YOUR CHILD FOR THE 2020s AND BEYOND

Nikki Bush and Graeme Codrington

PENGUIN BOOKS

Future-proof Your Child for the 2020s and Beyond
Published by Penguin Books
an imprint of Penguin Random House (Pty) Ltd
Company Reg. No. 1953/000441/07
The Estuaries No. 4, Oxbow Crescent, Century Avenue,
Century City, Cape Town, 7441
www.penguinrandomhouse.co.za

First published 2019

1 3 5 7 9 10 8 6 4 2

Publication © Penguin Random House 2019
Text © Nikki Bush & Graeme Codrington 2019

Cover image © ibrandify/Freepik

All rights reserved. No part of this publication may be reproduced,
stored in a retrieval system or transmitted, in any form or by any means,
electronic, mechanical, photocopying, recording or otherwise,
without the prior written permission of the copyright owners.

PUBLISHER: Marlene Fryer
MANAGING EDITOR: Ronel Richter-Herbert
PROOFREADER: Laetitia Sullivan
COVER AND TEXT DESIGNER: Ryan Africa
TYPESETTER: Monique Cleghorn
& Ryan Africa

Set in 11 pt on 15.5 pt Minion

Printed by **novus print**, a division of Novus Holdings

978 1 77609 453 0 (print)
978 1 77609 454 7 (ePub)

*To my late husband, Simon, for the gift of our sons
and for doing the parenting dance with me.
It's not the same without you.*
Nikki

*To my three amazing daughters, Amy, Hannah and Rebecca,
who challenge me to be more than I think I can be.*
Graeme

CONTENTS

About this book... 1

Acknowledgements... 9

About the authors.. 13

Foreword... 15

Chapter 1 – Wake up, the world has changed!........................... 17

Chapter 2 – How your child develops................................... 29

Chapter 3 – Trends that will change your child's future............... 73

Chapter 4 – Jobs of the future.. 101

Chapter 5 – Developing X-factors for success in our children......... 141

Chapter 6 – What can school do for your child?....................... 225

Chapter 7 – Building a Talent Profile................................. 251

Chapter 8 – Build a values-based family brand........................ 273

Chapter 9 – A call to action.. 297

ABOUT THIS BOOK

Future-proof Your Child for the 2020s and Beyond is a revised and updated edition of *Future-proof Your Child: Parenting the wired generation*, a bestselling title for the past 10 years for parents of children up to the age of 12. The first book focused largely on globalisation and the coming tsunami of change. At the time of publication it was a ground-breaking book, combining the art and science of futurism with the art and science of parenting.

A parenting book that focused on globalisation, megatrends and predictions about the future took many people by surprise when it was published – it was not your typical parenting self-help book. Those predictions, which were not intended to be prophecies, have held up remarkably well – at least, we think so. The picture of the world we painted turned out to be largely accurate, and our advice to parents about what is required for children to thrive in the future remains mostly unchanged.

Our own copies of the first book are littered with ticks that indicate either that the world we described happened, or is in the process of happening. With so many indications that the foundations for the tsunami of change have now been laid, we felt that it was important to update the book. There are four other key reasons for this update:

1. We have a much clearer picture now of the 2020s, and we are even more convinced than before that this is going to be one of the most important decades in human history. Today's young children will come of age in the 2030s, and we want to share some ideas of what *that* world is going to look like.
2. We need to address the challenge of how to prepare our children so that they can achieve growth and relevance in a world of continuous disruptive change where irrelevance is one of the biggest threats. This revised edition therefore shifts its focus from globalisation to disruption as its key theme.

3. Parents are even more time-poor and stress-rich than ever before, and so we've tightened up the book, making it shorter, sharper, more accessible and easier to read. It seems that a decade of short-form journalism, tweets and memes required us to adjust our style – hopefully not by dumbing down our content, but by repackaging it for today's parents. We have also removed some reference material from the book itself and made it available to readers online via our website: www.fpyc2020.com. This allows us to update it regularly. The book is now supported by videos, podcasts and online resources.
4. Now that our own children are teenagers and adults, we both feel that we have even more insight into what does and doesn't work when you are parenting younger children. Some of our children might have kids of their own by the end of the 2020s, so we've also snuck in a few additional references that apply to grandparents. And frankly, we're still trying to build up the courage to write the definitive *Future-proof Your Teenager* – look out for that book sometime soon.

The most important aim of this book is to help our children achieve relevance and growth in a world of continuous disruptive change. And we know this must be done with less time at parents' disposal than ever before. We realise that most of us are parenting for only two to three hours a day. That is our reality. And that is our challenge.

Interestingly, looking back on the last 10 years, both our families have experienced their fair share of disruption because, firstly, families are made up of human beings and people are always changing and growing. Secondly, because external forces disrupt our lives either by design or default. We have experienced and have had to adapt to everything from migrating to a new country and the death of a spouse, to adoption, a special-needs child, the creation of a multiracial family, shifts in employment and incomes, new schools, leaving school, moving homes, children entering the world of work, and more.

Throughout this book, we share stories of our own parenting experiences to illustrate what we are talking about. You can read a bit more about us and our families in the Acknowledgements and About the Authors sections that come up next. We are human. We are real. We do not have picture-perfect lives. We make mistakes. Life happens. However, we constantly aim to keep the human in the middle, to honour who our children are, and who they are in the process of becoming – and not just what they do. Their journey is evolutionary, and it will take the rest of their lives. As they grow up and adapt to the world, so must we.

Ten years on, we are still of the firm belief that in the future world of work, in a very high-tech world, a combination of both tech and people skills will be a winning formula, and that 'who you are' is going to be far more important than 'what you do' or 'what you sell'. This is true for one simple reason: with the magnitude of disruptive change coming our way, what we do and what we sell will be changing all the time. This book outlines that changing world and the X-factors our children will have to develop – beyond a report card from school – to make sure they are future-fit.

Future-proof Your Child for the 2020s and Beyond, like the original, remains a book for parents with children in pre- and primary school. While we cannot give you exact instructions for the perfect parenting journey, you will find frameworks on how to think about the future and guidelines for the mission ahead – of raising your children in an Age of Possibility, the likes of which we have never known.

Our aim is not to scare you, but to inform you: to sketch a picture of the future so that you are not caught off-guard. And, as parents ourselves who are future-proofing our own children for a world that is increasingly starting to resemble a sci-fi movie, we want to assure you that family, and keeping the human in the middle, is at the heart of all that we do.

You may be asking yourself some of the very same questions we have been asking ourselves:

- What will the world of work look like when our children enter it?
- What jobs will be available for our children? And what jobs won't exist any more?
- How will robots and automation change the world of work and the jobs available in the future?
- What subjects should my child study at school?

- What should my child study *after* school?
- Should my child study at all?
- Is school still relevant?
- If our children are going to work on a computer for most of their lives, why are they still being taught to write? Or do mathematics?
- What moral issues will our children face down the line?
- How do we, as parents, compete with the noise and excitement of 24-hour attention-grabbing screens?
- How do we engage our techno-savvy, immediate-gratification-craving, low-attention-span children?
- How do we connect with our wired and weird children?
- When should I buy my child a smartphone?
- How much time should my child spend doing on-screen activities each day?
- What is my role as a parent today?
- What will the future look like?
- Why do I feel so overwhelmed?
- Why has everything changed?
- How the hell did all this happen?

If any of these questions resonate with you, then read on as we try to give you a framework that will enable you to answer them for yourself. Just some words of warning: fasten your seatbelt, hold on to your hat, and read with an open mind. Let yourself entertain a world of possibilities to understand how we got 'here' and where 'here' actually is.

We want the contents of this book to change the way you think about your role as a parent of young children in the 2020s and 30s. Our focus is on the foundation phase and primary- to middle-school years, and the future of today's children as they enter the workplace of 2030 and beyond. The topics discussed will be revealing, some facts may be startling, and the advice will hopefully be meaningful and practical. **It is a call to parents to act wisely and courageously early on in their children's lives to ensure that they are resilient and emerge with a consistent world view** – one of the biggest challenges facing parents today.

ABOUT THIS BOOK

Chapter 1 provides a framework for understanding what's changing in the world, and why.

Chapter 2 will help you understand some themes in child development and early learning that, we believe, are important basics and essential to your child's success at school and in life.

Chapter 3 looks at the future of the workplace, and how your children might build a life of meaning and relevance within and beyond traditional careers – those that are part of *your* frame of reference. Flick through this chapter, read what grabs you and go back to it over time when your interest is piqued by something you hear, see or read: you will be able to connect the dots here.

Chapter 4 focuses attention on the jobs of the future – jobs that don't exist yet, and jobs that will disappear. This chapter also provides great conversation starters for discussion at your child's school or in your organisation. Keep your mind open to new possibilities. This is very important.

Chapter 5 delves even deeper, looking beyond academics and existing information to the character and personal qualities that will be required for success in the world of the 2030s and beyond – what we call the X-factors for success. This is where the book starts to get deeply practical, as we propose (literally) hundreds of activities, ideas and suggestions for you to do with your children. It's this chapter that you will revisit again and again, which is why you need your own copy next to your bed and not one circulating through your book club. We can't tell you how many parents told us this about the first edition of *Future-proof Your Child*.

Chapter 6 is a brand-new chapter, which discusses the changing face of education, how to select a school (or not), and supporting your child's educational process.

Chapter 7 outlines the process to develop a 'Talent Profile' – this is a new kind of CV or résumé, and is done by both parents and children to help define who they are, who they want to be, what they can do, and why. It's a whole new way of thinking about who you are.

Chapter 8 looks at what you can do at home to create a solid family base for your children – one on which they can build their Talent Profile, which, in turn, will launch them into the world of work and give them freedom of choice.

Chapter 9 is a call to action: to conscious and deliberate parenting with a view to ensuring that your children will not just survive, but thrive in the future, and that you will have peace of mind having provided them with a stable foundation in a changing world.

This book is *not* a complete and comprehensive parenting manual. We do not deal with discipline issues, or with health and safety issues. We do not deal with issues of parental relationships, nor do we deal with issues of family dynamics. Although all of these issues are critical, they are not what this book is about.

The intention of this book is threefold: firstly, we want to give you a glimpse of the big picture – the Age of Possibility – so that you can understand the backdrop against which you are parenting today. Secondly, we want to equip you to be an effective parent of young children, today. This part of the book is the most practical, as it deals with the issues parents are currently facing. Thirdly, we want to help you to understand the future and what it holds as our children grow up. We want you to be future-literate.

As parents, it is our willingness to change our perspective, to reconsider our world view, to resolve to learn new things and to stay connected to our children – despite the noise, clutter and chaos – that will make the greatest difference.

ABOUT THIS BOOK

Whether you are excited or scared by the future, this is our world, our new normal. Take the time to become familiar with the changes taking place so that you can incorporate them into your parenting, creating future-fit children as you go along. We'll be with you all the way, as we are for our children, too.

We trust that you will find *Future-proof Your Child for the 2020s and Beyond* relevant, accessible, practical and inspirational. Come and journey with us as we take you forward into the future to help you make the best choices for your children now!

Nikki Bush & Graeme Codrington
April 2019

ACKNOWLEDGEMENTS

Graeme

When Nikki and I discussed the idea of updating this book, I could not believe that nearly a decade had passed since we first wrote it. It seems like yesterday that she and I poured hours and hours, over many months, into research, capturing our experiences and those of others, and engaging in many debates around the content of the book. As I reread it, I was thrilled at how well it has stood up after a decade of even more change than we predicted. So, firstly, I want to acknowledge the hard work Nikki put into the original project. She really did lead the work, and would not accept anything but perfection from each sentence on every page.

For the updated book, I again want to start by acknowledging how much I have learnt from, and been changed by, my three wonderful daughters. Amy and Hannah, my older daughters, are now in their late teenage years and equipped with amazing minds and beautiful souls. I learn so much from them, and I value their views and insights. Our youngest daughter, Rebecca, has been diagnosed with autism – something we were blissfully unaware of as I wrote the first edition of this book. Learning to see the world through her eyes, and acquiring the parenting skills required to deal with disability and children who don't fit into society's 'norms', has been both a painful and enriching journey. I am a very different person – and parent – because of it. A better one, I hope.

I continue to be amazed at my wife, Jane, and her seemingly boundless ability to give of herself to others. But especially her ability to be three very different versions of a mother for our three very different daughters. I stand in awe of her, and continue to grow to love her more and more each day.

I once again acknowledge the teams that stand behind and alongside the work I do, including my colleagues at TomorrowToday Global, the team at Penguin Random House, and my extended family and friends, each of whose fingerprints are deeply embedded in this book. Of course, as far as the book is concerned, the most important of these is Nikki. Her attention to detail, her deep expertise and her passion for these issues have once again made this book better than I could ever have hoped.

Finally, I thank everyone who has read this book over the last 10 years, especially those who have contacted Nikki and me and shared how the book helped them navigate parenting the wired generation, providing us with valuable feedback and further insights in the process. We hope that this update for the 2020s and 30s inspires and assists the next generation of parents even more.

Graeme Codrington
April 2019
www.graemecodrington.com

Nikki
When we wrote the first edition of this book, it was not a series of prophecies about the future, but a well-researched set of possibilities. As the years have gone by, we have been able to, with increasing speed, put a tick next to each one as that particular scenario or possibility has become a reality. The level of accuracy about the future has been astounding. What seemed so 'off the wall' then has now become our new normal, and still the world is changing at a most unprecedented pace.

To keep the audiences at our talks up to date with the latest trends and shifts that will impact directly on their children's future, a new edition of the book became essential, just as parents and children continually need to reinvent, adapt and adopt to remain relevant and to thrive in this fast-changing world.

The first edition of *Future-proof Your Child* was not written in quiet seclusion on a mountain top or gazing over the ocean, but rather while I was a busy working mother juggling speaking engagements, meetings, fetching and carrying my two children (who were then in primary school), watching them play sport, helping with homework, being the class mom and, of course, being a wife, too. It took a year to research and write the book, in collaboration with Graeme and his extensive knowledge of trends and future scenarios, which he has so generously shared with me.

With the second edition, I still haven't managed to hide myself away to write in quiet seclusion! I still write on the run, at a desk in the middle of an open-plan, busy house (just like any normal 21st-century parent) in between speaking engagements, international travel, media interviews and more. But now both my sons are in their early 20s – one at university and the other launching himself into the adult world of work: the very world we sketched in the first edition! Where has the time gone?

There are two big differences, though, apart from the fact that my sons have grown up and are now both over two metres tall, dwarfing their mother. Firstly, this edition is written on the back of 12 years' work with parents, teachers, business leaders and the media – listening to, and responding to, their concerns, and having researched and written hundreds of parenting articles on the topic of future-proofing children, and having given over 2 000 media interviews. It only took eight weeks to pull this edition together with Graeme, so seasoned are we in this topic and in the writing itself.

Secondly, as I sit writing this book, I find myself with one son at university and the other on the verge of overseas work and travel. I am a tenant, not a homeowner, and a single parent after 26 years of marriage after my husband's tragic death in late 2017 during an armed robbery in our home in Johannesburg. My life changed irrevocably in just six minutes.

Disruption doesn't just happen 'out there'. It is not just being driven by information technology or biotechnology, robots or artificial intelligence. Disruption happens all the time, in our homes and in our families as individuals grow up and change (even adults), and as family structures are altered due to death, divorce, remarriage, blended families, special-needs children, financial and work pressure, and more.

There were many moments in the past year, having lived through a traumatic tragedy and journeying through grief, when I found my ability to write new content incredibly difficult, if not impossible at times. This book has been part of my journey to healing and finding that wellspring again.

As I said with the first edition, few books are written in a vacuum, and this one is no exception. It is the distillation of years of generous sharing of information and experiences from many experts in their field, too numerous to mention here. I would like to thank them all for my education and for the great work they are doing in the world.

We were thrilled that Penguin Random House, and Marlene Fryer and Ronel Richter-Herbert, in particular, were excited to entertain a revised and updated edition of *Future-proof Your Child*; thank you for seeing the value of this information for 21st-century parents.

To my co-author, Graeme, thank you for dancing with me again – it has been another stretching and enlightening experience weaving together our two strands of expertise and insights. I know that this book is not directly linked to the core work you do, but I believe it is very much an expression of who you are. It also reflects the importance you place on your role as a parent to your three girls.

To my amazing friends and family who have given me so much food for thought over the years, thank you for your love, support and encouragement. You have helped me get back on my feet and recentre myself so that the inspiration could flow through me once again. My work in the field of parenting and raising human potential is an expression of who I am. It feeds my soul. It's good to be back on my bicycle!

And, lastly, thank you to the many parents who have attended my presentations, read my books and articles, and listened to or watched my many media interviews about parenting in the 21st century, validating this work. You are the reason we needed to update this book!

Nikki Bush
April 2019
www.nikkibush.com

ABOUT THE AUTHORS

Nikki Bush is South Africa's parenting thought leader. She is a prolific speaker and author who is fondly referred to as the Creative Parenting Expert. She has helped hundreds of thousands of parents to build fabulous relationships with their children by turning very ordinary, everyday moments into extraordinary memories by creatively responding to everyday challenges. Nikki helps today's busy parents future-proof their children despite their busyness. Her wisdom, creativity and practical ideas are the solution for parents who are long on love and short on time.

Nikki's influential work is fuelled by her passion for play, connection and relationships. She is a sought-after speaker from Johannesburg to Hong Kong, from Cape Town to Polokwane, in America, neighbouring countries, and more. She is the co-author of three bestselling books: *Future-proof Your Child*, *Easy Answers to Awkward Questions* and *Tech-Savvy Parenting*, as well as a number of ebooks, including *Parenting Matters* and *Talent Re: defined*.

Nikki is the industry icon and go-to person for the media on anything to do with child development and parenting. She has racked up over 2 000 media interviews in just over 10 years, including a weekly slot on SABC 3's *Expresso* (for seven years) and Radio 702 (for almost five years). She is a guest lecturer at Henley Business School, Wits Business School and GIBS.

Described as a sane voice in a world of confusing opinions and choices regarding parenting and child development, Nikki is much loved and respected for offering real, practical parenting solutions for the 21st century.

Nikki was married to Simon for 26 years, until his untimely and tragic death in late 2017. Her two sons, Ryan (born in 1995) and Matthew (born in 1999), although now young men, are still a constant source of adventure, wonder and surprise. Parenting has been a huge part of Nikki's personal journey, and her children are undoubtedly the inspiration for her work in changing the world one parent, one teacher, one business leader at a time.

Graeme Codrington is a researcher, speaker and strategist on issues related to the future of work. He has five degrees in five different faculties from five different universities, including studies in commerce, theology, sociology and leadership. Graeme's work experience is just as varied, from audit articles at KPMG to IT-solutions development and training, and two years as a professional musician.

He now works for a company he co-founded, TomorrowToday Global (https://www.tomorrowtodayglobal.com), as a full-time strategy consultant, leadership developer and professional speaker. He is on the adjunct faculty of four major business schools and speaks to over 100 000 people in at least 20 different countries every year.

Graeme has been married to Jane Booth, his childhood sweetheart, since 1991. They have three daughters: Amy (born in 1999), Hannah (born in 2001) and Rebecca (born and adopted in 2005).

He is the author of a number of books, including *Mind the Gap* and *Leading in a Changing World*. His work with his team at TomorrowToday has given him a clear view of what needs to be done to prepare the next generation for the future.

FOREWORD

Parents have traditionally drawn a great deal of wisdom and experience from their own family experiences. There is familiarity and comfort in your family of origin, even if your own experience of being parented was not ideal. But the world is very different from the one in which you were raised. Technological advancements, new societal norms and the rapid pace of change create a new set of challenges – and opportunities – for parents today. These changes require parents to have a nimbleness of mind, a generosity of spirit and a preparedness to be active participants in the lives of their kids.

Parenting is no longer something you do *to* children, as in the days of authoritarian parenting. Nor is it something you do *for* children, as occurs in the era of overprotective or helicopter parenting. In the current age of cooperation and collaboration, successful parenting is something you do *with* children. Your ability to bring them along with you for the ride into an exciting and ever-changing future will undoubtedly be a marker of your parenting success.

It's easy to feel overwhelmed as a parent, not just with the day-to-day tasks of putting food on the table and managing behaviour, but also with keeping kids' spirits up. The growing complexity of issues parents face on a daily basis, from 'What's the right type of diet for my child?' to 'Is my child becoming addicted to their digital device?' can rob you of the confidence you need to be the loving, decisive parent that you want to be.

Fortunately, there's a robust international parenting education community that is currently helping parents make sense of the proliferation of research and providing wise guidance for those who want to stay ahead of the education and parenting game. Astute professionals such as Nikki Bush and Graeme Codrington are leading the way for all of us in the changing parenting landscape.

This book takes the reader on a wonderful journey into the future, covering consumer, educational and societal trends, and providing insights into the future of work and what these possibilities will mean for the children of today. Reassuringly, it's evident that there is a great deal you can do as a parent to prepare your child to capitalise on the evolution of the marketplace in terms of jobs and careers. The authors also give a timely message to schools to continue to adapt their teaching and learning to prepare students for the future.

Most importantly, Nikki and Graeme stay grounded. The parenting advice in this book is based on evidence-based child-development practice, while reminding us to raise kids with our hearts as well as our heads.

A great parenting book knows exactly where it wants to take the reader – it provides a map for guidance and includes plenty of detours to different places on the way. And in this, Nikki and Graeme have succeeded spectacularly. They are clear in the belief that parents play a vital role in preparing children for future success in a changing world. Crucially, they reveal how to pitch your parenting style and family life to maximise your kids' future success. They also provide wonderful practical parenting tips, tricks and techniques that will add fun and excitement to your family life.

My advice to readers is to read *Future-proof Your Child for the 2020s and Beyond* twice. Read it through the first time as quickly as you can. Then read it a second time using a highlighter to mark actionable steps and discussion points you pick up along the way. This is definitely a book to mull over and revisit time and again.

Let this book educate and entertain you, but also let it fill you with confidence, strength and self-belief that you can prepare your kids to take the first steps towards a truly remarkable future.

Michael Grose
Parenting educator, speaker and bestselling author of 11 parenting books, including *Anxious Kids: How children can turn their anxiety into resilience* (Penguin, 2019). Founder, Parenting Ideas, Australia's leading provider of parenting education for parents and schools (www.parentingideas.com.au).

Chapter 1

Wake up, the world has changed!

'We are not merely experiencing an era of change, it is a change of era.'
Leonard Sweet, *SoulTsunami: Sink or Swim in the
New Millennium Culture*, 2009

A hundred years ago, if a grandmother had gathered her grandchildren around her one late Saturday afternoon beneath the huge old oak tree in the back garden, the young tykes would have sat listening, spellbound, as Granny shared her wisdom and insights about the world. The children would have asked her how the world works, and would carefully have noted her answers – after all, this was the world they would soon enter as adults themselves, and her experience of it was invaluable to them.

Today, if that same scene played itself out, it is much more likely that it would be Granny, holding a smartphone in her hand, who'd ask the children, 'So, my dears, how does this thing work?'

Today's adults have lived in a world that spans not just two centuries, but the cusp of a millennium, too, yet there is a real sense that our past experience is inadequate preparation for what lies ahead. If we feel only vaguely confident about our own future, those of us who have children or grandchildren can sometimes feel overwhelmed by the task of preparing a new generation for a world that does not yet exist.

The difference, possibly, between today's parents and the generations of parents in the past is that now we know for certain that the world our children will inhabit will not be the same as the one we have lived in. It will not just be different in small, subtle ways, but in significant, markedly different ways. We know for certain that we *don't know* what the world will be like when our children are grown up.

In the first edition of this book, we spent many pages explaining the enormity of the coming change. Change was a key theme. Much of what we predicted has now happened, and change is our new normal. The globalised world with its few physical boundaries, its increasing technological capabilities and computing power, the sophistication of the internet and the development of social media platforms, such as Facebook, has enabled change and trends to move at incredible speed from one country, and one company, to the next.

This can be seen in a variety of ways. The media, for example, is now ubiquitous: on our phones and always with us. News comes to us in sound bites from all over the world, but we consume it only in headlines and one-liners, without analysis or the luxury of time to lend perspective. It is a constant stream of hype and clickbait headlines.

Similarly, we now know that foreign governments (Russia, China and America have been especially implicated) and international PR agencies (such as Bell Pottinger) alike have deliberately interfered in the politics, elections and public discourse of nations. They use the powerful technologies that connect and enable us to distort, agitate and misinform us. Multinational companies now dominate every part of the planet, which means that decisions impacting our local environment might be made on the other side of the world. And those decisions and their implications now move at warp speed around the globe. The world really is more 'VUCA' (volatile, uncertain, complex and ambiguous) than it ever was before.

As we look ahead to the 2020s and 30s, one theme stands out above all others: *disruption*. By this we mean that the way the world has worked up until now is going to change – and not just incrementally or predictably. The change is going to be deep and structural and result in new ways of doing things – the 'rules of the game' are being rewritten, whatever 'the game' happens to be. We are no longer absorbing change incrementally, but at a magnitude that is shaking up entire industries, destroying some in the process, and reshaping the way we do things both big and small.

It is estimated that around two-thirds of the jobs our children will do in the 2030s have not yet been invented. According to McKinsey, 30 per cent of the jobs that new graduates in the UK started at the beginning of 2017 did not exist the year before! That fact alone should make you sit up and think.

> Since we wrote the first edition of this book, Amy, who is at university, has started a part-time job as an au pair, a fairly traditional student job, while Ryan, after completing his degree, got his first full-time job with a virtual- and augmented-reality filming company. This is how we realised that we have to prepare our children for both the known and the unknown. There are even under-30s who are taking their first sabbatical or voluntary retirement to upskill and then re-enter the world of work in a different way.

The well-known examples below have become icons of disruptive change. They are symbolic of what the future holds, and are the types of businesses our children will either create or be employed in one day:

- Uber, the world's largest taxi company, owns no taxis. Both the Codrington and Bush families use Uber as a matter of course, both locally and internationally. On a recent trip to Australia, Nikki engaged with an Uber driver about the impact Uber and similar app-based taxi companies have had on the world – has Uber really 'stolen' business away from traditional taxi companies, or has the overall number of people using taxi services just grown? Two things emerged from this conversation. One, people who never caught taxis before now use them on a regular basis instead of driving their own vehicles. Graeme and Nikki are both a case in point. Two, there is a generation of young people who are no longer buying vehicles and taking on the attendant costs of petrol, insurance and repayments, but who, instead, are using services like Uber during the week, and sometimes hiring cars from an Uber-type car-rental agency over the weekend. Uber is not a taxi company – it is a disruptor of the way we think about cars and transportation.

- Netflix, the world's largest movie house, owns no cinemas and is in the process of redefining the television industry. It has spearheaded on-demand viewing of TV shows, movies and documentaries on any device, anywhere, anytime. This will have implications that extend far beyond on which screen to watch your favourite shows; it will influence how advertising works (or doesn't), how stars get discovered and promoted, and how families and friends spend time together.
- WeChat, the world's most powerful smartphone app (as we write this in 2019), showcases the possibilities of creating an all-encompassing ecosystem that allows for fingertip management of almost every aspect of our lives: from entertainment to banking, travel management to funeral services, shopping to conference calls. The fact that it happens to work best inside the authoritarian system of China is slightly disconcerting, especially when the Chinese government began experimenting with allocating citizens 'social credits', which then affect what they can and can't do in 'real life'. Suddenly, science fiction and reality become blurred.
- Tesla and SpaceX are the brainchild of Elon Musk, the eccentric engineer-inventor. His goal is to convert the world to clean energy sources and battery power, along with his vision of space travel and colonising Mars. Whatever you may think of the man, you have to admit that there is nothing 'business as usual' about him or his impact on a variety of industries. Richard Branson's Virgin empire impacted industries as diverse as music, health care and airlines. Musk is pushing the motor-vehicle, space-travel and energy industries to confront their orthodoxies and 'change the game'.
- Probably the biggest workplace trend of the next decade will be automation and all the ways in which machines, robots, software, algorithms and apps will be able to do many of the tasks that we humans do now. As we will see later in this book, this will affect even the most qualified professionals, and change the 'rules of the game' for us all. While speaking at an international conference for auditors and accountants in 2016, Graeme witnessed the unveiling of Auvenir,

automated auditing software that can reduce the hours that human auditors spend on a client by around 90 per cent. Needless to say, the audience was both astounded and scared stiff by the implications.

LIVING IN THE 2020S, PREPARING FOR THE FUTURE

For many people, the 2020s has always been the 'proper future'. Hollywood filmmakers placed their futuristic movies in the 2020s, filling our minds with majestic visions of technological marvels or dystopian nightmares of a world gone wrong.

Now, here we are.

And so we find that we're still fluctuating between the two grand visions of heaven and hell.

We're here, in the 2020s, but it's not entirely clear where 'here' actually is, or how quickly we'll get to where we're going. What we mean by this is that, in the last 30 years, during which many of today's young parents were born, we have been creating the building blocks with which a new world will be constructed. But what we have at the moment is more promise than reality.

The 'Fourth Industrial Revolution', as many people like to call it, promises a world consisting of smart objects, artificial intelligence, automation, virtual reality and bio-engineering. But you will still have to deal with your child's regular snotty noses and daily rush-hour traffic. It's easy for the excitement of a shiny promised future to dull quite quickly on a Monday morning as the reality of our lives – especially as parents of young children – hits us.

The biggest difference between previous industrial revolutions and the Fourth Industrial Revolution is that this one won't take decades to evolve, and this is why it matters to you and your children. We are not going to go through gradual change, but rather exponential and disruptive change. A tsunami of change is closer now than ever before.

This is both an exciting and a challenging time to be a parent, because there are no blueprints; we are given a blank piece of paper on which to write the future with our children.

Advanced technology enables us to do different things and to do things differently. The possibilities of what happens next are both exciting and scary, for example, in the following fields:

- Medicine: We are on the verge of curing a variety of major diseases, including malaria, cancer and Alzheimer's, and we are postponing ageing dramatically and helping people live younger for longer; yet we also have the potential to create monster clones or to unleash a global pandemic or pathogen.
- Energy: Clean and green energy sources are becoming ever more affordable and accessible, with amazing new energy alternatives about to be unveiled (e.g. see https://www.iter.org for an amazing nuclear fusion plant in France that will go live before 2030). And yet we are facing a tipping point in climate change that, if not averted, will result in a global environmental catastrophe.
- Technology: 3D printers and advanced robotics promise cheaper, easier manufacturing of everything from household objects to food and spare body parts. Yet the military could use the same technologies to create even more powerful weapons to wage even more devastating wars than ever before.
- Natural resources: Many parts of the world are running out of drinking water, while sea levels rise and glaciers melt. Food supply needs to change, with a shift away from planet-harming red meat to more plant-based diets. At the same time, we are developing 3D printing technologies that can print meat using stem cells. A ban on single-use plastics is set to be implemented in many parts of the world before 2020. All of these point to significant game-changing shifts in how we live, eat and consume, and are fuelling innovation and rapid change in key industries with which we interact daily.

What will this century bring? The 2020s will give us a real sense of not just the technologies we will have at our disposal, but also society's willingness, or not, to work together to use them for the good of the planet and its people.

19-Year-Old Makes Over $1 Million Hunting Software Bugs

On 1 March 2019, *PC Magazine* ran a story about an Argentinian, Santiago Lopez, who became the first person to surpass $1 million in rewards on HackerOne, a bug bounty platform that offers money in exchange for finding security vulnerabilities in the IT systems of participating companies. Lopez is an ethical hacker who started this line of work at the age of 17, and was self-taught by reading blogs and watching YouTube video tutorials online. Since joining HackerOne, he has found more than 1 670 security flaws in the products and services of Verizon, Twitter and WordPress, and in the software of government offices.

There is good news in all of this, which is that the future that is unfolding does not have to overwhelm us. As humans, we have what it takes to not only survive, but thrive in the world that is emerging. We just need the resilience to survive this period of disruption and chaotic change on our way to that world. Alvin Toffler, futurist and author of the classic *Future Shock* (1972), was deadly accurate when he said: 'The illiterate of the 21st century will not be those who cannot read and write, but those who cannot learn, unlearn, and relearn.'

If we asked you, 'What have you learnt in the last 12 months?', we are sure you would be able to supply us with an answer. Because it's almost impossible to live in our world without learning new things on a regular basis. But what if we asked you, 'What have you unlearnt in the last 12 months?' What attitudes, behaviours, habits or perspectives (world views) have you deliberately and consciously attempted to remove from your life in that time? And do you have any plans to relearn attitudes and habits in the next 12 months?

Now think about preschool children – specifically those under the age of three, when the brain is at its most plastic and elastic – soaking up every new experience like a sponge. They can cope with change and continuous learning; in fact, every day is an adventure of epic proportions.

Admittedly, they do take an afternoon nap, which helps to keep them balanced (maybe we should all take a siesta after lunch). These young explorers are actually carrying within them an intuitive blueprint for success in the 21st century. Consider some of the characteristics with which they are naturally imbued. Preschoolers are:

- inquisitive and curious about their world and how it works
- natural explorers
- physical learners (they create understanding and meaning by trying things out for themselves – by doing)
- original thinkers and highly creative (anything is possible)
- insatiable learners (they can't get enough of learning)
- not afraid of failure (no matter how high the couch is or how far they may tumble)
- desperate to master what they are doing and to develop to their next level
- sometimes selfish, but mainly collaborative and keen to be with others
- adaptable and resilient.

As parents, we can build on these natural skills and character traits, nurturing them and ensuring that we enhance them for the road ahead. But this means changing our approach to parenting.

For example, rather than attempting to give our children 'The Answers' to their questions, we need to teach them how to think, how to discern, and how to look at various scenarios for themselves in order to prepare them for an unknown and uncertain future. In essence, as 21st-century parents, we have been called to a new way of 'being' with our children. Parenting is (and always has been) more about 'being' than 'doing' anyway.

THE AGE OF POSSIBILITY

Out of the chaos of disruption something very exciting is emerging: a new era. This new era is characterised by connection, individual power, creativity and opportunity like never before. We call it the **Age of Possibility**. Despite the somewhat negative feelings many people have about the world right now, there has never been a time in history with more possibilities. Our birthplace, class, gender or background no longer restricts us. These factors still have a huge impact on where we start in life, but not on where we end up. Some people still have it easier than others, but there has never been a more opportune time in history for individuals to change both themselves and the world around them than now.

An example of this is how the young people of today have influenced the world on sustainability issues. Recycling, the eradication of single-use plastics and a shift away from meat consumption are all trends that started with young people and spread to their families, communities and, now, countries. Today's millennials are much more health-conscious than children of previous generations. Perhaps it's because they have more choice in the matter, or because their parents set the example. Or perhaps they're just fussy! But the number of children on lactose-free, gluten-free, high-fibre, low-GI diets is vast, as is the number choosing to become vegan or vegetarian.

The young people of today are quick to latch on to causes. Their focus is not only on their personal health, but also on the health of the planet. Almost instinctively they have come to realise that the planet is in trouble and that, in order for them to have a future, they must do something to fix it. They are prepared to put a great deal of emotional pressure on adults to make sure that the issues that concern them are appropriately addressed.

> When Hannah was five, the Codrington family was driving along a highway and got stuck behind a delivery van. As the truck downshifted on a steep hill, it belched forth a cloud of acrid diesel smoke that went into the vents of the car. Hannah was disgusted by the pollution. As the family car overtook the truck, she indignantly waved her finger at the van driver,

> admonishing him for 'pollutioning' the air. Then she turned to Graeme and stunned him by saying, 'Daddy, which company is that, 'cause I don't think we should buy from them any more.'

The playing fields have been levelled, and everyone now has the opportunity to use their potential to shape the world. It is up to individuals to use this potential or not, and how they use it will be dependent on their set of values and world view.

As in all revolutions, there is chaos and change, disruption, dislocation, relocation and reconnection. The youth are not immune from all of this; in fact, they are often the expression and embodiment of it all. Every change brings with it hidden opportunities and danger – whether it be a transition to a new era; a move to a new house, a new job or a new country; a new arrival in the family; or a change in school for your child.

The symbol on the left is the Cantonese symbol for 'change' or 'crisis'. Like many Chinese pictograms, it encompasses multiple meanings. In this case, the symbol is made up of two parts: the top part on its own means 'danger'; the lower part on its own means 'hidden opportunity'. So change or crisis embodies two elements: either we can focus on the danger, the downside or what may go wrong, or we can direct our energies into the hidden opportunity, the upside.

This truly is an amazing time in human history. Never before has anyone, born anywhere, in any circumstances, had as many opportunities to go anywhere, do anything, become anyone they want to be. It most surely is an Age of Possibility. *The* Age of Possibility. While this is an exciting thought, it is an equally daunting one, too. Our choices will make all the difference. We will not be swept along by the tide of history. But will we make the right choices? How do we know? How do we decide?

If these are powerful questions for our own lives, they become urgent and emotive when we consider our role as parents. We shape the critical formative years of our children and set them on paths for the future. Are these the right paths? Are we doing the best for our children?

As parents, we are shaping the individuals of the future, which is why it is so important for us to understand what the implications of these changes are, and the impact they may have on our children. For it is our belief that *parents*, rather than schools, will primarily be responsible for ensuring that children develop the critical factors that will enable them to succeed in the future.

As a parent or grandparent, consider how you responded when your youngster asked, 'What should I be when I grow up?' Our children will join the working world from 2030 onwards – what will it be like? We have very little idea what the 10 most in-demand jobs will be in 2030, or even if some of today's most sought-after jobs will still exist. We simply don't have enough information to know this, and sometimes our minds can even shut down, as it's too overwhelming to even think about it.

The question of a future career is linked, of course, to considerations about what subjects our children should study at school. And whether the schools that we've selected for our children will deliver on the hopes we have for them. As we meet our children's teachers, so burdened with administrative and curriculum overload, we wonder whether they are capable of helping to shape our offspring effectively. And whether the subjects on offer will lead to success in careers we can't even conceive of today. Again, this can be overwhelming, and some parents might simply avoid thinking about it.

But for now, let's forget about studies and careers. The factors that will actually feature more significantly in our children's development are key life experiences, personal skills and relationships. But which experiences? And how can we ensure that our children have these experiences? Do they have to experience what we did to get where we are? This gets tough. Once again, shutdown or avoidance!

At this point, we haven't even considered how much pocket money we will give our children, or how old they will have to be before they get their own smartphone. And what about the additional pressure on children when a smartphone is added to their list of responsibilities? And then, how can we protect them from inappropriate content on the internet or on any number of interactive media sources? How old must they be before we talk to them about sex, drugs and global warming?

Even more daunting, what do we *say* to them when we talk about these issues? And, perhaps most daunting of all, how do we help prepare them to make their own decisions within the next few years?

Living in the Age of Possibility will not help our children if our outdated parenting prevents them from utilising the options and opportunities it will bring. As parents, we need to keep up.

> 'Global warming, racial tension, Third World rage, rapacious epidemics, and myriad other global woes vie with less dire but no less unnerving phenomena – from information overload to media manipulation – to convince us that the apocalypse is about to pounce. Indeed, it will pounce on the unprepared, but there's no need for us to be caught unawares, if we will only learn from today's children. For those of us who grew up before computers became ubiquitous, the world is like a foreign country and we are its immigrants. Our kids – the 'screenagers' – are like those of any immigrant, fitting themselves more naturally into this terra incognita than we can.'
> Douglas Rushkoff, *Playing the Future*, 1996

Chapter 2

How your child develops

'If I had my child to raise all over again, I'd build self-esteem first, and the house later. I'd finger-paint more, and point the finger less. I would do less correcting and more connecting. I'd take my eyes off my watch, and watch with my eyes. I'd take more hikes and fly more kites. I'd stop playing serious, and seriously play. I would run through more fields and gaze at more stars. I'd do more hugging and less tugging.'
Diane Loomans, *101 Ways to Build Self-esteem and Teach Values*, 2003

Irrelevance is one of our deepest fears as human beings, and becoming irrelevant in a world of disruptive change is a very real possibility and a challenge for our children in their lifetime. It's something we need to address with vigour and intention as we support our children's development, and as we gradually release them into the world after building the skills, attitudes and values in their early years that will stand them in good stead for the future. To achieve this, we not only need to have a picture of the future world our children will inhabit, but also a solid understanding of the developmental stages they need to go through in order to become healthy, well-adjusted young people and adults.

The good news is that these developmental stages have not changed much, even in a fast-paced world. The first decade or so of our children's lives actually unfolds reasonably predictably, and what our children need from us and from the world around them is quite simple.

What *has* changed is how parents support and guide their children through these early phases of development. As parents, we have less time, are more pressured, and maybe are filled with more fear than previous generations. Too many choices, too many conflicting opinions, too many distractions, too many dangers – it can be overwhelming to be a parent in the midst of the cacophony that is our modern world. So, let us help you to step back for a moment and gain a bird's-eye view of what the first decade of your child's life will look like, and what you can do to future-proof them now.

STRONG FOUNDATIONS

Every tall tree is supported by deep roots. Every towering skyscraper has strong foundations. The Burj Al Arab, that beautiful, sail-shaped hotel on a man-made island off the shoreline of Dubai, is underpinned by 230 piles, 40 metres deep and 1.5 metres wide. It took five years to build it, three of which were spent on the foundations alone!

Similarly, children need strong foundations to support them as they grow. The wider and deeper the foundations, the stronger and taller the structure that can be built on top of it. You need to dig deep with your children, and build solid foundations. On top of those foundations, your children will continue to build themselves over time.

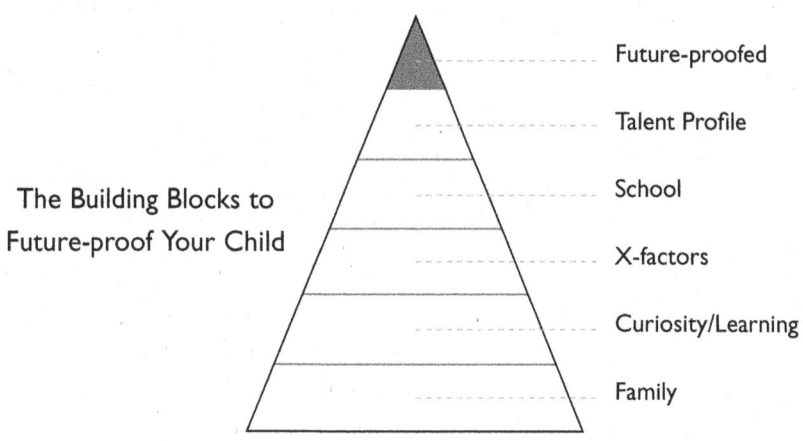

As illustrated on the previous page, the foundation for every child begins with family. And family today is whatever *your* family looks like. Family could mean a single parent with a child, or something completely different. There are no limits as far as gender or size are concerned. For a child, what is important is that the parent claims their family as 'our family': 'In our family, we ...' Family is the 'we', and within the 'we', children discover the 'me'.

Families have never looked more different than they do these days. Gone is the old picture of 'working dad, stay-at-home mom, 2.4 kids and a dog'. What has not changed, though, is how important it is for the parent/parents, caregivers and extended family to bond and create a sense of 'our family'. Every family is different. Children don't need a 'normal family': they need a sense of belonging; the confidence they gain by being a member of 'my family'.

In our fast-paced, high-tech world, we seem to have forgotten the vital importance of a solid family foundation, whatever the unique make-up of your family might be. Once that foundation is established, parents and children can work as a team to put the other building blocks in place that will future-proof them.

Interestingly, these days adults tend to direct and instruct children to such an extent, both at home and at school, that they are at risk of losing their own sense of curiosity about the world they live in. And as curiosity is the driver of all learning, this is a problem. When you are always being told what to do and how to do it, where is the sense of ownership and engagement in your own developmental process? How can you be intrinsically motivated in this situation?

Leadership expert Stef du Plessis contends that people only support that which they help to create. He is a specialist in change and culture in the workplace, but his theory holds true in homes, families and schools, too.

Once our children have a solid foundation, which encompasses self-confidence, a sense of security and self-acquired knowledge, they will begin to exhibit some of the characteristics that will be vital for their success in the future world of work. We'll come back to these in Chapter 5, when we talk about what we call the X-factors for success. When your children are keen to discover the world around them, you can begin to shape these X-factors in them.

The next building block for success is school. By the time they are 18, your children will have spent more time at school than they have with you. You need to see school as a vital partner in developing your children, and we'll give you plenty of advice on how to do so in Chapter 6.

The next building block will only truly begin to emerge in your child's teen years, but when your child is as young as eight years old, you can start to help him or her develop what we call a 'Talent Profile'. Essentially, this is a live and constantly expanding showcase of who they are, what they can do, and how they are already contributing to the world. Your child's Talent Profile will obviously change and grow over time as they develop in their own unique way and acquire a strong sense of self. We deal with Talent Profiles in detail in Chapter 7.

The culmination of building a successful Talent Profile results in the ultimate goal of parenting: your children have acquired the freedom, the confidence, and the necessary skills and abilities to be independent and make their own choices as they launch themselves into the world. Even though we cannot guarantee anyone's success or happiness, including our own children's, we can give them the best possible foundation for finding success and happiness for themselves, in their own way.

Digging deep and laying strong foundations require consciously spending time 'building' your children to prepare them for being independent in the future. It might seem like a strange thing to think about when you hold your baby in your arms, or watch their first teetering steps, but the ultimate goal of parenting is always to prepare your children to leave the nest, and to live independently of you. This is not a task you start when they're teenagers or young adults – it is something you work on from the first day. Helping your children to become confident and competent to navigate the world themselves – with you as a safety net – is what parenting is all about.

To achieve this, you may need to take a long, hard look at yourself, your knowledge about child development and your parenting style. In this chapter, we will introduce you to some essential basics about child development, how children learn, and how you can support and foster growth rather than hinder it.

We want you to have peace of mind that you have equipped your children as best you can in heart, mind and body, so that not only *you* believe they can thrive without you, but that *they* believe it, too. And this means that they need to be engaged in their own process of development and are invested in their learning journey. As parent and child, you need to learn to dance together, as well as apart.

SOME THINGS HAVEN'T CHANGED

As we have said, constant change is no longer just a phase – it has become our 'new normal'. Even childhood is changing, with our children increasingly drawn into the fast-paced world of multitasking and time urgency. However, it's comforting to know that children still go through the same basic developmental stages. Not *everything* has changed!

This is important for parents to remember when they have young children who may seem older than their years. Research indicates that two factors heavily influence the development of your child: technology (noise) and consumerism (clutter). So, it often appears as if our children are growing up faster, because they:

- are too connected to the digital world, own a lot more stuff, or want more stuff
- are busier, suffer more stress and are under more pressure than previous generations of children
- are exposed to people with a much wider variety of opinions and world views
- have less time for self-discovery and play.

How our children connect the dots in the future will depend on how they connect the dots developmentally during their foundation years. This, in turn, is dependent on their parents, teachers and carers, who should ensure that their development is not negatively affected by an overload of technology and consumerism, particularly in their early years.

With this in mind, it is important for parents to have a basic understanding of how children learn and develop in order to guide their developmental process appropriately.

> 'We spend the first 12 months of our children's lives teaching them to walk and talk and the next 12 months teaching them to sit down and shut up.'
> Phyllis Diller, *How To Be*, 2014

If you are the type of person who enjoys frameworks and theories, we'd highly recommend that you pause here and look up two very significant theories on childhood development, or alternatively browse through a brief summary below:

Piaget's Four Stages of Cognitive Development
Piaget identified the four key stages through which children proceed to acquire new knowledge, namely:
1. Sensorimotor stage: ages 0–2: learning through their physical senses.
2. Preoperational stage: ages 2–7: development of language.
3. Concrete operational stage: ages 7–11: development of logic, social skills and reasoning.
4. Formal operational stage: ages 12+: abstract and hypothetical thinking.

Erikson's Stages of Psychosocial Development
Erikson identified eight life stages we must all progress through, and each one is built around a key set of life tasks, namely:
1. Trust vs. Mistrust: ages 0–1½: learning to trust the regularity and security of my environment.
2. Autonomy vs. Shame: ages 1½–3: learning to assert my own will, but within a context of the norms and standards of my family and community.
3. Initiative vs. Guilt: ages 3–5: learning to take responsibility for my development and my mistakes.

4. Industry vs. Inferiority: ages 5–12: learning what I am good at, and what I am not good at.
5. Identity vs. Role Confusion: ages 12–18: learning who is 'on my team' and who isn't, and discover what I was made to be/do, and what I will struggle with.
6. Intimacy vs. Isolation: ages 18–40: learning who to love, and who will hurt me.
7. Generativity vs. Stagnation: ages 40–65: learning to care for others and to make a contribution to the world, while continuing to grow and develop myself.
8. Ego Integrity vs. Despair: ages 65+: learning what to do with my wisdom, contributing to society and enjoying the fruits of my life.

Understanding that each of these stages is necessary and a building block to the next stage, and knowing what each stage entails, can be a valuable asset in planning and guiding the development of your children, and anticipating how they will change next, just as you start to think you've worked them out!

CHILDREN ARE STILL MULTISENSORY HUMAN BEINGS

Children learn via their senses: hearing, sight, touch, taste, smell, movement and balance. The sensory system is the part of the nervous system that receives and processes information in the brain. Through this process, the brain will grow and develop. How your children interpret sensory information will shape their experience of the world. At the same time, their sensory system is shaped by their experiences of the world. An amazing thought!

It is important to know this, as parents act as their children's sensory gatekeepers, especially during the first seven years of life when children do not have emotional and psychological filters to protect them. In other words, they are unable to tell the difference between what is real and what is not, nor can they distinguish between tangible reality and virtual or digital reality.

For example, it is unwise to allow children in this age bracket to watch TV or engage with online content without limits or supervision. Firstly, they cannot differentiate between programming and commercial content (this must be taught); and, secondly, if the programmes contain inappropriate content, such as violence, antisocial behaviour, or anything that induces fear or sensory overload, they cannot protect themselves.

They also have no way of knowing what is appropriate or inappropriate behaviour (unless the shows they watch are specifically designed to teach these values). Thus, they experience everything as 'real' and 'right'. Such experiences influence their reality and world view, whether we are aware of it or not.

PHASES OF LEARNING

Children are constantly moving in and out of three basic phases of learning: the concrete, the semi-concrete and the abstract. These phases are explained in the table below:

The three basic phases of learning

PHASE	EXPLANATION	EXAMPLE
Concrete *From birth*	In the early stages: A child needs actual objects to touch, taste, see, hear and smell. A child learns through his or her senses. A child uses his or her tongue to obtain an understanding of texture and shape, as well as the taste of objects. Movement is essential for learning in this phase.	**A real apple.** The way a child personally experiences an apple will give it a meaning. The way a parent or teacher talks about the apple with the child as he or she holds it, and points out the properties or characteristics of the apple, will also help the child to verbalise his or her thoughts and discoveries about the apple. This is learning in the concrete – on the outside the apple is red, round and smooth with a waxy feel to it; inside, it's a different colour and texture, and it's crunchy, juicy and tastes sweet! All this information will be stored in the child's brain to be used whenever he or she next experiences something red, crunchy, round, smooth, juicy or sweet.

PHASE	EXPLANATION	EXAMPLE
Semi-concrete 3+ years	As the child gains experience, he or she is able to relate pictures, objects and models to actual objects with which he or she had some contact at an earlier stage.	**A picture of a red apple.** Now that the child has experienced a real apple, a picture of the apple will have meaning. The child can access everything he or she has experienced about a red apple and apply it to the picture. The child is using his or her memory.
Abstract 6+ years	At this stage, symbols, letters and numerals are able to be interpreted and understood.	**The word 'apple'.** Having had concrete and semi-concrete experiences of apples, the child will find learning to recognise the word for apple much easier because he or she can make real associations based on personal experience with apples. The child will also create categories and develop analytical skills. 'Apples' can be categorised as 'fruit', even if they are red, green or yellow, and small or big.

Source: Adapted and expanded from *Bridging with a Smile* by Doreen Maree and Margot Ford, 1995.

While this is an oversimplification of the learning process and the extraordinary brilliance of a human's complex brain, it does give parents a good idea of how their children learn. In fact, from birth right up to the age of 12, children's primary way of gaining an understanding of their world is through concrete, real-life learning situations. In other words, they learn through personal experience.

The three phases of learning are clearly manifested in a child who is learning to count. In the concrete phase, they should be given real objects to count, and be encouraged to touch each object as they count. In the semi-concrete phase, they can count just by looking at the objects in a picture. In the abstract phase, actual numbers have meaning, and a child no longer needs the visual clues or pictures to count, for example, the number 6 versus a picture of six ducks.

The senses of touch, movement and balance are integral to concrete, active and personal learning experiences. Right from conception, it is actually *movement* that wires the brain for future, more sophisticated, cognitive functions. There is a natural progression from one developmental milestone to the next that is driven by the connection between the brain and the body via a special substance called myelin.

Parents' awareness of myelin is usually limited to ensuring that the correct fatty acids are in their infant formula. The formation of myelin – the fatty coating of the nerve fibres of the brain – starts in utero, peaking at around one to two years of age and continuing until around the age of five.

Myelination starts in the head and works its way down the body, and from the centre of the body outwards. Myelin increases the speed of nerve-impulse transmission, which means that messages can be relayed more efficiently between brain cells. In highly myelinated neurons, impulses travel at 100 metres per second.

This means that your child will develop in a predictable way. Physically, your child will gain control of his or her neck, then trunk, then arms and legs, and finally, fingers and toes. As the muscles develop physically, the child will also develop sensations, emotions and perceptions as myelin increases.

REACHING THEIR MILESTONES

Parents are usually unaware that physical developmental milestones or phases are all in line with myelination development. In fact, milestones can't be reached until sufficient myelin is laid down. Head and neck control precede rolling, for example. The quality of a baby's physical development forms the basis of all learning and academic achievement later on, because it is intrinsically linked to the development of the neural pathways in the brain. For this reason, occupational therapists often say thoughts that never possess the body can never possess the mind.

It's a myth that the sooner a baby reaches his or her milestones, the more intelligent he or she will be. In fact, research shows that there is an enormous correlation between incomplete developmental phases in babies and academic underachievement later on. In other words, repetition is required at every phase in order to build a strong cognitive network in the brain. The speed of moving from one milestone to the next is much less important than complete mastery of each milestone.

LEARNING THROUGH REPETITION

Repetition is essential for good and comprehensive development to take place. For example, a baby should perform in the region of 50 000 crawling movements to wire the brain in preparation for the fine-motor skills of reading and writing. Effective myelination takes place through repeated body movement.

'Screen time' (TV, computers, smartphones, digital games, etc.) often involves passive experiences that are largely semi-concrete or abstract. These must therefore be balanced with real experiences. Remember that an elephant and a mouse can be the same size on a screen. Children will not comprehend their true size until they are able to compare themselves physically to these creatures, whether by visiting a pet shop, zoo or game reserve.

Similarly, playing an on-screen game that involves racing cars doesn't provide a child with a real concept of how to judge speed, space and distance. Although all digital experiences are certainly not bad – the same principle applies to books and picture cards, after all – nothing can replace real-world experiences. There is the possibility that full-body, virtual-reality experiences with haptic feedback devices might come close to simulating reality in the future, but it might be cheaper, and easier, to provide real-world experiences for the foreseeable future.

Parents can definitely facilitate their children's learning – and foster a love of learning – by offering them rich life experiences, characterised by visits to interesting places and exposure to different environments. For example, how does a child understand the sea without having experienced it, or visualise the texture of grass without having crawled on it?

Children also need plenty of free play, undirected by adult supervision, which enables them to potter and ponder and even to get bored, accessing their inner world, which is full of innovative and creative thoughts. Many 'play' experiences provided for children today are contrived, prescribed, organised and supervised to the detriment of a child's natural development.

The role of parents in the foundation phase of life is to give their children numerous varied experiences, and to provide for as much repetition within these experiences as possible.

> 'Learning is experience. Everything else is just information.'
> Albert Einstein

BASIC UNCHANGING NEEDS IN THE FIRST SEVEN YEARS

The basic developmental needs of children in the foundation phase are listed on the following pages. We should also understand how the world in which we live now could interfere with children's developmental needs if parents and teachers are caught unawares.

The basic needs of children for optimum development in the foundation phase, and potential threats

A CHILD'S DEVELOPMENTAL NEEDS	HOW THE WORLD IS INTERFERING
Children need freedom to explore, to find out how the world works, and to discover how they fit into the world.	Children increasingly live in a 'barbed-wire culture' with limited access to the outdoors, playgrounds and nature due to societal threats, parental fears, parental busyness and high-density living. Technology and screen-based entertainment encourage sedentary behaviour, resulting in children turning into sedentary screen slaves. Lack of parental presence or role-modelling is also negatively affecting this need.
Children need plenty of physical movement to develop the neurological pathways that wire the brain for more sophisticated functions later on. Physical exercise also develops resilience, perseverance and social skills.	The body is, in fact, the architect of the brain. Too much sedentary activity fails to stimulate the visual, vestibular and proprioceptive systems, which are the foundations for reading, writing and maths later on in a child's life. Childhood obesity and diabetes are on the rise due to a lack of exercise and physical movement. Too much screen time has been identified as a contributing factor to this state of affairs.
Children need to eat a healthy diet, since their development and mental and physical performance are influenced by their intake of water and nutrients.	Much of our food today is depleted of nutrients for a variety of reasons – from overprocessing to sterile soil, among many others. The side effects of added growth hormones and antibiotics are also cause for concern. Most food advertisements on TV promote junk food rather than broccoli – the opposite to a healthy eating plan. They encourage snacking on convenience or fast foods, which are high in salt, sugar, trans-fatty acids, colourants and flavourants. Such foods, while convenient for busy parents, contribute to obesity, diabetes, and food allergies and intolerances, as well as concentration and behavioural issues, and even personality disorders.

A CHILD'S DEVELOPMENTAL NEEDS	HOW THE WORLD IS INTERFERING
Children need plenty of rest. Sleep is essential and important: • for physical growth and a strong immune system; • to balance intense periods of physical activity, which characterise a healthy childhood; • to enable the body to balance sensory overload and prevent stimulation from overwhelming the child; and • to enable the child to process and consolidate what he or she has learnt and experienced each day.	Children have so much packed into their day that it is often difficult for parents to keep a regular routine, including bedtime. Sometimes a child's routine is governed by a parent's diary, and parents today are very busy. Children can battle to fall asleep after watching TV or playing on-screen games. The fast-moving light rays in these games negatively affect the melatonin levels in the body, which are necessary for good sleep. Stress, anxiety and fear can also affect a child's sleeping patterns. We underestimate how contagious parental anxiety is for children.
Children need to develop their imagination and creativity in order to have original thoughts that will help them to solve the problems of the future that are not yet problems. A strong imagination and creativity are very useful in subjects such as languages, art, maths, design, technology, and more.	Excessive TV viewing and on-screen activities are limiting this development in an alarming way. On-screen activities are replacing real-world playtime, affecting social and emotional development, in addition to limiting creative and imaginative play. Children are being overscheduled from a very young age with extracurricular activities from lunch time until dinner time, with little opportunity for rest, free play, alone-time and reflection. Boredom is actually very beneficial for children's creativity from time to time. Even creative art programmes are often so outcomes-based that there is little room for imagination, creativity and originality. In many instances, these programmes are being replaced by creative craft programmes, which is far from ideal because of their prescriptive nature.

A CHILD'S DEVELOPMENTAL NEEDS	HOW THE WORLD IS INTERFERING
Children need to play in the real sense of the word. Play is the language of childhood. It's a way to learn more about the world and find meaning. Children also need play dates in home environments. Remember that they learn the most important things in the sandpit, or swinging from the jungle gym, and not in the classroom. Most of what children really need to learn is caught, not taught, from you, their parents.	Many preschools today are falling into the trap of teaching via semi-concrete or abstract worksheets instead of providing a play-based curriculum through which children discover and learn for themselves through their own physical experience with their world. Parents demand worksheets as proof of learning and as a tangible outcome for their hard-earned money. Some parents push their children into competitive sports and fast-tracked learning experiences at the expense of play. Many children are enrolled in too many extramural activities from a young age, or spend their afternoons in aftercare due to working parents, which means that play dates in social settings are difficult to arrange. As adults, we question whether children as young as seven or eight still enjoy childhood pursuits and freedom in the traditional sense of the word. The majority of children report that friends do not visit or play at one another's houses during the week, and that socialising is limited to certain weekend time slots in and among family activities and shopping.
Children need real-life, real-time experiences, especially in the first seven years of life. It is only around the 12th year that the brain is able to handle abstract learning with ease.	On-screen activities transport children into a virtual world that is not real. This is fine in moderation and when balanced with plenty of concrete play experiences, and socialising with other children. On-screen activities should not be a young child's default setting.

A CHILD'S DEVELOPMENTAL NEEDS	HOW THE WORLD IS INTERFERING
Children need to develop social and emotional skills in order to build solid relationships with themselves and others. They learn this best by copying their parents and caregivers. They also need conversation, face-to-face contact and human touch. Emotional intelligence is a better indicator of how well a child will do in life than his or her IQ. (See the marshmallow experiment on page 169.)	Children are being bombarded by thousands of messages from advertisers and marketers telling them that satisfaction is based on the consumption and ownership of 'things' rather than on relationships. On-screen activities are replacing conversation and affecting relationships, even among siblings. Many families spend family time watching one screen or another instead of engaging in face-to-face conversation. As a result of more working parents and fewer parents at home with their children, there is less conversation taking place between the parent and child on a one-on-one basis, as well as less spontaneous interaction. Much day-to-day living is scheduled to fit in with the demands of work.
Children have a driving need to feel that they belong. This is natural for all human beings. If children don't feel this sense of belonging within the family, they will look for it elsewhere.	This fundamental human need is being exploited by marketers and brands selling the latest in 'cool'. If you don't have it, you can't or won't belong! Owning or wearing the right 'things' now defines who you are and whether or not you fit in. Of course, what's considered cool changes daily, forcing children into a cycle of conspicuous consumption. This also forces children into wanting to be 'the same' as everyone else instead of being unique individuals. Our jam-packed schedules are threatening time spent together as a family and can impact on a child's sense of belonging.

A CHILD'S DEVELOPMENTAL NEEDS	HOW THE WORLD IS INTERFERING
Children need to develop and own a healthy set of values. In a world of continuous, disruptive change, these will be their anchor and guide. Sound values help us to feel more secure in the world. They assist us when we have to make decisions or take action, even in the sandpit. Values are caught and not taught. They are demonstrated through our words and actions and it is, therefore, essential that we be consistent in this regard. Children will do what we do and not what we say. Children need a set of values against which to measure other value offerings.	Will children get their values from their parents or peers, as in the 'old days'? Or will the brash, noisy marketers, brands and media win their hearts and minds first? Some values being conveyed to our kids through various media include: • Adults suck, kids rule. • Don't worry about anyone else's feelings, just look after yourself. • Win at all costs. Yet children are also hearing the opposite – and sometimes from the same channels, such as: • Because every minute of every day you are a part of everybody. They must find this rather confusing – and who should they believe?
Children need to feel safe and secure in order to access their learning potential. They need to be calm and have a steady heartbeat for optimum learning to take place. Children need information to be presented to them in many different ways to appeal to their different intelligences and learning styles in order to encourage and activate learning rather than inhibit or stifle it.	Constant exposure to inappropriate content via news programmes, reality TV, kids' programmes and on-screen games do not lead to feelings of safety and security. When a child is stressed for any reason, his or her heartbeat increases, which can affect the workings of the brain. Even fast music or computer-game soundtracks that play above the heart tempo of 80 beats per minute will affect a child's brain. At this point, the thinking brain shuts down and all input goes into the emotional brain (limbic system), where the child's values, culture and beliefs sit. The child is now totally open to suggestion without any protection.

A CHILD'S DEVELOPMENTAL NEEDS	HOW THE WORLD IS INTERFERING
Children need boundaries. Of course, this does not mean living in a straitjacket. But it does mean that establishing a regular routine (boundaries or rules by which we live) provides a certain amount of predictability, which can bring sanity into your household.

Routine provides a feeling of safety and security for children, which is an optimum environment for learning. Routine does not mean inflexibility. Within routine there is plenty of flexibility and room for creativity.

Children need to know that this is what we do, when we do it, how we do it, what is expected of them and what is expected of us. Routine provides this reliability. | With so much on offer today, parents need to be consistent in the boundaries that they set for their children. Where possible, choices for goods and services should be based on children's developmental needs and the family's values. Parents must learn to overcome pester power.

Children thrive on routine from the earliest of days. This does not mean inflexibility. In fact, it means quite the opposite. With parents being so busy and overscheduled themselves, routine is often overlooked or sacrificed for convenience. |
| Children need their parents and they need their time. The importance of parental input cannot be overemphasised. Children need as much time and attention as we can give them, and preferably in a way that they recognise as loving and supportive. It's not about quality time or quantity time — it's about both! | Due to economic factors and changing family structures, we are not giving children the time or attention that they need. Yet parents are the facilitators of their children's lives and play a pivotal role. As far as possible, therefore, they need to be present and accessible in the limited time that they do have available.

Parents fill a leadership role. When they are absent, children will step into the gap and take control. There is never a leadership vacuum. |

THE DIFFERENCE BETWEEN PRESCHOOL AND PRIMARY-SCHOOL YEARS

In a nutshell, from a learning or cognitive development point of view, the preschool years lay the foundations for the perceptual skills required to learn to read, and the primary-school years are about reading to learn. If you can read, you can learn anything. It is a gift for life.

From an emotional and social point of view, the preschool years are about socialising children so that they can get used to being part of a group and get along with others. In the primary-school years, they can stretch their wings and build conscious friendships, for example, by choosing to befriend a specific child. They can also participate in activities of their choice, whether sporting or cultural or both, and in this way learn what they like or dislike, and what they are good at or not good at.

During the children's early years, teachers and parents are able to observe them at both work and play, and in this way can pick up clues about their specific learning style and in which of the multiple intelligences their strength lies.

LEARNING STYLES

By the time your child is ready for primary school, you may have a good idea of his or her natural intelligences and preferred learning style. Do you have a visual, auditory or kinaesthetic learner on your hands? Is your child more left- or right-brain dominant? Is your child logical and orderly, or creative and imaginative, or a daydreamer? What's your child's concentration like? Is he or she outgoing or reserved?

For more detailed and helpful information in this regard, you can have your child's dominance profile tested. It's a quick process that does not require your child to draw or write anything, but it will give you valuable insight into how he or she absorbs, processes and uses information. The test can also provide you with excellent guidance about the type of education or school system that will best suit your child, as well as the most effective study methods – and much more.

Children are born with a predisposition to receive information in a certain way. They absorb information through their senses, and some senses will be stronger in some children than in others. A child's preferred sensory modality will determine his or her natural learning style – whether the child is a visual, auditory or kinaesthetic learner. The benefit of understanding your child's learning style is that it will help you, the parent, to present information to him or her in a more effective way. It will also assist you to both motivate and discipline your child appropriately. This understanding will enable you to protect and nurture the relationship you have with your child instead of becoming frustrated, exasperated or angry.

How children *receive* information about their environment and how the world works is actually more important than how their brains *process* it, because how they receive the information determines the quality of the information they have to process. On the next page are some guidelines to help you determine your child's natural learning style. Some of these clues will be obvious from babyhood, while others will only reveal themselves as your child moves into toddlerhood and early childhood. Some children are clearly strongly dominant in one sensory modality, while others may utilise a combination of modalities.

VISUAL LEARNERS

- As babies, visual children enjoy looking around them and often make noises when they see things of interest. They may also be quick to notice things that are out of place.
- Visual children need to see to learn. Simply telling them about something doesn't help as much as showing it to them. As long as visual input is provided, such as a picture, the information is likely to be absorbed.
- Visual children tend to look upwards, towards the ceiling, in a learning situation, which indicates that they are accessing the visual part of the brain.
- Visual learners benefit from sitting in front in class so that the chalkboard and teacher can be clearly seen.
- They also need to summarise their work in their own words.

KINAESTHETIC LEARNERS
- As babies, these children like contact – to be touched and carried around. They also enjoy movement (being rocked, going for a walk in a stroller, etc.).
- In a learning situation, the eye movements of kinaesthetic children tend to travel downwards, towards the heart and hands.
- Kinaesthetic children need to touch, feel and experience. Learning is hampered if there is no physical involvement, or no opportunity for movement, or no triggering of their emotions.

AUDITORY LEARNERS
- As babies, auditory children love making sounds, and start 'talking' earlier than others. They also like musical mobiles.
- Auditory children's eye movements tend to travel towards the ears in a learning situation.
- When auditory learners are told about something, they listen and learn well. They love being asked questions about the tasks they are busy with.
- Auditory learners like to listen first and then to discuss the issue afterwards.

A good teacher will present the same information in all three ways in a single lesson in order to capture the attention of every different learning style represented in the class. When executed effectively, this is one of the benefits of true outcomes-based education.

If information is attractive to your child's learning style, learning becomes fun, and your child will have a better chance of grasping new information, as well as understanding, storing and being able to retrieve it for later use. In other words, if you present information to children in their preferred way of learning, it is more meaningful to them. When information has meaning, it is easier for the working memory to grasp and work with it. In turn, it becomes easier to store the information in the long-term memory.

Having said that, we must do our best as parents to develop children who are whole-brain learners. We should accept their learning strength when, and if, we have been able to identify it; however, we should also ensure that they continue to develop all of their learning styles. Focus on the one they're best at, but continue to push to develop the others at the same time. Remember our triangle analogy – the broader and deeper the base, the stronger and taller the structures are that can be built on it.

SCHOOL READINESS

Before we know it, the small children who entered our worlds, made us parents and changed us so much are ready to step into the world of formal education. We enter into partnerships with other people who get to shape our children's lives over a period of 12 years or more. Education is one of the most important things we will do for – and with – our children.

THE SCHOOL-READINESS JOURNEY

We wait with great anticipation for the day our children are able to read and write. But we don't often appreciate the really important stuff – that the foundations for all these sophisticated tasks, including reading, writing, maths and spelling, are laid down long before your child even enters primary school! This happens in ways that are seemingly unrelated, such as playing shape- or colour-matching games, building puzzles, threading beads, stacking blocks, catching balls, playing imaginary games and climbing trees.

In fact, play is one of the most effective vehicles for early learning. Play is the language of childhood – it is how children learn in a fun, incidental and stress-free way, as opposed to abstract, worksheet-based systems that are more appropriate from primary school onwards. Young children need plenty of exposure to concrete learning apparatus (toys and games), movement and outdoor equipment (such as jungle gyms, scooters and sandpits), and creative opportunities (drawing and painting on large sheets of paper). In addition, they need to socialise with other children as well as adults, while also spending time alone.

School readiness is a journey that starts from birth and takes seven years. It is a process that cannot be completed the year before a child enters formal education. A school-ready child should be able to cope socially, emotionally, physically and perceptually in a formal learning situation. To be 'school ready' implies that a child has reached a certain stage in his or her development, where it is felt that benefit will be gained from formal education.

However, a child does not become school ready alone. The child needs to be prepared for the first day at school – a highly memorable day in his or her life. Children need to build a mental bridge to enable them to move from life in the world they know to the greater environment of the 'outside world' with its emotional, social, normative, physical and intellectual demands.

A child's ability to learn easily and efficiently is influenced by early childhood experiences, such as the degree of bonding with a primary caregiver, physical or emotional traumas (in utero experiences will also have an effect), overall physical health, nutrition, socio-economic factors, the achievement of developmental milestones, sleeping patterns, and much more. A child's maturity will also impact on his or her school readiness.

The foundation for academic success is laid during the preschool years. From birth to the age of six, the brain is at its most pliable.
- By the age of three, 70 per cent of the brain is physically developed.
- By the age of four, 50 per cent of adult intelligence is already employed.
- By the age of five, your child will have a speaking vocabulary of around 10 000 words – adults only commonly use about 20 000 words!

School-readiness testing is done at least once, to ensure that your child is ready for school; either before entering Grade R or Reception, or Grade 1. If children are not emotionally or academically ready, being kept back at this stage can be beneficial for the child's long-term development, but each case is judged on its own merit.

Veteran preschool educator Martie Pieterse says that unique demands are placed on children when they start 'big' school for the first time, including being able to:
- be away from their family and home
- communicate with and relate to strangers
- hold their own in a group and assert themselves

- handle conflict and criticism
- switch from spontaneous and informal play to a more formal way of learning and working
- work without being continuously praised
- work on their own
- work quietly and calmly
- express their needs in words
- use basic language and writing skills in order to learn to read, write and draw
- concentrate on and complete tasks.

From the above list, it is obvious that the role of parents and teachers in a child's development should not be underestimated.

> 'Remember, even if your child has all the necessary physical skills in all the areas of development, but still does not have the inner skills such as independence, perseverance, resilience, the ability to concentrate on a set task, endurance, self-discipline and daring, she is like a brand-new car without an engine.'
> Martie Pieterse, *School Readiness Through Play*, 2001

During the foundation phase, children will acquire and develop a large array of perceptual skills through their interaction with people and the world, their play experiences, and their early childhood education programmes. Perception is about becoming aware via one's senses, which convey messages to the brain, which in turn then interprets these messages. It is how babies and young children learn.

The child's perceptual skills are acquired through experimentation, self-discovery and personal experience – by learning through play as opposed to being taught or interacting with a flat screen. Each child will acquire these many foundational skills in their own time, but they will follow a general, age-appropriate developmental timetable. Play is the rocket fuel of brain development.

According to the American Academy of Paediatrics in *The Value of Play Report 2018*, play leads to changes at the molecular, cellular and behavioural levels, promotes learning, our ability to adapt and problem-solve, and drives our social skills and positive behaviours.

Once again, let us remind you that children learn all perceptual skills by doing, through real experiences with the world, and with concrete apparatus such as games and toys, long before they shift to abstract letters, symbols and numbers. While there is an enormous amount of educational content available on the internet, on devices and in app stores, please ensure that your child gets a three-dimentional, multisensory experience of the world first and foremost.

> 'The time available at home, in school and beyond is becoming scarce. The need for highly diarised childcare and extra-curricular after-school clubs has resulted in children's lives becoming increasingly organised, time-bound and task-focused. For many children around the world, play time has become a set of highly structured activities rather than an experience they have chosen and directed themselves. 47% of children's time is now focused on structured activities and 27% of children's free time is spent on unstructured play.'
> *The Value of Play Report 2018* by The Real Play Coalition

For your interest, here is a comprehensive list of perceptual skills that children start acquiring in the preschool years and perfect in primary school – they form the foundations for literacy and numeracy:

- **Auditory (hearing) perception:** The way in which the brain gives meaning to what the ears hear; vital for all forms of auditory learning.
- **Auditory discrimination:** The ability to hear and discriminate between differences in sound; vital for speech development and spelling.
- **Auditory memory:** The ability to remember what the ears have heard.
- **Body image:** The way in which a person perceives his or her body.
- **Body awareness:** The awareness of the body, its parts and how they function.

- **Classification:** The ability to group objects according to kind or class.
- **Discrimination:** The ability to recognise similarities and differences.
- **Eye-hand coordination:** The way in which the eyes work together (coordinate) with the hands and fingers; vital for sewing, threading, drawing, writing, etc.
- **Figure-ground perception:** The ability to isolate and focus on an object/figure that may be in the foreground or background of a composite picture; vital for reading, writing, spelling and mathematical ability.
- **Fine-motor coordination:** The ability to coordinate the movements of the small muscles of the body, namely eyes, hands, fingers, toes and tongue; vital for writing, speech, sewing, etc.
- **Form perception:** The ability to recognise and name shapes and forms.
- **Form constancy:** The ability to recognise a form or shape, regardless of size, angle, position or colour.
- **Gross-motor activities:** Activities involving large muscles of the body, such as the neck, back, buttocks, arms and legs.
- **Gross-motor coordination:** The coordinated movement of the large muscles of the body.
- **Gustatory (taste) perception:** The way in which the brain interprets messages received through the tongue.
- **Olfactory (smell) perception:** The way in which the brain interprets messages received through the nose.
- **One-to-one correspondence:** The ability to match similar objects or groups to one another.
- **Phonics:** The sounds of the letters of the alphabet.
- **Spatial relationships:** The ability to recognise the position of two or more objects in relation to each other and the observer, e.g. above, below, next to, left and right; closely related to laterality (awareness of left and right), directionality and language.
- **Tactile (touch) perception:** The way in which the brain gives meaning to the messages received through the sense of touch.
- **Visual (sight) perception:** The way in which the brain gives meaning to what the eyes observe; vital for all forms of visual learning.
- **Visual discrimination:** The ability to recognise similarities and differences by sight; vital for reading, writing, spelling and mathematics.

- **Visual memory:** The ability to remember what the eyes have seen.
- **Visual sequencing:** The ability to arrange objects, symbols, words or numbers in a logical order.
- **Visual seriation:** The ability to place objects or thoughts in an orderly series, e.g. from most to least, small to large, lightest to heaviest, darkest to lightest; essential for mathematics.

Source: Adapted from *Bridging with a Smile* by Doreen Maree and Margot Ford, 1995.

THE RISK AND PROMISE OF TECHNOLOGY IN THE EARLY YEARS

The world is going digital. Along with our children, we are surrounded by more and more screens every day, which can both be incredibly useful and very distracting. While it's becoming ever easier to default to a screen due to convenience, choice and speed, there is both a risk and a promise inherent in technology that is particularly important to understand in the context of early childhood development.

Nikki and tech guru Arthur Goldstuck have written an entire book on this topic, called *Tech-Savvy Parenting* (2014), which is a must-read. We don't want to take up a lot of space going into the ins and outs of tech and kids, so here are some brief pointers to consider if you have children in preschool and primary school, taken from Nikki's 'What the BEEPP?' checklist. These pointers can help you to test whether or not you are overusing tech/on-screen devices with your children. Here is the acronym explained:

- B   Babysitter
- E   Emotional crutch
- E   Experience thief
- P   Pacifier
- P   Prompt

DEVICES AS BABYSITTERS

How often do you use technology to babysit your child so that you are free to do other things? Young children need and want you in their lives. When you are absent, even though they are occupied, there is an emotional void that a screen cannot fill. Do you see me? Do you hear me? Am I important to you? These are three questions they ask of you, non-verbally, every day. When sidelined to a device too often, they are not getting 'yes' answers to those questions. They might assuage their pain with a device, but it's no substitute for you!

DEVICES AS AN EMOTIONAL CRUTCH

Is technology or a screen being used as an emotional crutch to put your child to sleep or to get them to eat? Many parents report that their children can do neither without the aid of a screen or device. This means that they are not developing the self-regulation skills and self-discipline for the basics in life. If they cannot fall asleep without the aid of a digital tablet now, imagine what kind of tablet they may need in the future!

DEVICES AS EXPERIENCE THIEVES

Is technology an experience thief, stealing or displacing real-life experiences that are essential for your child's development? What is technology displacing, keeping in mind that young children learn best through concrete learning experiences with real people, real toys in real time, in order to provide them with multisensory experiences of the world? Tech has so much to offer – just make sure you create solid foundations first.

DEVICES AS PACIFIERS

Do you use a screen to pacify an upset child? While it most certainly will shut a child up, it also shuts them down, and then they don't get to experience and reconcile their emotional world. You do not want an emotionally stunted child, so beware of how you use devices to manage your child.

DEVICES AS PROMPTS

Is your child reliant on technology to prompt them on what to do next? Children are losing their initiative and creativity because they are becoming so used to being instructed by an adult or a program on a device. Help your child to develop their own initiative versus being helpless, which is something teachers today are increasingly witnessing in classrooms around the world. Showing initiative will help them to get a good job one day.

Looking at the above, it stands to reason that we need to take a balanced approach when introducing technology to our children. How much, what content and what type of tech they use will help shape them, at least to some degree. We need to determine the usage and ensure that it works to their benefit. Having said that, technology is not all bad and it definitely has a place in your child's development. In fact, children are finding increasingly innovative ways to play by combining their virtual/digital and physical play experiences. Making creations out of play dough, scanning pics of them into a game via an app and making them come alive in a virtual world is a perfect case in point of a multisensory and creative play activity being extended into the digital realm.

> In our respective families, we have had a common, invitational approach to our children's use of technology (TV, smartphones and gaming), while also providing boundaries by following these simple principles from early on:
> - Technology is not just another toy.
> - You have to ask permission.
> - We will limit your screen time.
> - You must be able to put it away (to avoid addiction caused by the dopamine rush).
>
> By the way, applying these rules becomes more difficult when you, as the adult, have to limit your own usage! Remember, you are the role model.

The rule of thumb for preschoolers is to limit their total on-screen time to no more than one hour a day. For primary-school children, that becomes approximately two hours a day. The question you need to ask yourself is, 'What else is my child doing to balance out their screen time? Are they having sufficient multisensory interactions with games, toys, children and adults?'

The regular lament from Grade R and Grade 1 teachers is that children enter school being able to do a 100-piece puzzle on an iPad but battle to complete a real 24-piece puzzle, as they don't have the spatial planning skills, or the ability to concentrate, persevere and finish the job.

In addition to the gift of learning how to read, learning how to pay voluntary attention to the task at hand and not being distracted by the lure of a screen is a very, very important skill to develop. Do not confuse your child's engagement with an on-screen activity with their actual ability to concentrate in real life. On-screen activities are designed to hold a child's attention via the constantly changing sounds and images and the varying speeds at which a game is played. Children also get addicted to the rush of constantly moving up a level, which gives them impetus to play more and keep going. This dopamine rush hits the pleasure centre of the brain, whether they are working through the levels of Reading Eggs or Mathletics, or playing a game of Fortnite or the latest version of SIMS or FIFA, for example.

The other thing to ensure is that you teach them to become healthy switchers. Can they easily switch from being involved with something on a screen to having a decent face-to-face conversation at the dinner table, where they make eye contact and show interest in other people? Do they realise that they get love and affection from human beings and not devices?

Devices certainly engage children of any age and keep them excited and focused, but children can never get enough of them, or feel fully satisfied by them, partly because of the pressure to keep going up a level, and partly because technology cannot fulfil their emotional needs in the same way a human being can. They are always left wanting more.

> Graeme's youngest daughter, Rebecca, has autism. She is verbal, but by age 13 has not yet learnt to read or write. Fairly typical of autistic people, she has difficulty reading social cues, facial expressions and body language. Graeme discovered a number of apps specifically designed to help Rebecca learn these social skills. In fact, one of the world's leading app developers for kids' games, Toca Boca, initially started by focusing on autistic

children and their needs, and then expanded their gaming repertoire to neurotypical children.

The games are designed to teach social skills through repetition and reinforcement, and Rebecca has found them both stimulating and extremely useful in her development. Technology certainly has its place in our children's development, but, in the end, they still need lots of time with their parents and with other people to analyse, apply and fully understand what the apps have taught them.

Having said that, if you do have a child with learning disabilities, technology can be incredibly useful in teaching skills and providing interaction with the world in constructive ways that were not previously available.

HAPPINESS AND FACE-TO-FACE TIME ARE CONNECTED

We are raising a generation of children who are suffering from the highest incidence of depression and anxiety in history. They do not have a sense of belonging and togetherness. While they are the most connected generation, they are also the loneliest. There are also links between feeling lonely and feeling irrelevant or invisible. Our children ask us three non-verbal and subconscious questions every day, to which they require a yes, yes, yes answer:

- Do you see me?
- Do you hear me?
- Am I important to you?

If there is a 'no' to a question on this list – because we are busy, unfocused, inattentive or out of touch with our children – they often resort to negative attention-seeking behaviour. A 10-year-old girl told us that when she feels invisible to her parents, she cries to get their attention, and it works. A 13-year-old boy said that he gets cheeky and then gets into trouble. Negative attention is better than none at all for a child. Freezing out a child is the worst form of punishment or torture you can inflict as a parent, and it can have destructive results.

One of the quickest ways to raise your child's happiness quotient, however, is to have face-to-face time with them. Engaging with them through play is also an amazing tool, because play is the language of childhood. It breaks down barriers between parent and child, and provides opportunities for sharing, teaching and learning while building emotional bridges. Play is a master love language; it is an act of service, of quality time spent with your child and a gift of your time. You get to use words of affirmation and encouragement and even physical touch (depending on whether you are having a physical play experience, such as having them do somersaults through your arms, or giving them an encouraging high five for trying hard or doing well).

According to the LEGO® Group's *Play Well Report 2018*: 'Play helps us learn, prepares us for the future, makes us happy, builds families and allows us to unwind.' *The Value of Play Report 2018* by The Real Play Coalition talks about low-play lives and play-poverty, which is happening across all socio-economic groups.

Nikki has been involved in educating parents and teachers about the power of play for over two decades. Over the years, she has observed that young children from disadvantaged backgrounds are rarely exposed to playing with basic wooden building blocks, despite all the learning benefits they offer. This, in turn, has a detrimental impact on the children's school readiness. The preliminary findings of *The Play Gap Report 2019*, based on an analysis of 40 countries, confirms her observation. The report indicates that, in some countries, children from disadvantaged backgrounds are more than 20 percentage points less likely to regularly play with blocks than children from socio-economically advantaged homes. This statistic also relates to the presence of books in children's lives and parents who read to their children, and also play with them.

Playing with blocks assists in acquiring language and early maths skills, helps with motor development, and promotes creativity, problem-solving and spatial awareness, among many other skills. Children need a wide variety of play patterns and a range of toys and games to support the depth and breadth of skills development. Neuroscience and childhood development experts around the world believe that in closing the 'play gap', a future skills gap can be avoided.

'[P]lay is increasingly under threat. Despite its vital importance in a person's early developmental journey, children's time and space for play is squeezed ... fewer play moments every day means fewer opportunities to develop the range of skills children need to strive in the dynamic, challenging economies of tomorrow.'
The Value of Play Report 2018 by The Real Play Coalition

FUTURE-PROOFING YOUR CHILDREN

While risks are inherent in life, parents can develop protective factors in their children to safeguard them. These fall into six broad categories, says psychologist David Verhaagen in his book, *Parenting the Millennial Generation* (2005): emotional, cognitive, academic, personality, social and family. Verhaagen's theory proves that parents have a greater role to play in their child's development today than at any other time in history, and that there is much they can do to help future-proof their children so that they can build a satisfying and successful life for themselves.

Verhaagen explains that the exciting thing about these protective factors is that most of them can be enhanced in some way: 'In fact, only two of the 21 – early temperament and high intelligence – are locked in. With the rest, the door is open ... if you increase the number of protective factors your child has, you will improve his chances of having a good life.'

Verhaagen advises that not all 21 protective factors should be tackled at once. Parents should work through the list, assess their child, and then select just three to five protective factors to focus on improving. These alone could make all the difference. It is a useful tool for parents that will enable them to assess their children's needs and take responsibility for their development.

Protective factors and their chance of improving

PROTECTIVE FACTOR	CHANCE OF IMPROVING			
	NONE	LOW	MEDIUM	HIGH
Easy temperament (easy, outgoing, curious)	X			
An average or higher intelligence	X			
A likeable personality		X		
Positive and supportive friends			X	
Talks about feelings openly and honestly			X	
Cares about the feelings of others			X	
Feels bad after doing something wrong			X	
A good sense of humour			X	
Believes good choices lead to good results			X	
A good overall student			X	
A strong interest in school			X	
Attends an excellent school			X	
Reads at or above grade level			X	
Feels a strong connection to family				X
A warm and positive relationship with parents				X
Good social skills				X
Enjoys support from members of the same religious faith				X
Involved in at least one positive group activity				X
A strong ability to cope with stress				X
Comes up with solutions to problems in life				X
Positive and realistic goals for the future				X

Source: Adapted from *Parenting the Millennial Generation* by David Verhaagen, 2005.

GIVE THEM TIME

All children have a natural developmental timetable, as we have already discussed. However, often this timetable does not match the hectic pace of their parents' lives. Do you ever feel that your child operates at a totally different pace to you, or that your child has absolutely no concept of time? How often do you find yourself using the words 'Hurry up!' or 'Quickly now!' when talking to your children?

With technological advancements and constantly improving connectivity, it is a fact that we are doing more in less time. Productivity has increased and we are busier than ever before. While technology has saved us time, it can also be said that it has stolen our time. Few of us are using our 'extra time' to meditate on a mountain top, or to play a game with our child, or to read one more bedtime story. No, no. The action list beckons. The more ticks on that list at the end of the day, the better we feel about ourselves. *The List* is often more important than precious moments of quality connection with our loved ones.

Children need time to learn, and they learn a great deal by doing things by themselves and for themselves. As parents, we need to be aware of adding in an extra 5 or 10 minutes here and there to allow for the development of our young child's independence, such as mastering how to do up a seatbelt in the car, to unlock a door with a key, or to cook a meal. Our children need to know that we believe they are capable.

What about creating time and space for special moments of quality connection to happen?

> Nikki distinctly remembers being in such a rush to get to playgroup and not be late for a meeting one morning that she nearly missed such a moment.
>
> Ryan, then three, had wandered away from the car while she was packing the boot and had picked a spring flower from the garden to give to her. She was about to tell him to hurry up when she saw the joy radiating from his face as he ran towards her with his gift. It was one of those 'magical mommy moments' that she will always remember.

> One of the gifts that autism has given to Graeme and their family is that they've learnt that Rebecca needs structure, certainty and consistency in her life. This means that Graeme has to carefully think through what impact certain activities may have on Rebecca. Their family has had to slow things down, prepare Rebecca mentally for what is to come, and be intentional about managing what might happen. Doing this has actually been good for everyone in the family. They are all more mindful of how they engage with the world.

Older children love talking in the dark. Just as you've tucked them in and kissed them goodnight and are heading purposefully towards the door to do some chores or work that you didn't have time for during the day, you hear 'Moooom …' Many fortunate parents have enjoyed some of the deepest and most extraordinary conversations with their children in the dark at bedtime. The warmth of bed and the comforting veil of darkness seem to encourage children to talk and share – if you make yourself available to listen.

We must try not to deprive our children of alone-time, when they are not being rushed from one organised activity to the next – time when they can simply potter around at home in a quiet space, contemplating life. Children, too, need downtime to allow them to assimilate all that they have learnt during the day. Just like an adult, they need to just 'be' – to take a break from the constant state of 'doing'.

And for our children to enjoy this luxury from time to time, we need to role-model it for them. Pottering and pondering is a key healthy habit to cultivate. CEOs of highly innovative companies take planned sabbaticals to do just this, and they say that the level of innovation and freshness in their organisations is a direct result of them 'taking time out'.

American psychiatrist Robert Shaw, a veteran with 40 years of experience in treating children and their families, states that parents are so caught up in the time-pressure 'epidemic' that they think they are doing their children a favour by filling their days with numerous extramurals to ensure that they don't 'miss out'. The values of downtime and relaxation have been negated in the pursuit of 'smarter, more socially adept and superior children'.

An even more serious consequence of pressure on children is highlighted by Shaw's fellow psychiatrists:

> 'The pressures placed on many children, while undoubtedly inculcating a constricting discipline in a child's life, probably have the unintended effect of delaying a child's finding herself and succeeding on her own terms.'
> Robert Shaw, *The Epidemic: The Rot of American Culture, Absentee Parents and Permissive Parenting, and the Resultant Plague of Joyless, Selfish Children*, 2003

MAKE THE TIME

Whether you work full time, half-day, are self-employed or have chosen to be a stay-at-home parent, there is no doubt that all parents are busy and time stands still for no one. The gap between our pace of life and that of our children seems to be continually widening. This means that we all need to be more conscious of making time to really focus on them, and to leave the outside world behind for a short while so that they don't feel caught up in our generally rushed and harried lives. It is so easy to become impatient if you cannot see and appreciate the miracle of a child's development, or how the presence of your children is so much a part of your own personal development.

Ellen Galinsky, the author of the *Ask the Children Study* (2000) on working and parenting, found that 40 per cent of children say that the time spent with their mothers and fathers is rushed. When children have less rushed time at home, they usually see their parents in a more positive light. They equate parent effectiveness with the amount of time they spend with their parents. Research shows that children want more time in which to interact informally with their parents via play and shared tasks.

A study by Dr Virginia Lewis of the Australian Institute of Family Studies shows that approximately two-thirds of children think that their parents work about the right amount of time, despite the fact that two-thirds of parents in the same study want to spend more time with their children.

The children in this study would like their parents to be available to them, but were more concerned with the *nature* rather than the frequency of the interactions. Children would certainly like their parents to spend more time with them, but they want them to be less stressed and less tired.

We need to find creative ways to connect with our children, no matter what our work scenario is, so that we touch them emotionally and stimulate them developmentally, even when we are on the run. In this way, we can banish the guilt that so often plagues us and robs us of the joys of parenting.

When we feel out of control, our response is to go into hyper-control, resulting in more and more helicopter and lawnmower parenting. These are terms coined to describe parents who hover over their children like helicopters, ready to swoop in at a moment's notice, or who go ahead of their children, cutting a clear, smooth path for them like lawnmowers through thick grass. Both these analogies describe parents who won't let their children experience failure, difficulty, disappointment or loss. This is precisely what we need to avoid if we want future-fit children.

Rather, we need to replace comfort with engagement, and fear with curiosity. Be curious about your evolving child and be curious about the world that is evolving around you. The future is arriving and changing, whether you like it or not. You might as well step into the flow and go with it. And don't feel the need to protect yourself or your children from learning opportunities that come their way every day; allow them to experience some of the stresses, disappointments and struggles of life.

We think it's time to reframe how we think about our children and start seeing them as the architects and storytellers of their own lives. We are the custodians and facilitators of this process. And who says we are always right? Do children not provide us with an opportunity to reassess what we think, believe and feel about life and how the world works? Do they not teach us valuable lessons about ourselves and how we are in the world?

Honouring the child and their capacity for learning and self-discovery is not about giving them carte blanche and no boundaries, but it is about helping them believe that they truly do matter, that the universe is all the richer for their presence, and that you are watching in wonder and awe at what they will do with their potential.

We have a responsibility to dig deep in the early years to help our children to develop solid, strong foundations – not just to help their school readiness and skills competency as they move through the education system, but also to ensure that they acquire appropriate mindsets, that learning has meaning for them and that we pass on the baton of responsibility of everyday life skills.

HELP YOUR CHILD DEVELOP POSSIBILITY THINKING

> 'The way you see yourself influences the way you see the world and the way you live. The way you see your qualities and abilities influences your actions and thoughts. It affects the way you approach life and what becomes of it.'
> Carol S. Dweck, *Mindset: The New Psychology of Success*, 2007

To end this chapter, and to prepare you for the eye-opening next chapter, in which we discuss the changing world of work that our children will experience, we believe it is imperative for parents to help their children develop their overall attitude towards themselves, and life in general.

As children grow and develop, as parents we constantly give them cues that we believe in them, usually via encouragement and praise. But here's the catch: *they* have to prove to *themselves* that they have abilities before they can start to believe in themselves on a deeper level, with self-knowledge and inner confidence. Children learn how to do things by actually practising how to do them, and the same process applies to learning to trust and believe in themselves.

There are plentiful challenges and little rites of passage that build the foundations for a child's 'I can' mindset. Many of these may seem innocuous to you, but don't be fooled – for your child, they are often powerful events or moments and can influence how they think about themselves and how they operate in the world. Consider these events:

- Mastering sitting, crawling, standing and walking as a baby and toddler.
- Learning to ride a scooter, then a trike, followed by a bike.

- Starting and settling in in preschool, primary and high school.
- Learning how to swim, hit or kick a ball – confidence is built gradually during practice sessions.
- Getting their pen licence (some schools present these when children graduate from using a pencil to using a pen).
- Doing chores, such as feeding the dog, emptying the dishwasher and learning to make their own bed.
- Learning how to make a sandwich or a cup of tea.
- Making friends and being included in groups.
- Making it into a team – either a cultural or sports team.
- Learning new games, from playing cards to dice or board games; whether the child wins or loses, they learn: 'I can.'
- Getting a learner's and then a driver's licence.

Children need countless opportunities to prove themselves to themselves. These are the layers of self-belief and self-confidence that are created by overcoming challenges and mastering skills on a daily basis. They need to inch their way up the 'I can' ladder by doing seemingly ordinary things over and over again.

> When Nikki's six-year-old nephew went on holiday with Nikki's family, without his parents, he learnt to make his bed by himself for the first time. When he saw his mom a week later, he beamed at her and, before he even greeted her, said, 'Mommy, guess what? I know how to make my bed!' It was a big deal. Being able to make his own bed was hot news – he could do it *by himself for himself* like a big boy.

You don't have to spend a lot of money on extramural activities for your child to build his or her self-belief, nor do you have to constantly tell them they're a superstar. Your child just quietly and regularly needs to *feel* a sense of mastery over life, at whatever stage they happen to be in at the time. This will entrench their 'I can' thinking into their DNA and help them to develop a growth mindset.

Let's get something straight in the early stages of your parenting journey: success is not a birthright, it's optional. It depends on whether or not we take the time to nurture a winning mindset in our child. Talent alone is not what makes great minds, first-class athletes or top performers in any discipline. Highly successful people have the ability to take the potential their basic qualities afford them and apply effort, persistence and self-discipline in order to improve themselves, even at the risk of failure.

Says Malcolm Gladwell in his well-known book *Outliers: The Story of Success* (2008): '[T]he closer psychologists look at the careers of the gifted, the smaller the role innate talent seems to play and the bigger the role preparation seems to play.' He believes that practice isn't what you do once you're good, it's what makes you good, whether you are Mozart, The Beatles, Bill Gates, grand chessmaster Bobby Fischer or a top Canadian ice-hockey player. The common denominator he uncovers is that before these people 'made it' or became world-class experts, they had all amassed 10 000 hours of practice over many years. Now that's a *lot* of repetition!

This is not necessarily brand-new thinking. Good educators, therapists, parents and employers have actually known this for years, and neuroscience is increasingly proving it. We know that the brain is adaptable and can continue learning well into old age. As long as you practise something often enough – a minimum of 200 to 300 times – you can create a new memory cell (an engram).

But, practise is not the only important thing. One's attitude and habits are also essential to success, as described in the concept of a fixed versus growth mindset, popularised by Carol S. Dweck in her bestselling book *Mindset: The New Psychology of Success* (2007), in which she describes how to nurture a winning mindset. Dweck makes it clear that parents, teachers and coaches pass on either a fixed or a growth mindset to children in the way that they frame success and setbacks.

Dweck says that to nurture a growth mindset, we need to tie success to effort – to doing good. We spend so much time telling our kids to be good, or doing things for them that they could do for themselves, that we often don't focus enough on their journey, on the *doing* – specifically doing things for themselves. Very importantly, we also need to reframe failure as a learning opportunity. You can find a comprehensive list of characteristics for fixed and growth mindset online via our website: www.fpyc2020.com.

In our opinion, fixed-mindset people believe that they are born with fixed abilities and traits that cannot be changed or improved. They often experience limited success, because they make little effort to develop themselves and tend to speak more than they act. They are very likely to brush off failure or place the blame on others. If they don't believe they will succeed, they sometimes don't even try at all. Their own fear and limiting beliefs end up stymying them.

Growth-mindset people, on the other hand, are action-orientated and take responsibility for their own successes (and failures). They are prepared to try and try again. They have 'opportunity eyes' and 'possibility thinking'. They are committed to their own growth and to continuous learning. Effort and change are comfortable bedfellows when it comes to success. Living with constant flux and change is stressful, so it will be easier for your child to cope if he or she has a more flexible mindset. A growth mindset enables human beings to be more nimble and adaptable, something that bodes well for your child in the workplace of the future.

We all have elements of both mindsets, but we can learn to change limiting mindsets. This requires doing and practise, not just thinking. It means that our children need to *do, do, do* to hardwire a growth mindset, as this will determine how they'll cope with failure and pursue success.

Choose a growth mindset for your child to enable them to thrive, not just to survive, in the 21st century, so that they can embrace all that is, all that they are, and all that they are in the process of becoming. To do that, you as a parent need to challenge and analyse your own mindset – you may need to make some mindset shifts yourself! Are *you* up for the growth challenge? Who are you in the process of becoming, and how will this, in turn, shape your child?

Successful people habitually and instinctively reflect on their experiences, learning and growing as they go. You need to help your children do just that – all the way!

'While we believe we hold the power to raise our children, the reality is that our children hold the power to raise us into the parents they need us to become. For this reason, the parenting experience isn't one of the parent versus the child but of the parent with the child. The road to wholeness sits in our children's lap, and all we need do is take a seat. As our children show us our way back to our own essence, they become our greatest awakeners. If we fail to hold their hand and follow their lead as they usher us through the gateway of increased consciousness, we lose the chance to walk toward our own enlightenment.'
Shefali Tsabary, *The Conscious Parent*, 2014

Chapter 3

Trends that will change your child's future

'If each future is unique, if every reality is different, then predictions aren't the point of futuring in any event. Predictions, after all, are answers to questions about the future. It's the questions that count, and each of us has to answer them separately, according to our separate journey through the world. And according to the separate choices we make ... The role of the visionary [isn't] to be a seer but to be a provocateur: to present a series of visions of the future against which those who want to prepare for the future can react. Nobody, after all, knows what the future holds; or who can really know what frames of mind, what receptivities, what structures you need to have in place to meet whatever does eventually come down the pike? And no one is less ready for tomorrow than the person who holds the most rigid beliefs about what tomorrow will contain.'
Watts Wacker and Jim Taylor, *Visionary's Handbook: Nine Paradoxes that will Shape the Future of Your Business*, 2001

'There will be more change in the next 15 years than there has been in the last 50 years.'
Bill Gates, speech at the London School of Economics, 2015

Mommy, Daddy, what must I be when I grow up? This is the classic question your child will ask when they begin to develop a sense of the future. And it's never been more difficult for parents to answer than in the present.

As a parent, you don't need to have a perfect understanding of the future, but you do need to have a sense of the trends and forces that are going to shape your child's world and, of course, your own world.

While many aspects of your child's early development have not changed, he or she is going to enter a world of no guarantees: a good education will no longer guarantee you a place at a tertiary education institution, a university degree will no longer guarantee you a job or a career, and a job will no longer guarantee you a consistent income. In fact, 47 per cent of all jobs will be vulnerable to automation, according to the seminal paper on automation in the workplace published in 2013 by the Oxford Martin School at the University of Oxford ('The Future of Employment' by Carl Benedikt Frey and Michael Osborne, https://www.oxfordmartin.ox.ac.uk/downloads/academic/future-of-employment.pdf).

The scary statistic in the attention-grabbing headline freaked people out to such an extent that they didn't read any further, thus failing to find that the report also predicted that many new jobs, in the fields of automation, robots and algorithms, would be created instead. The key to future success was to not be stuck in a job that would eventually be automated, but rather to develop skills that could not easily be done by machines. Change leads to disruption, which leads to new possibilities. So let's stay optimistic and keep an open mind.

In the next section of this book, we take a peek at what the world might look like in the 2020s and beyond, so that we can get a feel for what kind of future our children should be prepared for. And it's really just a glimpse of what we see coming down the line. Our intent is not to try to impress or surprise you with bold and expansive predictions, but rather to try to tease out some of the real-world implications of trends we already see altering our world. We are also not doomsayers – we don't believe that robots will replace humans in the workplace entirely. To the contrary, we are excited by what we see in the future. In particular, we focus on the world of work, as helping our children prepare for a career that will enable them to become financially and physically independent of us is a key factor in parenting success.

To reinforce our message that the world of work is changing rapidly, and that as many jobs are being created as are disappearing at any given time, here's a fun list of **20 great jobs in 2019 that didn't exist 20 years ago:**

1. Chief sustainability officer – the first CSO appointed by a publicly listed company was by DuPont in 2004.
2. Mobile app developer (the App Store was only launched in 2008).
3. User-experience designer (this is Sir Jony Ives, the third most important person at Apple's, job).
4. Content moderator for online platforms.
5. Professional podcaster or podcast producer.
6. Professional YouTuber, Instagram influencer or blogger. (Don't laugh – just look up what the top-10 YouTubers earn in revenue every year. In 2018, the channel Ryan ToysReview featured a seven-year-old boy reviewing toys. He earned $22 million that year.)
7. 3D printing technician or designer.
8. Uber, Lyft or Grab driver.
9. Airbnb host.
10. Drone pilot.
11. Home-produce sellers (using platforms like Amazon, Etsy and eBay to sell their wares).
12. Cloud architect (not in the sky, but for computers – we thought we'd better specify).
13. Virtual assistant.
14. Telemedicine physician.
15. Offshore wind-farm engineer.
16. Information/cyber-security analyst.
17. Data-protection officer.
18. Lean/agile consultant.
19. CrossFit coach.
20. Facebook, Google or Amazon developer.

(Okay, technically a few of these existed 20 years ago, but not anywhere near the present scale.)

In this chapter and the next, you should see a clear theme emerging from the picture we paint of the future: the 2020s will be filled with information, connection, globalisation and change. All of this will provide unprecedented opportunities for individuals, yet many may become overwhelmed by the scope of the change.

In response, we need to develop a strong sense of responsibility – not just to the planet and to each other, but to our own futures. For example, the technologies and trends that will shape our future can be used for either good or evil, and it's our responsibility to choose good over evil. The same is true of our life and career choices. The world we want to live in really is up to us – which is why we call it the Age of Possibility.

The problem, however, is that with so much change, it can feel as if we don't have any control over the rules that govern success or failure any more. We can't really cope with how quickly the world is changing.

Here are some alarming statistics that should make you take this section very seriously:

- In 2007 (when we wrote the first edition of this book), all the computers in the world combined had the processing capability (but not the speed) of a human brain. At the current pace of development, by 2025 a *single desktop computer* will have the same processing power as a human brain. By 2049, a $1 000 computer will exceed the computation capabilities of the entire human race!
- The amount of technical information in the world is doubling every six months. This means that for students studying a technical four-year degree, more than half of what they learn will be outdated by the end of their studies.
- By 2022, over 4 billion people will be connected to the internet. So will over 50 billion devices.
- Right now, there is a one-in-four chance that you have been in your current job for less than one year.
- At least half of the top-10 job opportunities for 2030 do not yet exist (see page 138 for a list of some of these).
- It is expected that today's learners will have more than 10 jobs before the age of 40, and a total of 17 in their careers (see, for example,

https://www.fya.org.au/wp-content/uploads/2017/07/FYA_TheNew-WorkSmarts_July2017.pdf for a 2017 report by the Foundation for Young Australians).
- At present, about 4 per cent of the world's population live and work outside their country of birth. By 2050, that number will have risen to 15 per cent.
- The fastest-growing job market in the world is that of freelancers; by 2030, half of all office workers will work on a freelance basis.
- In many industries and countries, the most in-demand occupations or specialties did not exist 10, or even 5, years ago (see the World Economic Forum's *Future of Jobs* report 2016 at http://www3.weforum.org/docs/WEF_Future_of_Jobs.pdf).
- Sixty-five per cent of children entering primary school today will end up in jobs that don't yet exist.
- Today's learners will not retire.
- And they will probably live to be well over 100 years old. In fact, half of all the people who have ever turned 80 are still alive.
- We have reached a point in human history where the problems we know about – from climate change and water shortages to pandemics and nuclear catastrophe – will either be solved in our children's lifetimes or will destroy our current way of life forever.

If you are sitting wide-eyed in your seat, then bear in mind that you can – and need – to take two important steps right now:
- Step 1: Understand the future (read and absorb this chapter).
- Step 2: Take action today (read and respond to the next two chapters).

THE BUILDING BLOCKS OF CHANGE AND GROWTH

Graeme's grandmother was born a few months before the start of World War I, in February 1914. Remarkably, she only passed away in December 2018, at the ripe old age of 104. If anyone had sat her down as a teenager in the 1920s and told her what the world would be like in the 21st century (and that she would be around to see it), she would have been incredulous.

Not only would the technologies have sounded fanciful, but the very nature of our lives and work would have been unbelievable to her.

Could she have imagined the nature and extent of international interactions, open-plan offices filled with diversity of every kind, the casual approach to dress and conversation, 24/7 operations, working mothers, smartphones, laptops, 24-hour news channels, online shopping (online *anything*, in fact), cheap airfares to anywhere, and a global mindset even her own grandchildren share? Would she have been able to imagine driverless cars, 3D printers, fitness trackers, nuclear fusion power, realistic talk of settling a Mars colony, and the possibility of genetically engineering her great-great-grandchildren? The list goes on and on. All of this was new in her lifetime. In fact, most of those are new in *our* lifetimes, too.

The amount of change Graeme's grandmother experienced in her century of life is almost nothing compared to what Graeme and Nikki's children have experienced in just the first two decades of their lives. And an even more remarkable decade lies ahead of us. The 2020s and 30s combined will see more change than all of the last century.

There is a very simple reason why we believe this to be true: society has spent the last few decades creating building blocks for change, and over the next two decades, those same building blocks will be changing the world as we know it. The science behind this thinking is called *complex adaptive systems*, but is more commonly understood by the phrase 'a tipping point'. When all of the pieces are ready, only then can they be combined to build the whole puzzle. That is when a tipping point occurs, and we rapidly enter a new era.

Let's bring this closer to home. Human beings are also complex adaptive systems. We can simplify this by describing how children master new skills in terms of the concept of together and apart. When children learn how to write, they generally acquire the new skill in disparate stages: first they practise the right grip for holding a crayon when they draw, and do threading and pegging activities to reinforce the neurological pathway for the pincer/tripod grip; then they start to draw shapes, and then different kinds of lines. Eventually they bring all of this together by learning to write specific letters and, eventually, complete words. There are so many different skills involved, all of which need to develop separately and are then integrated into one fluid movement.

Learning how to serve in a game of tennis is another classic example. A coach teaches a player how to serve in stages by focusing on different parts of the overall movement: first, learning how to accurately throw the ball up in the air; then the back swing. This is repeated over and over again. Then how to reach up to hit the ball, which is often practised against the tennis-court fence with no ball at all! Once the coach has introduced the corkscrew twist and foot movement, he or she brings it all together in a convergence of skills; all the different pieces of the puzzle now fit together. Seasoned players and tennis champions on TV make it look so easy, but that's because they've mastered the different parts and can do them all *at the same time.*

When we look back, we can see this in action with the emergence of the smartphone. In June 2007, Steve Jobs held up a small piece of glass on stage and announced the launch of the iPhone. But the world wasn't ready for it. In fact, in November 2007, *Fortune* magazine's cover article asked, 'Can anyone catch Nokia?' But even just one year later, it was clear that Nokia had faltered by sticking to keyboard-driven phones, and that smartphones were the future. Samsung entered the manufacturer fight, while Google launched an operating system called Android in 2008. By 2016, Nokia was basically dead, sold to Microsoft for a fraction of its former value.

The real point of this example, though, is why the smartphone emerged in 2007. Why not 2005? Or 2010? The answer is that four key technologies all converged at the same time: data storage, digital imaging, network capacity and lithium-ion batteries. In fact, if they had been concentrating, anyone could have built the smartphone in 2007. Nokia, BlackBerry and all the other established manufacturers had missed it. But Apple didn't – even though they weren't even a phone manufacturer at the time.

Today, we have a whole host of *converging technologies* that will form the basis of an accelerated, automated digital age. These include: the internet of things; continued improvements in data storage and communication, combined with data analytics, machine learning and quantum computing; autonomous transportation, robotics, virtual and augmented reality; a revolution in energy production that is clean and cheap, along with energy storage and distribution that reduces both cost and impact on the planet; biotechnology, genetic engineering, geo-engineering, as well as new wonder materials like graphene, along with new production methods that will fuel a global maker movement.

In fact, the list goes on and on: in every single field, industry and faculty, we are seeing remarkable breakthroughs every year, driven by our ability to use machines to help us learn and apply our knowledge.

We would recommend keeping an eye on three key groups of technologies, which could be the biggest building blocks of a new world:

1. **Renewable energy options** – as the price of alternative energy sources continues to plummet, the world will have access to better and cheaper energy sources, resulting in a significant shift away from fossil fuels.
2. **Synthetic biology** – our ability to both understand and manipulate our DNA and genetic code will unleash a new wave of medical breakthroughs.
3. **Computing-processing power** – significant leaps forward in this field, from quantum computing and neuromorphic chips to the software that will drive machine learning and AI algorithms, will allow us to learn how to work with machines to advance and apply knowledge in every area of human endeavour. (You can always google words you don't recognise, although we do expand on those we think you really need to understand!)

But what will the world be like when these technologies have shaped it? What can we tell our children today that, although it might seem fanciful and leave them (and us) incredulous, would nevertheless be helpful in preparing them for this yet unseen world? Let's look at a few key important implications of some of the major trends that will shape the future of work, as we try to answer these important questions.

MAJOR TRENDS IN THE FUTURE WORLD OF WORK

We wish we knew for certain what will happen in the future. We wish we could be completely confident about some of the predictions we make. The Hollywood producer and studio head Samuel Goldwyn once said: 'Never make forecasts, especially about the future.' He was probably right. Predictions are almost always wrong – either in their content or in their timing. For that reason, we are not planning on predicting specific events or activities.

Our focus will be on major trends and themes – some of which are already evident, and others which we believe will emerge within the next decade. As there is the risk of our grandchildren laughing at us if they should ever read this book in the future, we present an incomplete vision of what the world of work might look like in 2020 and beyond. Our intention is not to predict the future, but to assist this generation of parents *now* to help their children prepare for what possibly lies ahead for all of us.

We will also specifically not make predictions about future technologies – these will almost certainly turn out wrong, either in their scope or their timing. Although changing technologies are certainly key drivers of change, our interest is in how these technologies will drive change in the workplace. Later in this section, we'll speculate on some of the jobs that will be in hot demand by 2030. But our focus is not on the 'wow' effect of newly released technologies or conjectures about an unseen future. Rather, it's on what we need to know about the future to help our children today.

Far from trying to impress you with amazing facts and information about the future, we will instead point out the implications of some of the most powerful and obvious current trends in the hope that we'll get you thinking. And that that will convince you why it is so important to start future-proofing your children as soon as possible.

> 'Most people overestimate the effects of change in the short term, underestimate them in the long term, and fail to spot where change will be the greatest ... There will be evolution rather than revolution, and it will take years to work through.'
> Frances Cairncross, *The Company of the Future*, 2003

Whether you agree with our ideas or not, we hope that they will motivate you. You need to create some scenarios for the future, and to work out what these scenarios mean for you and your children *today*. Of one thing we are absolutely certain: the world of work that our children enter will be different from the world of work that we inhabit today. Let's take a look at the most important trends.

AUTOMATION, ROBOTS AND ARTIFICIAL INTELLIGENCE

> 'A widespread misconception is that AI systems, including advanced robotics and digital bots, will gradually replace humans in one industry after another … but what we've found in our research is that, although AI can be deployed to automate certain functions, the technology's greater power is in complementing and augmenting human capabilities … In essence, machines are doing what they do best: performing repetitive tasks, analyzing huge data sets, and handling routine cases. And humans are doing what they do best: resolving ambiguous information, exercising judgment in difficult cases, and dealing with dissatisfied customers. This [is an] emerging symbiosis between man and machine.'
> Paul R. Daugherty and H. James Wilson, *Human + Machine: Reimagining Work in the Age of AI*, 2018

In one of the most watched TED talks of all time, the economist Andrew McAfee talked about what future jobs will look like (see https://www.ted.com/talks/andrew_macafee_what_will_future_jobs_look_like). He correctly points out that 'just in the past few years our machines have started demonstrating skills they've never, ever had before: understanding, speaking, hearing, seeing, answering, writing, and they're still acquiring new skills. And they're still developing.' He goes on to say that robots will do many of the jobs we do now. But he then argues that this is the best news ever – and we agree with him.

Technological progress will help us to continue to increase output, with improvements in quality and volume, while decreasing prices. This is more than crass consumerism – it is how our world economic model works, and the improvements in productivity will fuel economic growth, create new jobs and stoke the flames of innovation around the world.

Even more importantly, when robots start doing our jobs, they'll be doing the jobs we don't want to do, which will free us from the drudgery of our working lives. This means that many of the jobs available today will not be available to our children – but many of the jobs available today are mindless, boring and soul-sapping. The jobs available to our children will require creativity, innovation and empathy.

We need to prepare ourselves and our children to work alongside the software and robots that will automate many tasks in the future. This automation is not restricted to manual labour or lower-level jobs; it will impact professionals, too.

It may take a complex system to replace them, but they are replaceable nonetheless, and here is an everyday example of this trend.

Let's look at doctors who work as general practitioners (GPs). They respond completely reactively to patients who walk into their consultation rooms. Their task is to apply a standard and fairly basic process of diagnosis. If they cannot do a simple diagnosis, they resort to blood tests. But they don't perform these blood tests – they send you to a separate company, where a different individual extracts a sample of your blood and sends it to a laboratory. There, a machine processes your sample and (if you're lucky) sends an electronic set of results to your doctor, who phones you and reads the diagnosis to you. Once a diagnosis is attained, the treatment is predetermined and not creative. (Who wants to be a doctor's guinea pig?) As soon as the technology becomes cheap enough to do self-diagnosis from home, the GP will basically become redundant. Like present-day accountants, the GP will probably still have a job for another decade or more owing to legislation around the scheduling of prescribed medicines. But that will be an artificial environment that cannot be sustained forever.

The 20th century was marked by the *automation of physical labour in factories*. This trend will continue, and even more labour-intensive work will be automated. But, even more importantly, the 21st century will be marked by the *automation of knowledge work* – utilising computerisation, thinking systems, artificial intelligence, webbots, and more. Jobs that depend on routines, or that follow a set of rules, or that can be reduced to an algorithm or 'recipe', will be replaced first.

First to go will be basic bookkeeping, basic research, computer programming and other, similar tasks, but it will quickly reach higher up the food chain, to accountants, quantity surveyors, registering attorneys, pilots and any other job that does not require creativity. (Remember, a creative accountant is one who should be behind bars!) These jobs used to be the pathway to a middle-class existence, but they will soon either be outsourced or automated.

DATA ANALYTICS AND DATA AS AN ASSET

One of the industries that will grow exponentially in the next few years is all the jobs related to dealing with data. Companies are beginning to recognise the value inherent in the data they own, and the data they are able to collect from their clients and customers. They will need data scientists, data detectives and data analysts to ensure that they gather the correct data, store it appropriately, and then extract valuable insights and information from it.

Although this includes the work of data administrators and security experts, it goes well beyond the 'nerds' who merely manage databases. The skills required will include the ability to make sense of huge data sets and to turn data into infographics that make it visually accessible, as well as the ability to analyse and interpret material creatively. This is a typical example of where art and science meet. These types of people are known as T-thinkers, and they will be in high demand. More about them in the chapter on schools.

INFORMATION INTEGRITY, TRUST, JOURNALISM AND 'FAKE NEWS'

In 2015/16, Donald Trump weaponised the concept of 'fake news' to undermine his critics and the American media during his campaign for the American presidency. We now know that many people around the world, including some directly funded by governments, deliberately generate false news stories and attempt to spread them via social media. The 2020s will see many different responses as journalists and ordinary people alike attempt to deal with this breakdown in trust. Our ability to confirm the veracity of information will be a growing industry in the 2020s. This means that our kids need to have strong reading and comprehension skills, as well as being critical thinkers, so that they are discerning when it comes to the information they access.

WORK-LIFE INTEGRATION

People are less and less willing to work themselves to the bone. They want to be able to work hard, but also to play hard and have time off as well. They are looking for a better quality of life, which entails work-life integration. We prefer this term to 'work-life balance' for two reasons.

First, we do not like the implication that work and life are opposites. Work is part of life, and our lives include work. Trying to create a separate box for our work experience is part of a mindset that today's young people want to move away from. Second, we do not believe that work-life balance is possible. On the one hand, balance means different things to different people. On the other hand, many people who think about work-life balance tend to think of it as an excuse for lazy staff members to be even lazier. This is *not* what the concept is about.

This new generation of talent will increasingly choose *more time* over *more money* as they strive to create meaningful lives. Time will become the new currency. In recent surveys, as many as a third of workers in the US said they would prefer more time off rather than more hours of paid employment.

A century ago, futurists were predicting the 'end of work'. A few decades ago, countries were experimenting with the 'three-day week'. We certainly do not predict this for the future. People will be working harder and for longer hours. But we believe they will demand more flexibility and more integration of their 'personal' issues into the work they need to do.

Most people make good use of workplace technologies to enhance interactions in their personal lives. The reverse of this will now also become more of a reality:
- If I answer emails on a Saturday night, can I go to the movies on a Tuesday morning?

- If I allow my smartphone to interrupt my family dinner time, will you allow me to let my family interrupt your executive-committee meeting time?
- If not, why not?

Children often present their parents with opportunities to make decisions about work-life integration that require a lot of soul-searching and introspection. They also give us reasons to break out of 'the system' and to make changes to our work-life integration that are more practical for the family unit. This will be different for each family.

> In 2012, before Graeme and Jane moved their family back to South Africa, Jane took a break from her career and studies to focus on homeschooling their three girls for four months while still in the UK. Their schooling included curriculum content, special, prearranged outings, and networking with people to facilitate both formal and informal educational outcomes. It was a short-term, very focused assignment for Jane, which she found challenging and hugely stimulating. Upon returning to South Africa, Jane then returned to formal employment.

> Going further back in time, when Nikki's eldest son, Ryan, was just three years old, she had had a particularly busy few months in her direct-selling job. Her team was doing very well, breaking sales targets each month, and Nikki was working towards earning an incentive trip to the idyllic tropical island of the Comores. The team was selling educational toys to parents as a means to educate them on the importance of playing with their children. Needless to say, Nikki was so busy working towards her goal that quality playtime with her own son diminished rapidly.
> One afternoon, when she was once again furiously multitasking – throwing a meal together in the kitchen, answering endless phone calls and completing countless orders – her son looked her straight in the eye and pronounced: 'Mommy, you so boring!' (Pronounced 'borwing'.) The truth

> cut Nikki to the core and, in that moment, she knew she was being called to make a very important decision, as much for Ryan's good as her own.
>
> Nikki spent the next four months considering her options. A threatened miscarriage of her second child cemented her decision to change direction, which opened up a whole new way for her to express her talents and abilities. Building on everything that she had done over the years, but in a more creative and flexible way, Nikki was able to remain true to her values as a parent and to her vision of herself in her various roles of wife, mother and businesswoman.

Such moments cause us to take a breather and to look deep inside ourselves. What do we want out of life? What kind of life do we want for our children? What kind of old age do we want? All these questions deserve serious thought, but they must also be framed in a relevant context. Today, looking back doesn't give us much guidance. We need to be forward-looking and to take our cues from what we know of the future – and not just our future, but the one our children will inherit, too.

We can create our own reality if we are prepared to take full responsibility for every move we make in this Age of Possibility. The choice is ours.

IKIGAI

Ikigai (pronounced 'eye-kih-guy') is a Japanese concept that means 'a reason for being', and is linked to the concept introduced above – creating lives of meaning beyond being work-driven. This framework provides a wonderful way to help our children think about their lives and future careers. While this becomes more important as they head into their teen years, it's never too early for us to start discussing these four questions with our children:

- What can you be paid for?
- What are you good at?
- What do you love doing; what are you passionate about?
- What makes a contribution to the world, and what does society need?

Only when all four of these areas are taken into account can we hope to find true fulfilment in our lives. People are going to be a lot more focused on finding this balance in the 2020s. And not just the younger generation or millennials, either. As the baby boomers (born in the period after World War II, from 1945 into the 1960s) head into retirement, they've already started to rethink what a good life looks like, and are influencing younger generations to think about this earlier in their lives.

It's telling that one of the world's top-rated business and leadership gurus, Clayton Christensen, has written books on this topic, including the bestselling *How Will You Measure Your Life?* (2012), and also emphasises these issues in his 2016 book, *Competing Against Luck*.

ON-DEMAND WORKFORCE

One of the biggest shifts taking place in the world of work right now is the number of people who are freelancing. For some people, freelancing is a 'side hustle' that allows them to earn a little bit extra on the side. But for an increasing number of people, working as a freelancer is now their full-time occupation. According to Upwork's fifth annual *Freelancing in America* report in 2018 (see https://www.upwork.com/i/freelancing-in-america/2018/), more than one in three Americans has already freelanced at some stage. This number is likely to increase in the 2020s.

Freelancing will change employment in more ways than might be immediately obvious. For example, we will see a proliferation of so-called 'third spaces'. Not the home, not the office, but somewhere in between – both home and office at the same time. The authors of this book are both users of third spaces, and with some really clever concepts emerging, the provision of such spaces will become a huge industry. A third space requires digital connectivity, the availability of good food, an ambience that combines both a social vibe and a mix of public and private spaces, and a range of ancillary services.

> Amy, at age 19, is already a member of the on-demand workforce, earning money by developing videos for training workshops. She doesn't have to meet the people for whom she works, as she is briefed and delivers the product remotely and online. Graeme has used the same platform for the creation of video jingles, and Nikki has had ebooks designed and set, all without ever meeting the people doing the work, and at incredibly competitive rates.

AN OUTPUTS-DRIVEN WORKPLACE

The days of nine-to-five jobs are almost over. Today's talented young generation want their outputs, and not their inputs, measured. Their approach to their managers is to know *what* is needed and by *when* it is required. Then they expect to be left alone to do it – whenever, wherever, however. It is not about being in at 9 a.m. and clocking out at 5 p.m., irrespective of how productive you are in this time.

Being measured on inputs provides little incentive for this young generation to work harder or be more productive. After all, if they do work harder and are more productive, more tasks will simply be poured into their spare time for the same returns. This is a tough logic to fault!

Perhaps this approach can best be summarised in a table from *The War for Talent* by Ed Michaels, Helen Handfield-Jones and Beth Axelrod (2001):

The philosophy of old and new pay

OLD PAY PHILOSOPHY	NEW PAY PHILOSOPHY
Pay for the job	Pay for the person and for performance
Job scope and seniority drive pay	Value creation drives pay
Pay what others in the company get (internal equity)	Pay what the individual could get elsewhere (market equity)
Set a range and hire within it	Break the compensation rules to hire the right candidate

This concept is not only applicable to office environments or among professionals, but can also be applied to manufacturing and primary industries. Probably the most famous example is Semco, a Brazilian manufacturer. Simply put, the concept works like this: a 10-*hour* mining shift becomes, instead, a 10-*ton* shift. The output of tons is measured against an agreed target. The workers have a set time in which to complete the task. When the task is complete, the remainder of the time becomes discretionary – workers can knock off early or continue to work and earn more money for additional output. For more on this, read the Brazilian maverick Ricardo Semler's books.

CAREERS AS 'PORTFOLIOS OF JOBS'

Charles Handy, the British management guru, coined the phrase 'a portfolio of jobs' to replace the outdated concept of a 'career' (see *Beyond Certainty: The Changing World of Organisations*, 1996). When he started to work at Shell in the 1950s, there was an expectation of cradle-to-grave employment with a single company. That is now a fantasy to which very few people adhere.

In 2007, the average 30-year-old had already had five or more jobs, and nearly half of 30-something professionals were not using their original qualification. As we update this book in 2019, it is obvious that change remains a significant factor in the world of work. People are moving between jobs more than ever before, and many employers have stopped looking at university qualifications when assessing job candidates. This trend will simply increase over the next few decades, with young people abandoning all thoughts of a traditional career in favour of a series of jobs, often spanning multiple industries and focus areas.

Many young people in their late 20s and early 30s are already developing multiple streams of income to create a life that is fulfilling, as well as to hedge their bets should one income stream dry up. One of Nikki's young friends double-majored in law and science, and started his working life in a law firm drawing up contracts. He then moved to an online retail company, where he was involved in procurement, and now runs a marketing agency connecting big brands to the young gamer community.

He also co-owns a gym with his wife, is a stand-up comedian in the entertainment industry, and reviews new gaming titles and tech gadgets for the media. His wife runs the human resources department of a retail chain, provides HR consulting to small- to medium-sized businesses privately, and is a personal trainer in the gym she runs with her husband.

Oh, and they have a child, too! Their focus is not on job security, as they don't believe it exists, but rather on creating a portfolio of careers in order to spread their income risk as the world changes.

SELF-EMPLOYMENT, ENTREPRENEURS AND MICRO-SOURCING

> 'Lifetime employment is over. Stable employment at large corporations is gone. The average career will likely encompass two or three "occupations" and a half-dozen or more employers. Most of us will spend sustained periods of our career in some form of self-employment. Bottom line: we're on our own, folks.'
> Tom Peters, *Re-Imagine!*, 2003

If we are changing jobs more often, then – for at least a portion of our working lives – it is highly likely that each of us will be self-employed at some stage. This is not a euphemism for unemployed – it is the new reality. People know that their skills can be used on a temporary basis at almost any company. Being an entrepreneur in the 21st century is not just about starting a company and growing it into a listed entity. It's about micro-enterprises that start up, offer a service for a period of time, and then perhaps shut down again as the owner-managers move on in a new direction.

Companies have been outsourcing for many years. They have been using temps for even longer. In the future, they will 'micro-source'. They'll employ the services of a small company to fulfil a specific function – usually within a limited time frame – and pay handsomely if the skills and inputs they require are rare and essential.

LIFELONG LEARNING AND MASSIVE OPEN ONLINE COURSES (MOOCS)

The previous trends will require another: that people continue with formal learning and on-the-job training throughout their careers. More universities and colleges will offer short courses and multiple-learning channels for 'mature-age' students, and more and more MOOCs will become available.

In fact, there are probably too many courses available already, and an industry will soon emerge that curates these and finds the best courses for you (we suggest that this could be a job opportunity in the future – see the next chapter for more details).

It will become commonplace for people to take time out from their careers to study extensively, often as a prelude to a major change of direction in career or industry. Their aim is not about the accumulation of certificates and academic qualifications, but rather about the continual need to keep up to date and relevant.

VOICE CONTROL AND REAL-TIME TRANSLATION

We have avoided referencing specific technologies in this list of predictions – although we were tempted! The list of emerging technologies that will shape the 2020s is as long as our arms. But these two technologies, along with automation and robotics, deserve special mention for the impact they will have on how we work.

The 2020s will see a significant shift away from keyboards and finger-based interfaces to voice control, and at the same time, real-time translation will also remove any language barriers that might exist between us and other people, and between us and machines.

This is really one of the most powerful and immediately applicable implications of AI, as machines learn how to communicate with us using natural language, and then help us to communicate better with each other. Just imagine a world without language barriers, and how this will boost globalisation and mobility.

A GLOBAL STAGE AND A MELTING POT OF DIVERSE WORLD VIEWS

The company of tomorrow will extend across traditional boundaries. It will be more diverse than ever before, and connect to an increasing diversity of suppliers and customers. We don't believe that an inevitable 'clash of civilisations' will occur in the future, but are cautiously optimistic that the next generation will find ways to integrate diversity into their world views.

We believe that today's young people will learn to see themselves as global citizens with a rooted cultural heritage. It is likely that a period of deep soul-searching on the issue of identity will take place. People will come to identify themselves as much with the companies they work for as they do with the cities or nations they live in, the languages they speak and the gods they worship.

The two paragraphs above remain unchanged from the 2007 edition of this book. As we update the book in 2019, we reflect that the rise of nationalism in the last decade is precisely what we predicted: people are struggling to come to terms with increasing diversity and globalisation. But we remain optimistic that after a brief period of nationalism, protectionism and even outright xenophobia, most people will continue to progress towards more integration and diversity.

We, as the authors of this book, certainly feel that this is a more desirable model and approach. Parents need to help their children see the value in diversity and difference – we will return to this topic with some practical suggestions in the next chapter.

PwC chief people officer Mike Fenlon affirms this view in a 2019 *Fast Company* article ('5 ways work culture will change by 2030' by Gwen Moran, https://www.fastcompany.com/90297816/5-ways-work-culture-will-change-by-2030): 'As a shortage of knowledge workers forces organizations to cast a wider net for talent, tapping new regions or underutilized demographic segments, cultures will need to focus on inclusion to create harmonious, productive work environments.

'Teams may be more far-flung, have different backgrounds, and have varied communication preferences. Tech solutions will play a role in this culture shift, facilitating collaboration across time zones, providing accommodations for people with disabilities, and even helping managers conquer their own biases.'

MOBILITY OF TALENT

The demand for skilled workers will continue to outstrip the supply on a global basis. The mobility of skilled labour around the world means that competition for talent now stretches across the globe. As a result, there will be an increase in creativity in recruiting, benefits, perks, retention strategies and 'employee value propositions' (EVPs) across all industries. This mobility will only add to the previous trend, multiplying the diversity factor in workplaces.

In addition, today's generation of young Americans will migrate overseas in significant numbers. According to the World Futures Society's *Forecast 2017*: 'For the first time in its history, the United States will see a significant proportion of its population emigrate due to overseas opportunities. According to futurists Arnold Brown and Edie Weiner, Generation Y, the population segment born between 1978 and 1995, may be the first US generation to have many of its members leave the country to pursue large portions of their lives, if not their entire adult lives, overseas.'

The US has experienced a century of being the land of immigrants. It will certainly be a different world: for Americans at home, and for everyone else, with more Americans abroad.

We predict that by the end of the 2020s, mass emigration will be true for the Chinese and Indians as well. Having saturated their own labour markets in the next decade, many Chinese and Indian firms will look to expand globally. They may focus, at first, on South-East Asia and then on Africa in their search for cheap labour (just as many Western companies outsourced to China and India in the 1990s and 2000s).

This should have the effect of boosting those economies and providing a much-needed increase in global productivity. Rather than fear China and India, we see their potential for uplifting the global economy – as long as they operate as our business partners and not our 21st-century colonisers.

THE ROLE OF WOMEN

> 'Among the world's most innovative countries and businesses there is an emerging cultural consensus on how best to strengthen their most critical resource: their people. And there is no greater indicator of an innovative culture than the empowerment of women. Fully integrating and empowering women economically and politically is the most important step that a country or company can take to strengthen its competitiveness.'
> Alec Ross, *The Industries of the Future*, 2016

Women are no longer just looking for jobs; they want to build careers. This requires a change in the workplace to embrace childcare, flexible working arrangements and disrupted career timelines. As women assume more leadership roles, we are also likely to see a shift in policies that support the new-look society that is developing.

An increasing number of women are earning more than their husbands or partners. If one parent needs to stay at home, increasingly it's the man, who is earning less than his partner. Parenting is a team effort, and 'the team' needs to find creative ways to share parenting responsibilities. Teams can consist of parents supported by various people who actively participate in the daily parenting process, from grandparents to paid au pairs or childminders (in addition to teachers, coaches and after-care personnel).

And let's not lose sight of the fact that there are same-sex couples these days, not just the stereotypical mom and dad. There is also an increasing number of women who choose to single-parent.

> A young couple known to both Nikki and Graeme are high-level financial directors living in London with their seven-year-old twin girls. Right from the start, they agreed that stability and emotional connection were essential to parenting their children, and so they arranged with their employers that Dad would start work later in the morning so that he could get the children ready for the day and do the school run, while Mom leaves work earlier in the afternoon to be with the children then.
>
> Both parents also work from home on days when one of the children is ill or there is a special occasion. They also go on weekend adventures or travel together so that they have quality time as a family without any distractions.

The #metoo and #toxicmasculinity movements are raising issues that have previously been disregarded, but that have disempowered women and allowed men to avoid taking responsibility for the destructive use of their power over women. These issues also shine the spotlight on current leadership in the world, as it remains largely male-dominated and does not reflect well on men or on human rights issues involving women.

AGEING POPULATIONS

While the world's population will continue to grow (it's estimated to reach nine billion people by 2050), the average annual growth rate will continue to decline. Most developed nations will soon have declining populations, with fertility rates below the replacement level. The countries most immediately affected by ageing populations include Japan, Germany, Italy and the Scandinavian countries. Other countries, especially in Western Europe and North America, will need to import young workers within the next few decades. China has recently scrapped their one-child policy to try to raise the birth rate and ensure a steady supply of younger workers into the workplace.

A key implication of this trend is that the age range of workers in some companies will span four generations, which will have huge implications for management and team interactions, as well as on the companies' customer base.

DEFERRING RETIREMENT

As the baby boomers head into their senior years, they are the most youthful in attitude, the healthiest and the wealthiest old people the world has ever seen. And they are not retiring. This is partly because they don't have the nest egg they'd hoped to have (due to their high consumption levels, a lack of savings or bad investments), and partly because they have longer to live.

> Nikki's parents are a case in point. They are still in good health, due to good nutrition, taking supplements and getting enough exercise, and in their 70s and 80s, respectively, are both still working. They very actively support all their grandchildren's activities and often assist with fetching and carrying, too. If one is to live longer, remaining an active, contributing member of society is essential from a mental, emotional and financial point of view.

Lynda Smith, a colleague of Graeme and Nikki's, has built a business around helping seniors to 'refire and retyre', and not to retire too soon. Not only in order to give them something to do in their later years, but also because they have so much wisdom and experience to offer the younger generations. They don't *want* to walk off silently into the night. They have a lot left to contribute, and nothing is going to stop them. A very simple example of this trend is to look at the average age of politicians in the world at the start of the 2020s – they're in their 60s and 70s!

A major possible consequence of this trend is a generational war. In most developed nations, wealth is disproportionately held by the older generation. For the first time in history, it seems unlikely that this wealth will be handed down to the younger generation – at least in significant amounts. And the baby boomers are unlikely to give up their positions of power, making it increasingly crowded at the top of the pyramid. In countries where large retirement expenditures loom (such as in the US), the younger generation will be expected to help fund the retirement of the older generation. This is likely to divide voters along generational lines as never before.

It is a trend that has already started in some countries. In Israel, for example, a political party was voted into office in 2005 with a mandate based solely on entrenching generational privilege, and the original Brexit referendum in the UK in 2016 was largely split along generational lines.

THE FUTURE ISN'T WHAT IT USED TO BE

We could go on and on, as there are so many megatrends and forces emerging. Hopefully those mentioned are enough to convince you that the world of work, as well as our personal lives, are about to undergo significant change. We therefore cannot continue to raise our children to merely repeat the lives we've been living. We need to avoid getting stuck in tight parameters.

Start by focusing on the words you use with your children; they are vitally important. Replace 'You should,' or 'Why can't you,' with 'Why don't you?' or 'How about this?' We live in a world of entirely new possibilities, and despite old opportunities falling away, there is hope and we are optimistic about the future.

Our children also require a new approach to their schooling and new options after school, as they'll have to learn skills we didn't need at their age. They need to see the world differently from how we view it. All of this is easier said than done.

Experience isn't what it used to be. In fact, by its very definition, experience is something you get just after you need it (think about that!). Experience is most valuable in an environment in which what happened yesterday happens again tomorrow – an environment in which there is little change or, at worst, in which change is predictable and the future is little more than an extrapolation of the past.

But in an environment of discontinuous change, such as the world of the 21st century, the easiest way to fail is to try to repeat, or simply improve, on past successes. 'Just as good' is the enemy of great, and experience is the enemy of innovation and adaptability in tempestuous times. Tomorrow is hardly ever a repeat of yesterday, so the danger lies in thinking that we understand what is happening because we've seen it all before. In fact, experience is actually what you get when you don't get what you want.

By listing some of the emerging trends (and it is by no means a comprehensive list, or even the most mind-blowing trends), we are trying to encourage you to leave yesterday behind and focus on tomorrow. For those of you with young children, tomorrow seems a long way away. Yet it will be here sooner than you think. You might not be able to plan for it, but you can at the very least prepare for it, starting today.

Two of our key themes – choices and responsibility – will be caught from, rather than taught by, you. Our view of the future is not a prophecy, but it is a possibility. It is your responsibility to try to discern the shape of things to come in the next two decades. Then you can choose how to respond to the challenges that lie ahead.

Are you simply going to hope that the future stays predictable and as similar as possible to what you know now, or are you going to embrace the fact that we live in a time when monumental changes are taking place? If you choose the latter, then it is your responsibility to stop doing what you have always done, to stop thinking the way you always have thought, and to start making the necessary changes to the approach you take with your children.

Chapter 4

Jobs of the future

'The sun is setting on the Information Society – even before we have fully adjusted to its demands as individuals and as companies. We have lived as hunters and as farmers, we have worked in factories and now we live in an information-based society whose icon is the computer. We stand facing the fifth kind of society: the Dream Society ... [It] is emerging this very instant – the shape of the future is visible today ... Future products will have to appeal to our hearts, not to our heads. Now is the time to add emotional value to products and services.'
Rolf Jensen, *The Dream Society: How the Coming Shift from Information to Imagination will Transform your Business*, 2001

'In business areas as far afield as life sciences, finance, warfare, and agriculture, if you can imagine an advance, somebody is already working on how to develop and commercialize it.'
Alec Ross, *The Industries of the Future*, 2016

You might have been raised to believe that a profession was the pinnacle of a successful career. Over the past few decades, ambitious parents dreamt of their children becoming lawyers, doctors, engineers, accountants, actuaries, architects, vets, etc. And some of these professions might still be safe bets for the next decade or so, but we are not convinced that all of them are great choices for the children of the 21st century. In this chapter, we explain why we think so.

In the Information Age, those with specialist knowledge were both sought after and well paid. However, the problem arises when many of the tasks they perform can be done by machines. As we head into the Age of Possibility, head knowledge alone will not suffice; you will also need a network, creative solutions and opportunities. Some universities are already adjusting accordingly. The University of the Witwatersrand's Medical School in Johannesburg, for example, has started to set entrance exams that do not simply test academic ability. It has been found that the ability to obtain distinctions in subjects such as science, biology and mathematics alone cannot predict whether a teenager will make a good doctor. A good doctor also requires emotional intelligence, empathy, resilience and other characteristics not measured by final-year school examinations (Matric, A-levels and the like). So, some very clever kids are being turned away from medical school – much to their disgust and dismay. But, the university has a point. The world of work is changing, and some of the old, established requirements for success are being adjusted.

In this section, we continue our predictions and are more specific about which types of jobs *we think* will be in demand in the future, and which will not. Again, our aim is not to impress you with almost unbelievable, wild and breathtaking predictions of super-sexy job titles and careers based on technologies that don't yet exist. Although that sort of fantasy thinking is exciting and we encourage you to indulge in it at some stage – just to stretch your mind – the task we have set ourselves is this: we want to help you to prepare your children and yourself for some of the possible futures that are likely to emerge if the trends we identified in the previous chapter are realised.

It is not expected that a great many jobs will disappear entirely, so our focus is on those jobs and industries that we think are declining – therefore offering fewer job opportunities – and those we see expanding in the next two decades. Although we don't expect you to agree with our analysis completely (especially if, as a parent, you have made your living as a lawyer, accountant, engineer or actuary!), we hope that we will provoke you into thinking about how you will secure your children's future.

Remember, your children are likely to still be working in 2080! Now there's a thought …

Resources to keep you updated

Most countries have a government department devoted to labour and employment issues, and many of these do long-term job forecasts. We highly recommend you consult the following:

- The US Bureau of Labor's employment projections: https://www.bls.gov/emp/
- The UK Department for Work and Pensions future of work papers: https://www.gov.uk/government/collections/the-future-of-jobs-and-skills
- The Australian government's Department of Jobs and Small Business: https://www.jobs.gov.au/
- The World Economic Forum's annual *Future of Jobs* report: http://reports.weforum.org/

Many universities and consulting firms also produce regularly updated studies on the future of jobs and work. We have found the following extremely valuable in formulating our predictions:

- A 2013 Oxford University study on 'The Future of Employment' – this is the most cited study on this topic in the last decade: https://www.oxfordmartin.ox.ac.uk/downloads/academic/future-of-employment.pdf
- Insead's Future of the Workplace research: https://knowledge.insead.edu/leadership-organisations/the-future-of-the-workplace-5396
- McKinsey's studies on the Future of Work: https://www.mckinsey.com/featured-insights/future-of-work
- Accenture's Future of Work resource page: https://www.accenture.com/gb-en/future-workforce

A simple search of your favourite local university website or the website of your most trusted professional services firm will no doubt produce a treasure trove of resources about how the world is changing, which you can share with your children. We highly recommend that you do this research on an ongoing basis. TED videos and YouTube channels are also useful – your children will probably prefer to consume this information in video format, and may be more open to a discussion if you watch the videos together, rather than if you just gave them something to read.

DECLINING INDUSTRIES

> 'The first wave of labor substitution from automation and robotics came from jobs that were often dangerous, dirty, and dreary and involved little personal interaction, but increasingly, robots are encroaching on jobs in the service sector that require personalized skills. Jobs in the service sector that were largely immune from job loss during the last stage of globalization are now at risk because advances in robotics have accelerated in recent years, due to breakthroughs in the field itself as well as new advancements in information management, computing, and high-end engineering. Tasks once thought the exclusive domain of humans – the types of jobs that require situational awareness, spatial reasoning and dexterity, contextual understanding, and human judgment – are opening up to robots.'
> Alec Ross, *The Industries of the Future*, 2016

Let us start our glimpse into the future by attempting to identify which jobs *might* be in decline. It's actually less important to know which jobs will disappear than to understand *why this might happen*. The jobs we list are therefore examples of the types of jobs that will decline in the next decade or two. The main reason for such decline is automation, but other issues also affect jobs, among them globalisation, changes in market demand, shifts in society and how we live, and changing demographics.

As we write this edition, the latest US Bureau of Labor Statistics report projects that the following 12 jobs will be the fastest-declining occupations in the period 2016–2026, and the report includes the percentage of the decline expected (we have consolidated some of the job titles for this list):

- Locomotive firers   -78.6
- Respiratory therapy technicians   -56.3

- Parking enforcement workers   -35.3
- Word processors and typists   -33.1
- Watch repairers   -29.7
- Motor-vehicle electronic-equipment installers and repairers   -25.6
- Foundry mould- and core-makers, metal pourers and casters   -24
- Computer operators and data-entry keyers   -22.8
- Telephone and switchboard operators   -22.6
- Mine shuttle-car operators   -21.9
- Postmasters and mail superintendents   -20.9
- Hand-grinding and hand-polishing workers   -20.5

Source: https://www.bls.gov/emp/tables/fastest-declining-occupations.htm (2018)

THE REASONS WHY

The main theme in this list is *robotic automation*, which will be the most important issue to consider for the 2020s. And one particular form of automation is likely to affect the types of jobs that people will have then – the force of *artificial intelligence*. For many people, the concept of AI is a mystery. They imagine humanoid robots, massive supercomputers in basements crunching data and intelligent devices interacting with us as if they were sentient. And since none of these are a reality yet, it is easy to dismiss the concept out of hand, thinking that it is either pure science fiction or so far off in the future that we don't need to worry about it now. In that case, it may be helpful to rather think of IA instead of AI – 'intelligent assistance'. A major change that will occur in the 2020s is that we will increasingly rely on intelligent devices and applications to help us do the things we can't do by ourselves.

We'll talk about growth industries shortly, but be aware that as far as automation is concerned, there are lots of clever people hard at work behind the scenes, designing robots, writing algorithms and training software systems to replace today's conventional jobs.

A GOOD EXAMPLE

To help illustrate the profound impact AI/IA can have on our world, and how it will change the way we do things in every part of our lives, consider the history of GPS navigation. The first digital maps were nothing more than screen-based versions of their paper counterparts – we replaced the old 'A–Z map books' with static maps on digital screens. Then GPS was introduced, and we built navigation devices that gave us directions after entering a destination. That was still a fairly static and clunky process. We then got rid of the separate devices and integrated these mapping applications into our smartphones.

Today, mobile map apps like Waze use real-time user data about drivers' locations and speeds combined with crowd-sourced information about traffic jams, accidents, road conditions and other obstructions to create the perfect real-time map with constantly updated and optimised route suggestions. The more people that use the system, the better it gets. All that data from all those users, combined with a powerful engine to make sense of it, enables the system to update directions in real time, rerouting drivers mid-course to minimise any possible delays and to smooth out the traffic experience for everyone.

The system also acquires knowledge over time, remembering congested areas, peak traffic times, and evaluating its own understanding of the routes it recommends and all traffic systems everywhere people use the app. Whereas the old approach simply digitised a static paper map, Waze has combined AI algorithms and real-time data to create dynamic, optimised maps that convey people to their destinations in the fastest time possible – and it just keeps getting better and better. It is 'intelligent assistance' underpinned by some clever 'artificial intelligence'.

Waze is also an example of how various aspects of a tech application can combine to produce an immensely useful end product for its users. The combination of high-speed mobile data (5G will arrive in the 2020s and be a game-changer), real-time crowdsourcing of user data from people's devices, along with geolocation, voice-activated controls, big-data analytics and sense-making algorithms will affect many industries, including the ones discussed below.

GENERAL PRACTICE PROFESSIONALS SUCH AS LAWYERS, FAMILY DOCTORS, MEDICAL SPECIALISTS, ACCOUNTANTS AND STRUCTURAL ENGINEERS

In a recent conversation with a friend, Graeme was talking about careers. His friend is an accountant, with his own small firm servicing other entrepreneurs and small family businesses. He makes a good living. As they talked about university choices for their daughters, Graeme's friend said he would happily pay for his daughter's studies, provided she doesn't pursue a degree in accounting.

This isn't the first time we've heard a parent say that they don't want their child following in their footsteps career-wise – we've heard it from musicians and authors, of course, but now increasingly from lawyers, accountants and other professionals, too. And not because the parents feel they've been unsuccessful in their career or the job has been too demanding – it is simply because they feel that future job prospects in their fields are bleak. And the main reason for this is the most important issue facing their industries in the near future: automation.

Take the family doctor. For most common diseases, the general practitioner does nothing more than diagnose, via a fixed series of observations (swollen glands, bloodshot eyes, high blood pressure or pain). If you know what to look for, anyone can make these observations. Doctors don't even do blood tests – a nurse usually takes a blood sample from our bodies and sends it to a laboratory. We could either utilise home blood-test kits, or go directly to the lab ourselves (and there won't be any human beings at the lab either – even now we have machines that analyse our blood, not a lab assistant with a microscope).

The doctors of the future will not be required to diagnose what is wrong with their patients, nor to prescribe the medicines they should take. IBM's 'Watson' computer is already proving to be much better at doing these things than human doctors are. Only doctors who go beyond diagnosis to real empathy and care will continue to practise.

Similarly, in the future, many surgeons will have to change their skill set quite dramatically. Robots are now much better than humans at performing certain surgeries, especially fiddly micro- and keyhole surgeries, as well as laser-based surgery, like cataract and cornea operations. Today's surgeon closer resembles a video-game controller than the 'scalpel and scissors' doctor of the past. Future doctors and surgeons will have to become a lot more comfortable partnering with robots and algorithms in order to do their jobs. If they don't, they will simply be replaced by machines. Or they could be replaced by another medical professional many kilometres away.

As an example, when surgeons use micro tools for keyhole and specialised surgery, they do not actually touch their patients. As long as we can trust the computer connections and networks, the surgeon could be thousands of kilometres away during an operation and it would make no difference. This is already happening where patients located in the US are being operated on by Indian doctors somewhere in India.

If offshoring and AI replacement can happen in *surgery*, consider how easily we could replace lawyers, accountants, engineers, architects and, basically, any other profession. The more advanced functions of these professions are a few decades away from being automated, but entry-level and many front-line functions will be done by machines by the early 2020s.

'Ross' is an artificial intelligence system that does legal research using IBM's Watson supercomputer. It searches through millions of pages of case files for data points that attorneys can use in court. It can analyse contracts to identify errors and problems, clause by clause. Ross can read 40 million pages in 15 seconds. This work replaces what entry-level attorneys do during discovery and the early stages of contract creation. Ross actually works through a spoken interface, where users simply speak their questions into the system. Ross then reads through the 'entire body of law' and responds with an answer and topical readings from legislation.

Ross is already in use in some of the larger law firms around the world. As Ross handles more of the grunt work, it will free experienced attorneys to tackle more cases, do more in-depth research and focus their efforts on the most important issues. Although Ross does not replace lawyers, the system does dramatically change what they are required to do.

For young people today, this poses an immediate problem: how do they obtain the training and initiation they need when they start in these professions if the jobs they might do as candidates and juniors will be automated? This isn't really a problem for your child to solve so much as it is an issue for each of the professions they might want to enter. The message for your child is threefold:

1. The professions are no longer 'safe havens' for clever kids. Even professionals will be threatened by automation, and will need to innovate to ensure they remain relevant.
2. In the past, becoming a professional was a way of being a specialist. These days, you need to be a specialist professional. A 'general practitioner' doctor, accountant or lawyer can easily be replaced by an algorithm. If your children show interest in a profession, make sure you push them to understand what specialisations exist within that profession – and nudge your children towards the more technologically advanced specialisations if you can.
3. Whatever your children study, add the following three areas to their subject list: business and entrepreneurship (how to actually run a business), technology and software development (in order to speak and understand the language of the machines) and communication (the ability to translate what the machines say and do into 'human' language will always be valuable).

FARMERS

Technology and automation will continue to replace labourers and managers alike in primary and secondary industries. Farm labour has declined by nearly 90 per cent in the last century as smart harvesters, drones, and computer-controlled irrigation and nutrition systems have changed farm work forever. But it isn't just labourers who are in danger of being replaced.

Most analyses of what jobs will look like in the next few decades claim that farmers themselves are likely to be replaced by artificial intelligence, data analytics and the application of data science to agriculture. Almost every decision that needs to be made on a farm can be made by machines these days.

Although some job creation will occur, these jobs will be for creative thinkers and technology experts. Precision farming will provide some opportunities, especially the computerised management of crops to suit variations in land characteristics. But automated tractors will drive across fields that are mapped according to pinpoint GPS coordinates. As the tractors progress, precise data about soil composition, water levels, required nutrition and other crucial factors will control how much seed, fertiliser, water and pesticides are needed in order to ensure optimum production.

Farm-equipment manufacturers will need high-level technical skills and creative farming experts on their team, and farmers will need computer programmers and system designers to help them farm. However, the specialised farming knowledge that used to be the domain of the professional farmer can now be managed by machines.

MINERS

Similarly, those working in the mining industry will find that machines more efficiently do many of the jobs that need to be done. Now that health and safety levels have been raised and human life is not as cheap as it used to be, it will be financially more viable to use robots for mining. Companies like Rio Tinto are already automating many aspects of mining, including using driverless trucks to transport the rock and minerals after they've been extracted. Machines are also being used to map underground deposits and find new ones.

CONSTRUCTION

The advent of 3D printing will soon progress to industrial scale and start to replace construction workers. But construction will change for more reasons than mere automation. We are about to enter the graphene age. A century ago, electricity, the internal combustion engine and concrete were changing the world of construction in a variety of ways. These new materials and powers allowed us to build skyscrapers and change our city landscapes forever.

But new wonder materials have been discovered in the past few years, with graphene being the most amazing. It's a single layer of carbon that is

200 times stronger than steel, but lighter than air. It also has many other properties, which means that as soon as we can find ways to make it cheaper, it will change construction forever. Those civil engineers, architects and construction engineers who don't keep up to speed with this development will be left behind very quickly.

PETROLEUM ENGINEERS, OIL RIGGERS AND REFINERY OPERATORS

Besides the threat of being replaced by machines and robots, engineers and operators in certain industries face losing their jobs simply because their industry is in decline. It is the end of the Age of Oil. The biggest industries that will see a decline, starting in the 2020s, are plastics, oil and postal services. Oil and petroleum might be the most surprising inclusion on that list, but it seems that we are coming to the end of the age of fossil fuels. This is evident in the reduction in price of solar panels and battery technology, and the increased investments in alternative energy solutions. Visit the fusion reaction project at https://www.iter.org and also read about Bill Gates's Breakthrough Energy Coalition at http://www.b-t.energy/ for more information.

AGENTS

Across almost every industry, the middle person in many business transactions will gradually disappear. This includes estate agents, travel agents, insurance brokers, investment advisors, logistics agents, freight forwarders, sports and celebrity agents, and any other intermediaries you can think of. This is called disintermediation, and it is fuelled by technology and increased consumer awareness as sellers and buyers connect with each other directly. Blockchain technology will further create a digital basis for trust and real-time, smart record-keeping, which will accelerate disintermediation in the 2020s. It will change the way we record, track and report on transactions and create a completely transparent system. Unless agents find ways to add more value than simply connecting two parties, and customise and personalise their service, they will become increasingly obsolete.

THE CURATOR OR SPECIALIST AGENT

While the need for the middle person is declining, there is still a role for the specialist agent. He or she will act much like a skilled concierge or curator when their clients need someone who:
- has specialist knowledge, e.g. a financial planner
- is a recognised authority on a subject
- has foresight, and can better predict a possible outcome.

To better explain this, these are the people who do stuff for us while we are doing our day job. For example, while we could manage our own financial planning and wealth creation, we can only do so if we take time off from our work or personal lives. Not everyone can or wants to do that, preferring to leave such matters in the hands of specialist agents, who spend their lives studying the markets and have acquired expert financial knowledge.

Another type of specialist agent may be someone who can help parents with parenting – a higher level of expert than a childminder or au pair. Nikki recently had a conversation with a parent who has decided that it is more beneficial to invest in this kind of expert than in enrolling her child in a more expensive school or an alternative education system.

TRANSLATORS AND INTERPRETERS

One of the most obvious applications of computing power and artificial intelligence is the way in which computers can recognise and interpret our voice instructions, and manage real-time translations between languages. Right now, these translations are quite mechanical and obviously computer-generated, but very soon they will sound completely natural. Google's Assistant app, launched in early 2018, is a great example of a computer that sounds human – it can make phone calls on your behalf without sounding like a machine at all. The need for humans to translate or interpret will become obsolete in future, unless it's a minority language that hasn't been coded yet.

RETAIL

When we wrote the first edition of this book, retail was the first item on our list of industries that would decline by 2020. And we were right. The past decade has been brutal for the shopfront retail sector, and this downward trend will continue. The need for shelf packers, cashiers, floor staff, shop managers, security personnel and other employees who make big stores functional will gradually reduce. Only shops or shopping malls that cater for a bigger experience and provide entertainment in various forms will survive, but even they will not look the way they do today.

It is interesting to note, though, that Kidzania, which is the number-one kids' entertainment and experiential learning franchise in the world, is a much sought-after anchor tenant in key shopping malls around the globe, as it brings new feet through the doors on a continuous basis.

As far as online shopping is concerned, although it may never fully replace bricks-and-mortar stores, they will also transform their look and the services they provide. This, in turn, will affect what staff these companies need to employ. For many people, their first jobs may have been as a shelf packer or a cashier in a store. Those entry-level jobs won't exist in the future.

In another aspect of retail, we will continue to shift towards a cashless society. The advances made in contactless payments (ApplePay and Google Pay, for example, and even cryptocurrencies such as Bitcoin) are ensuring their entrenchment in mainstream society. With that, fewer people are required to handle payments. And with self-service tills already a common sight in supermarkets and popular restaurants, the demise of the cashier is inevitable. Just google 'Amazon Go' on YouTube for a great example of how retail is changing.

BANKERS

Banking is one industry that will lose a number of jobs in the 2020s. At every level and in every function of a bank, automation and artificial intelligence will play more significant roles. Banks may even be replaced entirely by applications built on blockchain technology. Bit by bit, small FinTech (financial technology) start-ups will chip away at the services for which banks currently charge, from foreign exchange and cash management to home and student loans.

There will be a big demand for people who work in the FinTech space, as well as for cryptocurrency miners and managers, and for those who provide alternative payment systems.

REPORTERS AND JOURNALISTS (THE MEDIA)

There might not be many people who will mourn the loss of a few bankers from the planet, but we are sad about the imminent demise of reporters and journalists. As we write this update, the media is under threat from a number of directions. Most people expect to get their news free of charge on one of their devices these days, and don't see the need to pay for it any more, putting the survival of media houses at risk.

The media has also been under siege from politicians and third parties who spread false news and undermine the public's faith in the press and in journalism in general. However, the media is still a vitally important part of our free, democratic world, and we trust that it will survive into the future, and emerge in an updated, revived, more hi-tech format in the 2020s.

But whatever the media looks like then, it will probably have to cope with reduced staff. Perhaps we will see the emergence of superstar, specialist commentators who own and run their own channels. In order for the public to trust them, the information they share will have to be accurate and unbiased. No matter what the future holds for the media, one thing is for sure: the days of the trench-coated journalist with their trusty notebook and voice-recorder, chasing after a story, are over.

DRIVERS AND PILOTS, AND FREIGHT FORWARDERS

It is estimated that as many as 10 per cent of the world's employees are involved in logistics, from truck and taxi drivers to pilots and ship crews. Almost all of them could be replaced by driverless vehicles in some form or another. The technology for this will be ready by 2030, though it might take slightly longer for the public to be comfortable flying in a plane without a pilot, or boarding a bus without a driver. The world of travel, logistics, deliveries and transportation will need far fewer people to steer the vehicles, ships and aircraft, but a lot more people to write software, manage the systems by remote control, run security checks and, especially, monitor the driverless infrastructure we've created.

AIR-TRAFFIC CONTROLLERS

This is a fantastic example of a job that requires incredibly high skill levels, but will still be much improved when fully automated. Air-traffic controllers famously have the most stress-filled job in the world. It requires high degrees of focus, razor-sharp reactions and the ability to keep calm under pressure. All of these would be better done by machines – a Waze for air-traffic control! And, of course, their unions often go on strike around the world, crippling the global airline industry. These factors make it perfect for automation.

FAST-FOOD WORKERS

Fast food's big appeal is that it's consistent, reliable and fast. Menus are generic and the food is made to strict standards with little variation. This means the industry is ripe for automation. In California, for example, a robot named Flippy has been flipping burgers and placing them on buns at a CaliBurger location since 2017. Becoming a burger flipper might not be the dream job for your child, so you might think that this is no big deal. The reason why it probably is, is because flipping burgers and other menial restaurant work have been entry-level jobs for many people in the past. It is where they learn about business, teamwork and customer service, and get a foot on the job ladder. A great many entry-level jobs no longer exist.

CALL-CENTRE OPERATORS

The recurring theme found in this section is that those careers based on scripts that do not require (or do not *allow* for) creativity will decline. Automated systems, artificial intelligence, voice-recognition and voice-activated technologies will continue to replace human beings in contact and call centres and on helpdesks.

Note that we're not saying that *call centres* will decline. In fact, quite the contrary – they will proliferate. But they will become increasingly automated. The best-paying jobs are likely to be the technicians, programmers and scriptwriters who operate in that work environment.

TELEMARKETERS

Most people (apart from telemarketers, of course) will probably be pleased that this job will disappear – or at least they would be if only the annoying, unwanted sales calls weren't going to be replaced with even more annoying automated sales calls. Many telemarketing companies (especially small ones, which don't always play according to the rules) have adopted automated calls, which saves on staff-hiring costs and can engage potential customers at any time of the day or night.

If you're adamant that, at some point in your life, you were mis-sold payment protection or credit card insurance, it is unlikely that you will mourn the demise of telemarketers.

PHARMACISTS

Let's return to the medical world for a moment: we predict the demise of the pharmacist by the 2020s. Not to oversimplify, but in our health-care system, the role of the pharmacist is primarily to be a backup for the medical doctor. Pharmacists assess prescribed medicines and ensure that the person for whom they are prescribed knows what dosage must be taken, and won't have any allergic reactions or side effects to the medicine. But if an AI-driven medical computer can do this for us, and can even prescribe the correct medications based on our personal DNA and genetics, we won't need pharmacists at all.

MIDDLE MANAGEMENT, SUPERVISORS, SECURITY AND QUALITY CONTROL

By now, you will begin to see that many jobs that are under threat are concerned with controls and checks. Supervisors, quality controllers, security personnel, middle management and many other positions spend a lot of their time either passing information around or checking on other people and systems. The death of middle management was a concept we introduced in the first edition of this book, and it seemed rather far-fetched at the time. However, middle management is increasingly being made redundant in organisations around the world as AI takes over the roles of these people – supervisors, quality controllers, security personnel, etc.

AI-driven computers will perform all of these functions in future. Some of our clients are already reporting that they have removed middle management in their organisations.

SPORTS REFEREES AND UMPIRES

Almost every major sport in the world is bringing more and more technology into their games, aimed specifically at assisting – and, in future, replacing – referees and umpires. Players today are wearing digital trackers that provide coaches, referees and umpires with information and statistics about performance in real time. Might robots even become the sports stars?

FRONT-LINE SOLDIERS

If aircraft, ships and cars could be driverless in future, this will impact on the military as well. In addition, the military could potentially deploy robots in front-line combat situations in the future, which could save countless human lives. The military, in fact, is one of the biggest investors in robotic technology development. The military will offer job opportunities for drone operators, programmers or AI-developers, but old-school soldiers might be a thing of the past.

Look back to look ahead

If you don't think that the jobs we've mentioned above will disappear, take a quick look back over the past few decades at various jobs that were once in great demand, but are now almost extinct in most developed countries (people under the age of 35 might not even know what these are!):
- **Dockyard loaders:** Unloading a timber ship in 1970 took 108 men five days. By 2000, it took 8 men only one day. That's a 98.5 per cent reduction in man-days (540 to 8), owing to containerisation.

- **Typists (the 'typing pool'):** Typesetting began in the 1400s with the first printing presses. The trend away from typesetting to desktop publishing started in the early 1980s and was completed by the mid-1990s. The golfball typewriter made way for the personal computer, and thousands of typists lost their jobs.
- **Secretaries:** Individuals now do their own word-processing, with no need for secretaries.
- **Punch-card operators:** Prior to 1985, tens of thousands of people were employed as punch-card operators. They were made obsolete almost overnight as punch cards were replaced by other forms of digital input.
- **Fax-machine operators:** As the cost of fax machines decreased and they became commonly available, most people started handling their own faxes. Of course, fax machines largely gave way to email in the mid-1990s.
- **Telephone and switchboard operators:** Once a premier job, demand was reduced significantly by touch-tone systems and then, later, by voice-recognition technology and cellphones.
- **Film splicers and editors:** Digital formats of filming replaced the old cut-and-paste approach to editing film, both for home video and in Hollywood movies.
- **Draftsmen:** Manual drafting using a pencil and ruler was replaced by computer-aided drafting/design (CAD) in the 1980s.
- **24-hour photo processors:** There used to be an overnight photo-processing booth in every shopping centre in the world. Now there are none.
- **Stock-exchange floor brokers:** It wasn't that long ago that stock exchanges around the world were noisy places with floor brokers shouting out offers to buy or sell shares. This job has disappeared, along with many of the stockbrokers who worked in the back offices.
- **Video-store clerk:** Netflix isn't just changing how we watch TV, it will also be the final nail in the coffin of the video and DVD rental business.

GROWTH INDUSTRIES

'The defining characteristics of jobs that will not be replaced by machines are: creativity (research and academic jobs), complexity (strategy and management positions), dexterity (aero engineers, but also plumbers), and empathy and compassion (care providers, teachers).'
Dr Kai Fu Lee, founder of China's Sinovation Ventures,
at Davos in 2018

In addition to developing the skills that can allow us to collaborate with and compete against machines, it is also worth looking at which industries and careers are set to grow over the next two decades. These growth industries will emerge as some of the changes we have highlighted become entrenched in society – so, for every job that is lost, there is the potential of new jobs being created. Historically, this has happened in all previous industrial revolutions – so there is hope!

For example, let's consider driverless cars. We know that the technology that allows for autonomous cars to safely drive on our streets already exists. As the 2020s unfold, more and more countries will make driverless cars legal. We predict that during the 2030s, not only will driverless vehicles be legal, they will also start to become compulsory. When every car in a particular area is driverless, cars will be connected with one another and be able to communicate with other cars, resulting in the emergence of a 'hive mind'. Fatalities will decrease dramatically – around 94 per cent of all road accidents are due to driver errors.

Another benefit will be the reduction in congestion, as the cars will be able to calculate the optimal traffic pattern among themselves. A shift as significant as making driverless vehicles compulsory will happen at the same time: car sharing. An individual won't need to own his or her own car at all – driverless vehicles will be programmed to operate in an Uber-like system, with passengers simply occupying the next car that becomes available.

If all cars are required to be driverless and many are shared, this will result in job losses. Jobs that will be lost include those of chauffeurs, taxi drivers, traffic police, people who make and install traffic lights, panel beaters, insurance-company and car-financing employees, and car-park attendants, and there will be fewer nurses and doctors working in A&E at hospitals due to the reduction in car accidents. But, equally, many jobs will also be created. In any industry where robots and algorithms replace humans, there will be a need for people to design, build and install the robots/machines, and write the software.

However, this won't hold true for the 2040s, when machines might be so advanced that they are able to design and build other machines. For now, though, most AI relies on the creativity of intelligent people. Other industries could also benefit from the above scenario, including car manufacturers, which will require new designs for vehicles, advertising and media (we can picture a world in which a person could even use driverless cars for free if they're prepared to watch adverts in them), and pubs and restaurants (as people can safely 'drink and drive' again).

Apply the same exercise to any emerging technology: imagine what would happen if it became ubiquitous, and then list which jobs and industries will gain or lose by it.

The US Bureau of Labor Statistics Occupational Outlook for 2016–2026 predicts that the following 12 jobs will be the fastest-growing in the near future (we have combined a few job titles in our list):

- Solar photovoltaic and wind-turbine installers and technicians   +105%
- Home health- and personal-care aides   +47%
- Physician assistants and nurses   +37%
- Statisticians   +34%
- Physical therapists and aides   +31%
- Software developers for apps   +31%
- Mathematicians   +30%
- Bicycle repairers   +29%
- Genetic counsellors   +29%
- Information security analysts   +28%
- Operations research analysts   +27%
- Forest-fire inspectors and prevention specialists   +27%

Source: https://www.bls.gov/ooh/fastest-growing.htm (2018)

Here are some jobs and industries that we believe will grow in demand by 2030:

CLEAN AND ALTERNATIVE ENERGY INSTALLERS AND MAINTAINERS

We agree with the US Bureau of Labor regarding the growth of alternative energy industries, from the development of wind, wave and solar farms to generate energy, to redesigning and rejigging the distribution network, to the installation of private energy solutions in homes and businesses around the world.

DISASTER RELIEF, RECOVERY AND CLEAN-UP ENGINEERS

The impact of extreme weather and climate change could result in an increase in natural disasters, including extreme storms, droughts, floods and rising sea levels. This will see an increased demand for specialists in disaster management and emergency relief. There will also be room for creative solutions and new technologies to prepare for disasters, including opportunities for structural and civil engineers, app developers, surveyors, architects, politicians and town planners.

CARERS AND PERSONAL HEALTH-CARE ASSISTANTS

As more people live longer, every aspect of the health-care sector is set to grow. And while telemedicine, robotic surgical equipment and other forms of automation will change how some health care is delivered, as described on page 107, demand for caregivers is going to increase. Robots can take care of some of these tasks, but most people – especially the elderly – will prefer to have human carers.

The opportunities in the health-care sector extend far beyond front-line medical carers. Some estimates say that this sector will grow by more than 30 per cent over the next decade, adding millions of jobs around the world. This includes an increase in private hospitals, nursing and residential care facilities, and individual and family services. As the ageing generation of baby boomers rely more and more on social services, including adult day care and meal delivery services, managers of such businesses will be in greater demand.

> People of all ages are finding or creating jobs for themselves in elderly care in the developed world. Graeme's mom, who is in her 70s, is a case in point. She, along with a colleague of Nikki's, who is in her 40s, have earned a very good living doing this kind of work in the UK.

Employment growth will be driven by an increasing demand for health care and social assistance due to an ageing population and longer life expectancy. Also, as more women continue to enter the labour force, demand for childcare services is expected to grow.

Advances in medical science will result in new cures and treatments. This will happen at the same time as some diseases appear to be mutating, with the spectre of a global superbug emerging. Whichever way it goes – good or bad, or both – the need for medical and social services will increase exponentially over the next few decades.

SPECIALISED MEDICAL PROFESSIONALS

The role of medical research and drug development follows on from the previous section. Obviously, there will be continued efforts to cure some of the diseases that afflict humanity – from the killers like malaria, tuberculosis and AIDS, to the diseases associated with an ageing population, such as Alzheimer's, cancer and dementia. There will also be continued research into 'lifestyle cures', including sexual dysfunction, hair loss and weight control. And, of course, there will be a marked increase in work in the arenas of biotechnology and genetics.

In addition to research, there will be a high demand for medical sales representatives. But owing to the increasing complexity of medicines and the proliferation of options, these reps will need a high degree of medical training. There may also be a marked increase in information and technology that allows for home medical care and self-diagnosis, supported by travelling pharmacists and medical practitioners.

Another growth area will be in genetic research on plants and animals. For example, to feed everyone on the planet for just the next 40 years, we will need to produce as much food as we have done in the whole of human history up to this point! In order to do this, genetically modified plants that can grow in less than ideal conditions will become widely utilised. Research, new-style farmers, support staff, geneticists and ethicists will all be in high demand.

VETERINARIANS

It is unlikely that robots will perform surgeries on animals in the foreseeable future. Animal medicine is very advanced (linked as it is to experiments with drugs and procedures that will ultimately be used on humans), but the level of automation that is imminent in human medicine is not going to be available for animals for some time. There is a shortage of vets in the world at present, a situation that is unlikely to change any time soon.

EDUCATIONAL INNOVATORS AND AUTOMATORS

There is some debate about whether to include teachers on the list of declining jobs or under growth industries. There is no doubt that education and training will continue to be critical in the future of work, but we are convinced that this will manifest in very different ways to traditional concepts of schooling. It might mean fewer teachers in classrooms, but more people who are involved in managing educational innovation and automation. Jobs in education will be diverse, and will include curriculum developers, presenters of educational material, website designers, app developers, video editors, writers and animators.

EdTech (education technology) is a particularly fast-growing industry. From 2015, EdTech investments began to rapidly increase each year, surpassing $10 billion by 2019. It includes aspects of AI in education, such as individualisation of learning experiences, teacher assistance with admin, marking and scheduling, and online learning portals, which alone is set to surpass $6 billion by 2024.

CONTENT CURATORS AND MASSIVE OPEN ONLINE COURSES (MOOC) MANAGERS

In addition to educational innovators, a job that will emerge in the next decade will involve individuals who can find, filter and repackage information for the use of others, like creating internal 'universities' within companies. In particular, the market for MOOCs is bound to grow exponentially in the next decade.

At a conference in 2019, Antonia Cusumano, people and organisation leader at PwC, said that people will increasingly turn to dynamic resources for training and development: 'You're going to have 10 minutes on your bus ride home when you're commuting. You're going to pull up an app from one of the many businesses out there that are doing these mini-clips of video learning. I'd like to learn 10 minutes on C++ so that I can brush up on my coding. You're going to see learning shift to these little mini bite-sized chunks of information that you can get on the go and when you need it and at any given time.'

APP DEVELOPERS

Along with those who will write the automation software and build the robots that will drive much of the change that will happen in the 2020s, a particular subset of developers will be those who write, deploy and support the millions of apps we have available on our phones. Many of these apps are small and cheap, but an increasing number are big money spinners. The Apple App Store brought in $46.6 billion in 2018 alone.

GAME DEVELOPER

The most lucrative category of apps is games. The online and app gaming industry is already worth more than the Hollywood film industry, and is the fastest-growing and most lucrative entertainment industry in the world. Today's games are supported by large teams of designers and developers, and the people behind them possess a wide range of skills and expertise. Their jobs range from programmers to behavioural psychologists, marketing experts, kinesiologists (the study of human movement) and anatomists.

AUGMENTED-REALITY JOURNEY BUILDER

One of the specialist skills in the gaming industry, which will eventually extend to corporate and business applications, will belong to those who can design and develop virtual- and augmented-reality applications. The immersive nature of the VR experience means that it is not merely another type of screen. VR transports us to new worlds and different locations, and becomes a full sensory experience.

Designing meaningful uses of VR and AR requires a specialist skill set that will be in huge demand, and combines what has traditionally been considered to be two very different brain functions: the logical and the creative. Interestingly, Nikki's eldest son's first job (he has a BCom in strategic management) was selling virtual- and augmented-reality content. Already in existence are specialists who build AR journeys for people who want to cook just like Gordon Ramsay or Nigella Lawson.

DESIGN

We've mentioned 'design' a few times already. This set of career opportunities should come as no surprise to anyone. Almost every product, service and industry needs to be packaged and delivered to the market in new and exciting ways that capture attention. In a world of oversupply and proliferation of goods and services, only those items that compete successfully for attention and connect with consumers emotionally will be lucrative.

People who can design packaging, create advertisements, and develop connections through visual, auditory and other sensory design will become increasingly in demand. And specialists in 'UX' (user experience) are among the most sought-after professionals in the world right now.

Sir Jony Ives, for example, is Apple's chief UX designer. He was knighted for his contributions to technology, and is the third-highest paid Apple employee. Management guru Tom Peters reckons that designers will be in higher demand than MBAs. In fact, they already are – mainly because of undersupply, but still, Peters makes an interesting point.

> 'The MFA [Master of Fine Arts] is the new MBA [Master of Business Administration].'
> Daniel Pink, *A Whole New Mind*, 2006

> 'For every ten MBAs graduating in the USA in 2005, there was one job available. For every one Fine Arts graduate, there were ten job offers.'
> Tom Peters, *Re-Imagine!*, 2003

In our opinion, employment opportunities will grow for those people who design experiences for others. These include those involved in hospitality, tourism and customised adventure holidays. Those who are able to turn these services into exciting packages and market them effectively, using enticing design, will be very successful.

DATA DETECTIVES

These are professionals who will analyse data to provide insights that go beyond the obvious. It is one thing to extract an insight based on an existing set of behaviours, but it is something else entirely to dig into a pile of data and come up with something completely new. For example, Amazon and Alibaba, the online shopping giants, keep track of what their customers buy and then make suggestions based on those purchases. Who isn't familiar with the line: 'People who have bought this product have also bought the following'?

That's a fairly obvious set of information and is informative and compelling for users of their online shops. But what could a data detective discover if they took all that shopping data and looked at it differently? Could they discern that a customer was pregnant based on purchases they made over a few weeks? And if we combined your shopping activity with your travel schedule, could we make suggestions that would improve your health? The technology takes data from unconnected areas of our lives and seeks out patterns that we can't work out ourselves. It opens up a world of possibilities, tailor-made for each individual's needs.

INFORMATION AND ONLINE SECURITY PROFESSIONALS

If you're worried about all the data that's available for data detectives to investigate, rest assured – that's exactly why there will be an increase in the demand for much better online security. In addition to the current IT security expert, who guards our hard- and software against hackers, an array of advisors, consultants and security experts will help us manage and protect our online profiles.

SMART-HOME AND INTERNET OF THINGS DESIGNER, INSTALLER AND MAINTENANCE WORKER

The 'internet of things' is a phrase used to describe all the 'smart' devices we're connecting to the internet. A device becomes smart when we capture its data, share it via a network, control it remotely or give it some intelligence so that it can control itself. This allows us to automate the buildings we live and work in, and allow devices and machines to work in them without human help. It includes everything from remote-controlled doorbells with video links, to automated vacuum cleaners and lawnmowers that operate alone.

The plumbers, electricians and DIY experts of the future will be highly skilled, hi-tech people who can design automated systems, and then install and maintain them for us.

ARTISANS SUCH AS PLUMBERS, ELECTRICIANS AND WELDERS

Mike Rowe has coined the phrase 'dirty jobs' for electricians, plumbers, welders, tilers, etc., on his popular TV series *Dirty Jobs*. The world is desperately short of good, old-fashioned artisans and skilled tradespeople. Because these are not considered the most glamorous – or lucrative – jobs around, their popularity has waned considerably over the years.

The mikeroweWORKS Foundation provides scholarships for trades and advocates our need for them. Rowe connects the decline in blue-collar trades with the crumbling state of infrastructure in the US, but it is a global problem.

Although countries around the globe are experiencing unemployment crises, there is a paradox between unemployment and unfilled positions. For example, in 2018, the US Bureau of Labor announced that there were just over 6 million unfilled jobs available and only 6.8 million people unemployed, which either means people aren't prepared to do certain jobs or there is a shortage of specific skills.

We often hear that there is a shortage of software and app developers, as well as electricians. China Power & Light, for example, recently wanted to fill hundreds of positions for electricians, but the local population does not want to do that job. Instead, the Chinese are obtaining multiple degrees and then end up in customer-service positions, among other administrative jobs, for lack of anything better to do.

3D PRINT DESIGNER

It won't be long before every house has a 3D printer, or maybe even two. When our grandparents were young, they could not have imagined that there would be a fridge and freezer in every kitchen, let alone a microwave and coffee machine. We should therefore not be surprised to find that more and more people are installing 3D printers at home. As we write this update, 3D printers for home use are still novelty devices and can print plastic only. But sooner than we think, 3D printers for home use will be able to print out metals, polymers and a variety of materials – even food!

As 3D printers become more ubiquitous, we'll need experts who can create the designs that these machines require to function properly, to service them and to teach people how to use them (that is, teach older people – young people will just google a YouTube video on how to do it!).

DRONE PILOTS

Drones are not just for fun and games, or for taking some spectacular holiday videos and photos. Drones are being used in many industries, from the military to retail deliveries, from construction to movie-making. For example, should a natural disaster occur these days, drone data is invaluable for saving lives, surveying damage, and providing search-and-rescue operations with crucial footage of hard-to-reach locations. While many drones can fly autonomously, we predict that the job of drone pilot will become much sought after in many industries.

And when drones that are big enough to carry human beings are built, a whole new world of job possibilities opens up. This development might result in flying cars, and it is very likely that the first legal versions of airborne vehicles will require specialist pilots, much like planes and helicopters do now. (This is not just a prediction, by the way. Drones that can transport humans already exist, and they are relatively cheap to operate, don't require expensive infrastructure, like runways, and can stop in mid-air to drop off passengers or deliver goods.)

TOURISM AND HOSPITALITY

The rise of nearly two billion middle-class Indian and Chinese citizens with increasing levels of disposable income will lead to a global surge of tourists. It has, in fact, only just started – a veritable flood of tourists is expected in the next few decades. In addition to new countries entering the tourist market, baby boomers will become a generation of 'denture-venturers'. These are people taking a gap year in their senior years to globetrot. The difference between them and young adult backpackers is the amount of money they will spend and the luxury in which they can afford to travel.

In addition to all the obvious services – travel agencies (older people still prefer agents to manage their premium travel plans), travel insurance, financial services, airlines, cruise ships, rental agencies, food and accommodation providers, tour guides and extreme sport coaches, etc. – other requirements in future will include technology support, the shipping of purchases, security, translation and the provision of trusted information.

Travel will extend itself to parts of the world that are currently untapped, from remote deserts and ice floes to the ocean floor, and even into space. This will impact on construction, transportation and engineering, and the many more jobs required to design, create, maintain and utilise new areas of our world.

In addition to changes in tourism, the hospitality industry – including MICE (meetings, incentives, conferences and exhibitions) travellers, and restaurants and pubs – will continue to grow. Job growth will be concentrated in food services and drinking places, reflecting the worldwide increase in adult population numbers and dual-income families (often with fewer children and less discretionary time), as well as more sophisticated dining experiences.

LEISURE, SPORT, ENTERTAINMENT AND THE ARTS

Closely related to the previous section is the issue of how people choose to spend their leisure time and discretionary income. There will be an increased demand for all forms of entertainment, both passive and active, as well as for content in all manner of media that deliver entertainment. Job growth will also stem from public participation in the arts, entertainment and recreational activities – reflecting an increase in income, more leisure time, and an awareness of the health benefits of physical activity and personal fitness.

As for the arts, there will always be a need for artists and entertainers. Writers of books, movies, plays and TV shows will still be in demand, as will music composers and other types of artists. And in the greatest entertainment arena of them all, sports stars will be as popular as always. Jobs that require a high level of creativity and originality will be highly valued for decades to come, since they are the most difficult to automate and computerise.

eSPORTS PROFESSIONALS

Since the first edition of this book, electronic sports has seen a phenomenal rise. One of Graeme's business partners has a teenage son who is training to become an eSports professional – with the full blessing of his family. The top gamer in 2018 earned more than $50 million in prize money and endorsements.

eSports encompasses everything from first-person shooter games, where teams of players compete against each other, to drone-racing in stadiums. These competitions are hugely popular, and in countries like South Korea they can be played in packed stadiums with tens of thousands of fans paying to watch the games live. These 'events' could even be included in the Olympics soon, and the people who play these games will be as well known as the world's top sports stars.

In addition to the gamers themselves, other job opportunities in this burgeoning industry will include stadium builders, team owners and equipment developers. Add to that the promoters, agents, livestream video managers, commentators and game designers, and you have the potential for tens of thousands of people to make a living in this industry.

DENTIST

The previous section described the heady heights of a brand-new industry, but let's bring it down a few notches to those industries that might not be automated in the foreseeable future. On almost every list of jobs that are likely to be automated, dentists always come in right at the bottom. Some people joke that not even robots want to look in our mouths and fix our teeth, but the complexity and sensitivity of our mouths are the main factors here, as well as the customised service offered by dentists. No two mouths are the same, and no two dental procedures are the same, which means that dentistry is very difficult to automate.

HAIRDRESSER

Similarly, very few people will be comfortable with a robot styling their hair. This may change, of course, when someone unveils the Hal-dresser 2000 (see what we did there?), but we doubt it. It is a case not of what technology is capable of doing for us, but how much we are prepared to *let* it do for us. Hairdressers, make-up artists, stylists and pedicurists are likely to always remain in human form. Probably.

INFORMATION TECHNOLOGY

It should be obvious, but there is, and will remain, a huge demand for the people who design, build, install and maintain the IT systems that will result in the many forms of automation we mentioned. Sometime towards the end of the 2040s, we will reach what Google futurist Ray Kurzweil has called 'The Singularity'. This is when computers have enough processing power to mimic, and then overtake, human mental capacity. It remains to be seen, of course, whether they develop consciousness as we experience it. At that point, it is possible that machines will build other machines. Maybe. Until then, though, we're going to need millions of humans to be involved in thousands of different jobs in the IT sector. Becoming tech-savvy must be one of the easiest and most obvious ways to future-proof both yourself and your children.

Introducing MeInc.

Even if you are employed, you should be thinking of yourself as a free agent looking for the next opportunity, either within or outside your current organisation. If we think of ourselves as a business that is growing and developing, we might make different or more strategic decisions about our future.

ENTREPRENEURS AND INTRAPRENEURS

We've left the best until last in this list of growth industries. In addition to being tech-savvy, we should also instil an entrepreneurial mindset in our children; it is a foundational building block for being future-proof. By this we don't mean that every child should aspire to start and own their own business. In fact, only a small percentage of people are truly cut out to be entrepreneurs. But we do believe that an entrepreneurial mindset (they need to think of themselves as MeInc., no matter where they are in their careers) is vital, for four key reasons:

1. Because our children will live longer, they will work for many more years than we will. And they will also change jobs more often. There is no doubt that they will experience periods of un- or underemployment during their lives. If they save and invest their money wisely, they may even be able to afford optional working lives – working when they want to.
2. An entrepreneurial mindset is highly sought after in the world of work. This includes attributes such as resilience, creativity and proactivity. Entrepreneurs don't 'clock-watch' – they do what it takes to get the job done. They don't merely follow the rules – they try to work out what must be done and make it happen. They don't wait to be told what to do – they take initiative and are proactive. When this mindset is applied inside a corporate job, it is often referred to as *intrapreneurship*. And it gets rewarded, because it contributes a great deal to a company.
3. Freelancing – often called the 'gig economy' – is one of the fastest-growing sectors in the world of work. Companies are now micro-outsourcing all sorts of tasks to people outside of their organisations. It is

increasingly an option to earn a full-time living by freelancing for multiple companies. If you haven't been exposed to this world, have a look at the jobs people are asking for and the skills being offered on websites like https://www.upwork.com and https://www.fiverr.com.

4. A side hustle never hurt anyone. And for some people it might open the door to the next big thing in their lives. Many of today's young people aspire to this right from the start of their careers. A 2018 Gallup poll found that 77 per cent of US teenagers see themselves as future entrepreneurs, with 24 per cent of young people already having done some form of entrepreneurial work before leaving university (see https://www.gallupstudentpoll.com). Tim Elmore, researcher and author in this space, explains: 'The world is at their fingertips. With a smartphone in their hand, they have all kinds of information available, enabling them to see that they don't need a record label to become a songwriter or musician; they don't need a publisher to be an author; and they don't even need a company to create and sell a product. Thank you, GoFundMe. Ideas galore can be found online and they inspire a generation of "screenagers". The three elements of invention are now converging: (i) Opportunity—they see the chance to solve a problem and sell a product. (ii) Need—they need the money, after growing up in two economic downturns. (iii) Ambition—they're incentivized by the tools and recognition available.' (From https://growingleaders.com/blog/)

We believe that more and more people will prefer to work for themselves, and small companies and entrepreneurs will abound. But of course, being an entrepreneur is not for everyone. Some people flourish in more structured and predictable environments. Others simply don't want the stress of starting their own companies.

It is not within the scope of this book to guide you or your children in deciding what form their future employment should take. Understanding who you are and how you can be your best, however, is a critical factor for future success. The traits that will assist in making this decision will begin to emerge during the teen years. Thus, some form of assessment should be taken as early as possible so that decisions and plans can be formulated during the middle-school years.

Whether as an employee, intrapreneur or entrepreneur – and one will be able to bounce between all three in a web formation, not a linear journey – there is a set of skills, attitudes and characteristics that will help our children to be successful at whatever they attempt and wherever they find themselves. It is to this list of success factors that we will turn our attention to in the next chapter.

Jobs that will never disappear

With tongue firmly in cheek, we suggest that these 'jobs' will always be around:

- **Politicians:** We hate most of them. We adore a few. And we'll never get rid of them, no matter how hard we try.
- **Prostitutes:** Perhaps when they make androids as realistic as humans, this job could be automated. For the next few decades, however, the 'oldest profession' shows no signs of decline.
- **Artists:** Creative writers, comedians, actors, entertainers, painters, designers. Art changes and evolves with technology, so it will never disappear.
- **Religious leaders:** Many people will continue to look to religion to find meaning in their lives.
- **Criminals:** The crimes may change, but the 'profession' will remain.
- **Parents:** Okay, so it doesn't pay very well. Or at all. But there will always be a demand for someone to raise our helpless human babes.
- **Cyber-security experts:** When robots have finally taken over all the other jobs, we'll probably still want humans to keep an eye on the robots.
- **Professional sportspeople:** Even though robots will be able to run faster and further than athletes, it isn't going to be as much fun watching robots compete as it is watching human competitors strain every sinew and fibre of their bodies for our entertainment.

NEW CAREER OPTIONS

> 'Now, at both ends, there are jobs that are going to be fixed. At one end are people who are really special and specialized: Michael Jordan, JK Rowling, your brain surgeon – no problem, they're safe. They're not going to be outsourced or digitized. At the other end are people who are localized and anchored: your butcher, your baker, your candlestick maker, this cameraman here until they get a robotic camera, so they're all fine.'
> Thomas Friedman, *The World is Flat*, 2006

It should be obvious that the world of work in the next decade will look different from the current reality, and very different from the world we grew up in. In the next chapter, we will look at the key skills our children will need in order to remain relevant for this new world of work, and in the chapter after that, how schools and the education system need to adapt to prepare them for this changing career landscape.

Having said that, people's fundamental needs will remain unchanged for many decades. We all need to live somewhere, to eat, interact, connect, be entertained, and so forth. Jobs that are related to servicing basic and localised needs are unlikely to be geographically relocated, although the technology used to complete the jobs may change over time.

'Local' jobs – including artisans such as auto-repair technicians, plumbers and electricians; product and service providers such as restaurants and supermarkets; and amenities such as hairdressers, utilities and internet service providers – are all likely to remain in business for decades to come. Our children must be equipped to keep up with changes in technology, but these basic products and services will still be required to help local communities to function.

Equally, as the quote from Thomas Friedman points out, the most highly specialised jobs of today, especially those that require high levels of skill and/or high levels of creativity, are likely to remain in demand for many decades to come.

It is the non-creative, intermediary, middle-management type of jobs that will disappear before our children reach adulthood. There are four key insights we want to highlight now:

1. The old mindset that the professions were the 'best' career options, and that clever young people should aspire to become lawyers, doctors, engineers, accountants or other professionals, is outdated. Of course, if the child is suited to a professional career, and he or she takes account of the changing world of work and is equipped to counter the automation of their profession, and if he or she loves their profession, then they'll be properly future-proofed and ready to live fulfilled lives. But just being a professional won't be enough any more.
2. Automation, artificial intelligence, data analyses and machine learning will affect every aspect of our lives and impact the nature of every job in every industry. We must work to understand this fundamental shift in the world of work, and prepare ourselves and our children to partner with the machines and algorithms.
3. It appears that current high-wage and low-wage jobs are safest from the threat of automation. The jobs that are most at risk in the next decade are middle-wage jobs. Mid-level staff, doing mid-level work that is largely repetitive and 'part of the system', are most at risk. We don't want our children to get stuck in one of these mid-level jobs, doing mid-level work with mid-level skills.
4. Parents need to use their imagination and try to understand the emerging world of work so that they don't impose an outdated view of the world on their children.

It is not easy to predict what will happen in the future. Every time something changes in an industry, there are unintended, and unforeseen, consequences.

> A recent example that both Nikki and Graeme have experienced while travelling overseas is the automated baggage check-in systems at airports. Certain airlines no longer use conventional check-in counters and ground

> staff. Instead, travellers put their own baggage on a conveyor belt armed with sensors, which weigh, measure and print out luggage tags. Unseasoned travellers find it very tricky to peel off the tags and stick it on their bags, but there are staff members walking around who help these travellers with this basic task. They also deal with logjams that occur when conveyor belts grind to a halt because the sensors cannot 'read' a piece of luggage. The moral of this story is that during an industry shift, and while bugs are being ironed out in a system, more people are required, not fewer. Helping people adapt to change is a human job. Once we are over the initial adjustment phase, fewer people are required.

Bank tellers and ATMs (automated teller machines) are another good example of how we need to think about jobs of the future. ATMs were introduced during the 1970s and proliferated dramatically in the late 1980s. It was predicted that bank tellers would soon be made redundant. However, this didn't happen. But the job did change a lot.

Before ATMs, bank tellers spent most of their time either collecting cash from customers or handing it out. ATMs automated this process, and at the same time made the process much less costly to operate. In order to provide a better service, banks opened more branches, added more services and extended operating hours. They therefore needed more people, even though there were fewer tellers in each branch. Tellers today are focused on a broader range of customer services. Although the number of bank tellers is now starting to decline with the advent of app-driven banking, for a long time the number of bank tellers actually increased at the same time the number of ATMs increased.

Let's give another example of why a decline might not happen as expected. Let's take airline pilots. Very little of a pilot's time is actually spent flying the plane. In fact, planes can already do everything they need to do without a pilot, including taking off and landing. Yet there are two pilots, or three on long-haul, international routes, on each flight. This is really due to a social norm: would you want to fly in a pilot-less plane?

Science-fiction jobs that just might be a reality by 2040:
- **Corporate gene screener:** In the future, a genetic screen will be as common as a blood test is today. Employers will need technicians to collect and analyse DNA from potential staff members as they try to identify those with a propensity for drug abuse or other issues that could interfere with productivity.
- **Quarantine enforcer:** If a deadly virus starts spreading rapidly, few countries will be prepared to deal with it. Certain occupations will benefit from this misfortune. Nurses might be in short supply. And when people start dying in significant numbers, and neighbourhoods are closed off, someone will have to guard the gates.
- **Digital scrubber/undertaker:** There will be a growing need to remove online content about people either during their lifetimes or after death.
- **Algorithm bias auditor:** It was recently disclosed that certain job-advertising websites prioritised men over women. This gender bias was built into the system because most of the programmers at these companies are men. Algorithms don't write themselves, and someone will need to audit out bias and correct the system.
- **End-of-life counsellor:** With the likelihood that we will live a much longer life, we could reach a point where we choose to end it. To do so would require counselling and guidance.
- **Gene editor:** If we are able to manipulate our genes in future, we'll need experts who can edit our DNA as required.
- **Drone-traffic optimiser:** When drone-use starts to proliferate, and human-carrying drones become commonplace, a traffic-management system will need to be established.
- **Hydroponic vertical urban farmer:** We will soon start to produce food in new ways, including in indoor urban farms, which will require a new type of farmer.
- **Memory augmentation therapist:** Entertainment is all about the great memories it creates. Creating a better grade of memories can dramatically change who we are and pave the way for an entirely new class of humans. We will need doctors who are skilled in removing bad memories or destructive behaviour.

- **Asteroid mining companies:** While it is unlikely that human beings will actually travel to asteroids to mine them, we will need teams of people who manage the spacecraft, the mining equipment and run the companies that bring the materials back to Earth.
- **Mars colonist and space engineer:** Elon Musk has famously said that he hopes to die on Mars, 'just not on impact'. A whole range of skilled professionals will be involved in projects to transport humans safely to Mars.
- **Geo-engineers – weather-control specialists:** We are moving past the age of meteorology and climatology to one where true power brokers will control the forces of nature. This includes cloud-seeding, volcano-stoking, earthquake inducers, wind-funnellers and snow-makers.
- **Personal data broker:** In future, people will generate an income from their own personal data. In other words, instead of Facebook selling your data to Amazon, you will sell your own and make a profit from it. A personal data broker will monitor and trade your personal data on newly created data exchanges to ensure that you, their client, earn your deserved revenue.
- **Drowned-city specialist:** If climate change happens a lot quicker than anticipated, and considering that over half the world's population lives within five kilometres of an ocean, people's belongings will need to be rescued, and houses moved to higher ground.
- **Robot mechanic:** Middle-class families worldwide will be able to buy robotic personal assistants or companions. Sony already sells the Aibo, a robotic dog, for about $2 000. The dog doesn't need a vet – but he might need the occasional tune-up.
- **Animal guardian:** Should a gorilla have the same rights as a three-year-old child? There is a push to classify some non-human animals as 'persons' under the law. As our legal definitions change, we'll need specialised lawyers to represent animal interests.
- **Deep-sea city engineer:** An option for expanding our living space in the future is to go underwater or build on top of the sea. This will necessitate the building of floating cities or underwater residences.

- **Teleport specialist:** Imagine walking to a teleport station at the end of your block, dematerialising and then reappearing at your place of work. Cars would be gone, as would auto mechanics and petrol-station attendants, among thousands of other related jobs. Plus a whole new economy would develop around the teleporter. Okay, this scenario is a little far-fetched — cars probably won't disappear in 20 years. But hey, commuters can dream.

When we think about the technologies we've discussed in this chapter and whether they will come into existence in the next few years, we have to consider the political, regulatory, environmental, economic, societal and even religious implications of possible future scenarios before we can confidently predict that they will happen. It is an immensely difficult task, of course. And that is why some of you might think that it's not worth doing at all.

But you are misguided. It might be true that we can't accurately predict the future, but we can get a sense of what direction things are moving in. It makes it even more vitally important that we acquire the skills and mindsets that will allow us, and our children, to deal with anything the future might hold. We discuss this next.

Chapter 5

Developing X-factors for success in our children

'The past few decades have belonged to a certain kind of person with a certain kind of mind – computer programmers who could crank code, lawyers who could craft contracts, MBAs who could crunch numbers. But the keys to the kingdom are changing hands. The future belongs to a very different kind of person with a very different kind of mind – creators and empathizers, pattern recognizers and meaning makers. These people – artists, inventors, designers, storytellers, caregivers, consolers, big picture thinkers – will now reap society's richest rewards and share its greatest joys.'
Daniel Pink, *A Whole New Mind*, 2006

'Thomas Stanley has not only found no correlation between success in school and an ability to accumulate wealth, he's actually found a negative correlation. "It seems that school-related evaluations are poor predictors of economic success," Stanley concluded. What did predict success was a willingness to take risks. Yet the success–failure standards of most schools penalized risk takers. Most educational systems reward those who play it safe. As a result, those who do well in school find it hard to take risks later on.'
Richard Farson and Ralph Keyes, *Whoever Makes the Most Mistakes Wins*, 2002

So, whose job is it to prepare our children for the future, and what needs to be done? These are the questions we will attempt to answer in this section.

If even a fraction of what we have said so far comes to pass, it is critical for us to attempt to develop in our children the characteristics of successful, talented people from as early as possible. In this chapter, our aim is to be very practical and show you what you can actually *do* as a parent to create a solid foundation on which your children can develop their character, skills and habits.

There are five X-factors for success that will set your children apart in the future world of work. There is no single definitive profile of a successful person. Every book you read on success – and there are many! – will highlight slightly different characteristics, so we don't intend to create a similar list for you.

Instead, our goal in this section is to encourage you to think about what future success might require; to inspire you to be proactive and intentional in your parenting; and to provide you with highly practical suggestions about what you might do *with* and *for* your children to give them every chance of future success. Along the way we will supply references to a variety of works that we have found helpful, but these are by no means the only sources that we recommend on this important issue.

To make it in this new world, we need to 'model' talent for our children so that they can become talented. You cannot study to become talented, as talent is born of *who* you are, and *how* and *why* you do things; it is not necessarily just about *what* you do or know. Talent is based on the acquisition of X-factors, not grades. X-factors for success are not taught but mostly caught – via role-modelling and a process of osmosis – from parents, mentors, coaches and other significant people in our lives and those of our children.

The factors discussed in the next section are critical to your children's future success, regardless of what industry or field they select, and irrespective of their personalities and characters. We have given some very practical suggestions with which you can experiment. These lists should be seen as mere starting points for your own imaginative interactions with your children.

The most important 'talent X-factors' for developing exceptional young people include teaching our children to:
1. break conventions
2. be resilient
3. learn
4. know themselves
5. relate to others.

What follows are some tips for developing X-factors, some of which may turn into family rules. Bear in mind that the best rules are those that apply to each family member. For example, if your children are not allowed to make calls on their cellphones during family mealtimes, then neither are you!

1. BREAKING CONVENTIONS (CREATIVITY BY ANOTHER NAME)

> 'Curiosity is essential for progress. Only when we look to worlds beyond our own can we really know if there is room for improvement.'
> Simon Sinek, https://simonsinek.com, 2016

We cannot continue to do what we have always done, or just follow conventional rules, if we are to survive and thrive in the future. This is a time to connect the dots differently and to think outside the box, a cliché that refers to looking at a problem from a new perspective, without preconceptions. Because the world has never looked this way before, we must apply different thinking to a whole new set of problems and challenges. This may involve breaking old rules (when it makes intelligent sense to do so) and making up new ones, as well as piecing together information and experiences differently.

The concept of breaking conventions has nothing to do with bringing up children without limits or boundaries. Indeed, we believe that these are essential to raising children in a constantly shifting and changing world. Here, 'breaking conventions' means developing a way of thinking outside the dots.

A key defining factor of talented people, in any industry or arena, is their ability to break conventions, push boundaries, stretch the limits of performance and change the game. This may be the toughest skill to teach our children. The skills discussed will be helpful in building a foundation for breaking conventions.

Thinking outside the box

'Thinking outside the box' is most consultants' favourite phrase. It probably originated from the nine-dots puzzle of the 1980s. The challenge is to connect the dots by drawing four straight, continuous lines without lifting the pencil from the paper.

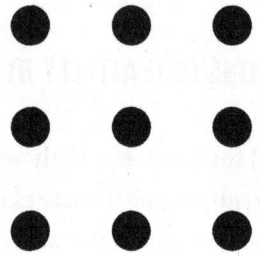

The puzzle is easily solved, but only if you draw the lines outside the confines of the square area defined by the nine dots themselves. Here is one possible solution:

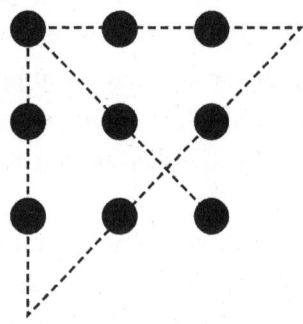

IMAGINATION AND PLAY

Great inventors, scientists and sportspeople never stop at the known limits presented by the world around them. They push the barriers because, as *Mind Power* specialist John Kehoe comments, whenever there is a conflict between will power and imagination, imagination always wins. All great discoveries have been made and records set by an individual posing a question, pursuing a dream or wanting to do the seemingly impossible.

This era we live in has also been called the Dream Society, in which products and ideas will be sold by the stories that are told around them, which strongly connect with people's emotions. In order to develop a company or product story, you will need to dream. (We highly recommend Rolf Jensen's 1999 book, *The Dream Society*.) One of the most sought-after skills in a new society will be storytelling. Successful companies will sell stories about products rather than the product itself. Good stories are memorable and they sell. Human beings love to be actors or players in a story, but most have never had the opportunity to be part of an unfolding dream.

So we need to create dreams in our businesses. Says Rolf Jensen: 'The future's realm of possibilities is always bigger than you imagine.' Whoever would have imagined, for instance, that there could be a market for Ice Age ice cubes made from imported pieces of the Greenland ice cap? By making this story the product in 1996, Copenhagen Airport single-handedly expanded the ice-cube market.

The Dream Society will demand the ability to visualise, to form images and ideas in the mind, especially of things never seen or not yet experienced personally. Imagination leads to original thought and is often driven by the dual thoughts 'Why?' and 'Why not?' Our children will need original thoughts and ideas to solve the problems and challenges of the world – problems that do not yet exist!

You hardly need to develop this ability in most children. The key is to ensure that you don't stifle it.

Tips for developing imagination

For all

- Tell stories. Tell the good old favourites – the fairy tales. Tell modern stories. Make up your own. Just tell stories. Avoid the shortened, abridged versions and look for the lengthy originals. Make sure your children *hear* stories. Note the word 'hear'. Television and movies strip away the creative, imaginative power of turning words into mental pictures.
- Tell ghost stories in the dark. It's great fun. Just make them up as you go along. These stories should obviously be age-appropriate and not unduly frighten younger children!
- Make up stories in the car. Each person gets to add another detail to the story.
- Keep a dress-up box at home for children to engage in fantasy play. They love different hats, old clothes, adult shoes, jewellery, pirate swords, masks, fireman and nurse outfits, fairy and king accessories, etc.

> Nikki once came upon her husband, Simon, with three-year-old Ryan on his lap, telling him an imaginative story about the small train engine embroidered on his slippers. Ryan was enthralled.

For younger children (1–5 years)

- Before going on holiday, instead of telling your children a bedtime story, tell them to close their eyes. Then make up a story, with the family as the main characters, going on a holiday to the exact place where you are heading. Obviously, this works particularly well if you are going back to a place you have previously visited. Get your children to visualise what you are saying and to imagine themselves helping to pack the car, on the journey, arriving at the destination, smelling the air on the beach, feeling the sand between their toes, etc. You could do something similar a day or two after your return from a holiday or from a visit to a particularly interesting place.
- Encourage your children's artistic efforts from the time they pick up their first podgy crayon. Never criticise their artwork or label it for

them. What looks to you like an aeroplane may be something entirely different to them. Encourage the process with comments such as 'I love all the colours you've used,' or 'Look at how you've covered the whole page with your drawing.' Stunting your children's imagination and creativity at an early age is interrupting a highly important, natural developmental process that will enable them to come up with original thoughts and creative solutions to life's problems at a later stage.

- Discourage the use of colouring-in books and worksheets in the early years. Large pieces of blank paper are the best canvas for a child's imagination.
- When choosing a preschool for your child, enquire if there is a creative art *and* a creative crafts programme, and ask what the difference is. Many schools churn out crafts at an impressive rate, but this is prescriptive. It does not allow children to exercise their imagination and creativity in the same way as art does.
- Always look at the art on the walls in a preschool. It will give you a very good idea as to whether or not children are being encouraged to use their own imagination. It's a good sign if all the art looks different. Also make sure that the children are being given large sheets of paper to work on. This is very important! Look for a play-based preschool programme, not one in which worksheets abound. Children in this phase learn best through concrete, real-life play experiences and not through abstract learning, which is boring and fails to stimulate the imagination.

For older children (6–12 years)
- Encourage your children to become avid readers. (Yes, we know some children are and some aren't, but give it a go – and persevere!)
- The *Harry Potter* series and *The Chronicles of Narnia* are examples of books and movies that could stimulate an older child's imagination.
- Encourage your children to express themselves through creative pursuits such as art, music and drama.
- Have fun by playing word-association and problem-solving games in the car instead of constantly talking on your smartphone, or allowing your child to watch Netflix on the way to school.

- Encourage your children to play app-based games on their devices (or on your phone until they get their own) that are free-flowing and encourage personal expression. Minecraft or dress-up games are good examples. We particularly like the games produced by Toca Boca (see https://tocaboca.com/).
- PlayStation and strategy computer games enable older children to play in an imaginary world. Play the odd game with your children; it's a way of accessing their world.

You will have noticed that play has been mentioned often in this section, so it would be appropriate to say a little more about it here. Play is the language of childhood. It is a child's work, the way children learn, and is the least stressful way of doing so. Play can help a child to achieve almost anything. It is often multisensory and appeals to a variety of different intelligences at the same time. From this, you will understand why play becomes a memorable experience and makes learning fun.

The philosopher Plato said: 'It is the essential nature of man to play.' We were born to do it; it is hardwired into the very core of who and what we are.

The definition of play from the *Collins Concise English Dictionary* is: 'To occupy or amuse oneself. To fulfil a participative role in a team. To give a dramatic performance. Fun and light-heartedness. Games and diversions.' Play is all these things and so much more. It is truly multidimensional with mental, physical, emotional and even spiritual significance. It reflects the holistic nature of our beings, our interconnectedness within ourselves and with our world as a whole.

Through play, small children begin to understand their physical world. They become aware of their bodies and learn to communicate. Play helps them to solve problems and enriches their creativity and leadership skills. Play, or stimulation through the medium of play, actually grows and wires their brains.

CREATIVITY

> 'You see things; and you say, "Why?" But I
> dream things that never were; and I say, "Why not?"'
> George Bernard Shaw, renowned Irish playwright (1856–1950)

We live in what some are calling 'the imagination economy', in which imagination, innovation and creativity are rewarded as never before.

We often think of creativity as an attribute of mad scientists, designers or artists. However, the ability to think out of the box and to employ original thinking to problem-solve are critical life skills for any career today. We would go so far as to say that creativity is a core element of our very survival! It is a vital way of expressing who we are, since we all do things differently and for different reasons.

THE BUTTERFLY OF FREEDOM

'Why do you fly outside the box?'
'I fly outside the box because I can.'
'But we *know* the box. We are *safe* inside the box.'
'That, my friend, is why I leave it. For you may be safe,
but I am *free*.'
Edward Monkton, *Happiness*, 2007

One of the myths that exists around giving children creative freedom is that no boundaries should be imposed. On the contrary: true creativity is being creative within set boundaries. If you say to kids, 'Go and play a game,' more often than not they will reply, 'I don't know what to play or what to do.'

But if you change the instruction to 'Try to create a game that uses these three balls and a stick,' you will obtain a much better result. Boundaries can enhance creativity because children are forced to use their imagination. In a room full of toys, no imagination or creativity is required to work out how to have a fun-filled afternoon – you just flit from toy to toy, window-shopping.

But having only one toy to play with for a few hours ensures that, out of necessity, creativity and the imagination are engaged to alleviate boredom.

> Nikki asked her son the following question when he was 11: 'If I gave you a box of LEGO® and said you have one hour to build a military vehicle without an instruction booklet, would you find that fun?' His eyes lit up. Excited, he said: 'It would be such fun because it's not what other people think you should build, it's what *you* think you should do. It's using your own ideas.' Much more fun than using a LEGO® kit with an instruction booklet!
>
> When playing with a friend's six-year-old daughter, Jenna, Nikki asked her to build a fairy castle out of a bag of wooden blocks, with the specific instruction that it was to have two towers. Jenna tackled the project with gusto, taking great pride in showing Nikki her masterpiece 15 minutes later.
>
> It was a stimulating and absorbing whole-brain exercise. It required Jenna to use her left brain to problem-solve by designing within the parameters of a bag of blocks and two towers, but allowed her right brain to be as creative as it liked.

School encourages creativity within very specific norms and structures, and few worthwhile things have been invented within standard norms and given structures.

> **'The Wright brothers invented the airplane because they were willing to fly off a cliff hundreds of times. Edison invented the light bulb because he played around with all those different filaments. The truly creative person has an insane devotion to an idea, banging away at it from all sorts of angles in all sorts of ways. School doesn't permit this ... Teaching to the test, the inflexibility of [curriculums] and policies, and the mass production of students, stifles creativity.'**
> Roger Schank, *Coloring Outside the Lines*, 2001

It is up to parents to create spaces for creativity to develop.

Tips for developing creativity

Children are full of wacky ideas. Take them seriously. Ask a lot of questions about them, and get your children to think them through and to verbalise them. Just as you play games with your child, you can play with his or her ideas, too. Fantasy play in which children make up their own roles and rules is great for creativity.

Here are some more very doable ideas:

For all
- Don't always answer all of your children's questions. Help them to find the answers for themselves.
- Let your children be bored. You don't have to jump up and respond every time they say, 'But there's nothing to do!' Let them solve this 'problem' themselves, without your help. Just give them permission to go and play.
- Create reasons for different family celebrations, in addition to the usual birthdays or religious festivals. For example, have a Rugby World Cup dinner just because dad is a rugby fanatic and it is World Cup month.
- Play word games in the car instead of talking on your smartphone, or becoming frustrated with the traffic, or allowing your children to play on your phone or listen to the news on the car radio (usually fairly negative content).
- Cook or bake together.
- Grow a garden together.
- Play a wide variety of games – some with toys and some without.
- Prolong childhood by allowing children time to engage in unsupervised free play. Children need time out in nature or at home to be alone with themselves. This enables them to process all the input they receive in order to create meaning. Children today move so quickly from wearing fantasy costumes to dressing like adults, and from playing like children to acting like adults. They need the time and freedom to be children. A longer childhood is preferable in terms of adjusting to adolescence.

- Don't overschedule children with too many organised, supervised, prescriptive activities. Play dates and free play are essential to their development.

For younger children (1–5 years)
- Provide your children with plenty of opportunities to create their own artwork in their own way. From shaving cream on the bathroom mirror or on the glass of the sliding patio-door, to pavement chalk for use on the driveway, to paper, paint, pastels, play dough, etc. But there are two rules – Rule 1: Your child should work on the surface provided, and nowhere else; Rule 2: Do not interfere with your child's creative process. Encourage the process more than you praise the outcome, for example: 'I just love the colours you are using'; 'Do you have a name for what you have painted?'; 'I can see how much thought you have put into your drawing.' Don't ever label children's works of art for them. Allow them to tell you what they are all about (what looks like a fish to you may be the sun to them). You should not disturb or unsettle their creative process.
- Look for a preschool that runs a play-based curriculum, pays attention to creativity and movement, and is not dominated by worksheets and prescriptive art. (As mentioned previously, it's always a good idea to look at the art on the walls when shopping for a school. If every child's art looks different, it's a good sign that children are being allowed to express themselves.)
- Turn ordinary time or activities into special experiences that reinforce your connection with your children while, at the same time, stimulating their skills. For example, lay the table together, play games in the car, or do spelling homework in shaving cream on the bathroom mirror.

For older children (6–12 years)
- Serve a 'perseverance breakfast' (or lunch or dinner) for your child who has been working really hard to improve a grade (or a skill) in recognition of his or her effort. A little creativity can go a long way to

engender excitement and anticipation in children in what would normally be rather mundane situations.
- Create family adventures and holidays together. The older children become, the more involved they can be in the planning and decision-making.
- Encourage your children to put together plays with their friends and siblings for special occasions.
- Organise creative birthday parties for your children – you do not have to do what everyone else is doing. If you want a good party, just base it on play. For example, plan a Mad Food Party with a cryptic menu. Children might end up ordering a knife, fork, spoon, salt and pepper for their first course, and ice-cream with mayonnaise and rice for their main course, etc. Children are attracted to, and delighted by, creativity.
- Encourage your children to play with shape games and to make their own picture or design out of shapes without copying a picture card. Construction toys such as LEGO® are great for creativity when they are used without instructions and children are left to pursue their own ideas.
- Encourage your children to play with apps that develop their creativity, including meme generators, painting programs and image manipulators.
- Ask your children what they think about current world problems and if they have any solutions. You will be amazed at how creative their solutions can be!

EXPERIMENTATION

Children are naturally adventurous. The best way to learn at a young age is by trial and error (personal experience), so experimenting comes naturally to them. We slowly shut down our children's curiosity because we fear their health and safety will be compromised, and as we become irritated with their constant tinkering that fails to fit into our busy schedules. This is a serious error on our parts, since the skills of experimentation and investigation are both critical for success in the 21st century, and are essential characteristics in talented people.

> Hannah is crazy about the reality TV show *MasterChef* and really enjoys cooking. When the family goes on holiday, they have *MasterChef* competitions on a few of the evenings, encouraging experimentation with new food dishes. Sometimes it doesn't quite work out as planned, but most often something delicious is produced – and consumed.

Tips for developing an experimental mindset
For all
- The easiest way to encourage an experimental mindset is to consciously experiment on an ongoing basis. For example, tell your family: 'Tonight we are going to experiment with some new tastes and smells as you prepare an extraordinary dinner with unusual ingredients. You can even start with dessert first!'
- Do actual experiments with your children. Safe and fun science experiments are available at all good toy stores. These can do many things, from firing rockets, to testing wind speed, to building a home volcano. Various books packed with ideas for science experiments can also be purchased at good book stores. Your local library might have a useful selection of ideas, too.
- Ensure your children have a variety of different construction toys and brain-teaser games. These allow them to experiment through trial and error with different solutions to find the one that works. A tower made up of blocks will fall down if the base is not wide enough – but you only learn that through experience! This is a safe way of allowing children to experiment and, the more they are encouraged in this area, the more confident they will be when challenged by real-life situations that require creative solutions.

For younger children (1–5 years)
- When driving to preschool or the shops, take a different route. Take random turnings and see where you end up. Make sure you get your children involved in the fun of this experiment.

- Let your children bake with you. Baking is always a wonderful experiment. Next time you use the same recipe, add another ingredient just to experiment, such as raisins to bran muffins.
- Make jelly. It's the perfect science experiment, changing as it does from solid to liquid to solid.
- Making fruit smoothies also fascinates children, as different ingredients create a different result in taste and appearance.
- Play dough, slime, crystal growing, etc., are great for experimenting.

For older children (6–12 years)
- Eat out at a variety of different restaurants, exposing children to food from different countries.
- Teach your children to test the swimming-pool water to learn about acidity and alkalinity.
- Water-skiing and snow-skiing demand physical experimentation to develop the necessary skills to master the particular environment and equipment.
- En route to your family holidays, try to stop at a different national monument or tourist attraction each year.
- Encourage your children to plan family days once a quarter. Give them a budget, but very few other limits to restrict them. The only rule should be that they should do something none of the family has ever done before.
- Ask your children to suggest a new app every fortnight. Try it out for two weeks and give feedback to each other. Then also discuss which apps you should be deleting from your devices, and why.

> In Graeme's family there is a simple rule at restaurants: you have to try at least one bite of every new food that is on the table. You can't say, 'No, I don't like it' until you've actually tried it! Because of this simple rule, Amy, at age six, discovered that she was a sushi fan. And she even mastered the use of chopsticks. But Amy doesn't like tomato sauce. That's Rebecca's favourite, and she'd have it on anything. As long as you

> try, you can then make your own decisions about your likes and dislikes. But you can't decide until you've tried. By the way, why *can't* you have tomato sauce on cornflakes? Rebecca would like to know.

INITIATIVE AND PROACTIVITY

A core characteristic of talented people, which is most prized by their managers, is the fact that they go beyond what is expected of them without being told to do so – they take the initiative and are proactive. This connects specifically with the aptitudes of experimentation and imagination, but it also refers to leadership in that talented people make determined efforts to find solutions to problems.

At times, modern parents have been labelled as helicopter parents – they are overprotective of their children and hover over them. Ironically, children who are mollycoddled and raised almost risk-free are at greater risk than children who enjoy more freedom. Children need a certain amount of risk in their lives to help them to solve problems and develop personal initiative and coping skills.

This starts from toddlerhood. For example, allow small children to navigate the stairs so that they can learn how to do it for themselves. Children who are always carried up and down stairs, for fear that they will fall, are at greater risk of falling down the stairs because they haven't had the chance to experiment and work out the skill for themselves.

This is not to say you should be negligent, but you need to find the balance between allowing your child to develop and use his or her initiative, and protecting your child from all the bumps and bruises that accompany learning.

Tips for developing initiative and proactivity
For all
- Let children try things for themselves as much as possible. It means that they will sometimes fail, and we have to be ready for this. We can't always rescue them when we see failure looming, and, while securing their health and safety, take the time to help them fix their failures (if

that's possible) and debrief their learnings. This can be tough. Should you resist the urge to rebuild your child's tower of blocks when it tumbles to the floor, or refrain from talking to her coach if she never gets to play in her preferred position in a team? There's no right answer. You need to determine how much struggling/challenge your children can cope with. But here's a hint: it's probably a lot more than you imagine, and just a bit more than they did last time.
- Allow children to help you prepare and cook meals, lay the table, make beds and do everyday household chores. Non-verbally, you are expressing your belief in their capability by encouraging and permitting their involvement, instead of sending them to watch TV while you do it all by yourself. This instils an 'I can' mentality, which fuels initiative and proactivity.
- Say 'yes' to as many of your children's ideas, suggestions or requests as possible when it comes to showing initiative and being proactive. If it is not convenient or practical at that particular moment, then say, 'Yes, but not right now.'

For younger children (1–5 years)
- Teach your children how to do things for themselves, such as fastening their seatbelt, doing up their own buttons and tying their shoelaces. Make sure that you give them enough time in your busy schedule to do these things without rushing them, showing irritation, or winding up doing it for them anyway because you have run out of time.
- Give children the responsibility of watering plants and feeding pets.
- Encourage your children to become involved in art and other creative outlets, such as drama, music or pottery.

> As Rebecca is autistic, she is much happier with structure, routine and predictability. Even so, Graeme and Jane work hard to help her develop initiative and be proactive. This can include simple prompts phrased as questions that help her to get ready in the morning. So, instead of telling her to brush her teeth in the morning, they ask, 'Rebecca, have

you done everything you need to do before you go to school?' This places the onus on Rebecca to think through what needs to be done. It turns into proactivity over time, as Rebecca feels that she has taken responsibility herself.

When Nikki's boys were 15 and 11, respectively, they were on holiday with their aunt and uncle when their aunt was rushed to hospital at five o'clock in the morning. Ryan and Matthew were left with a baby of six months and a seven- and 10-year-old for over 12 hours, and they had to cope – from nappy changes and bottle feeds to making meals for the older children and keeping them entertained and as calm as possible, while they were not sure what was happening with their mom. These sorts of situations test your children's initiative and resourcefulness. Make sure you have passed on life skills to your children so that they can cope without you.

For older children (6–12 years)
- Teach your children to pack their own school bag from Grade 1 so that it becomes habit. In this way, they learn to plan ahead and prepare for the next day, which shows initiative and proactivity.
- Encourage your children to do homework when there are gaps in their daily schedule, such as half an hour between extramural activities. This will save them time later and teach them effective time-management skills.
- Give your children the opportunity to make decisions or to help you with the decision-making process. If you are planning a holiday, for example, ask your children what they think needs to be packed.
- From time to time, ask your children how they think things should be done. Then try them in the way your child suggested for a change.
- Teach your children to switch off lights when they leave a room that will not be in immediate use thereafter. (The energy crisis has provided a great opportunity for implementing this lesson!)

2. RESILIENCE

'Resilience is knowing what to do when you don't know what to do.'
Jean Piaget, *Child Psychology*, 1986

Resilience is simply defined as successful adaptation to risk and adversity. Some would define it as survival in the face of multiple challenges, while others would describe it as coping with trauma. Resilience is the new mantra for the millennial generation. As members of an era experiencing unprecedented levels of change and shift, they will need to be the most resilient generation ever. Resilience and constant flexibility will help millennials to adapt and survive.

There is a lot of debate about whether or not resilience can be taught. Some experts assert that you either have resilience or you don't. Others argue that various skills can be learnt that result in resilience. We believe that you can nurture resilience in yourself and your children, realising that your resilience quotient is impacted upon by a multitude of factors, including personality, health, self-esteem and environment.

In *The Secure Child* (2003), Stanley Greenspan describes a study of Hawaiian children who had grown up in adversity. Those children who managed, despite the difficulties they encountered, all had one thing in common. The 'hidden strength', as Greenspan called it, was neither physical nor intellectual. It was access to a nurturing and supportive relationship with a relative or other person in the community. According to Greenspan, resilience emerged not as a state of mind, but as a reflection of the relationships available to the child.

Annie Greeff, author, educator and trainer, explains that we are born with an innate capacity for resilience, a so-called 'self-righting capability' that enables us to adapt to changing circumstances and to develop:
- social skills
- problem-solving skills
- analytical thinking skills
- autonomy
- a sense of purpose.

Resilience also involves:
- having strategies for getting the best out of yourself – assuming that you live in a multiple-intelligence world and it is possible to develop the full range of your talents
- loving learning
- being able to keep going when things get tough
- being resourceful (having a good, full 'tool kit' of techniques)
- adapting and responding to circumstances
- having self-knowledge, or knowing yourself.

Research shows that resilience leads to happiness. One of the traps that parents of millennial children have fallen into is striving to keep their children happy and stress-free from an early age, which does not help them to develop resilience. In fact, overprotection is a form of deprivation.

> 'The idea that a child should avoid misery at all costs distorts both the reality of life and the ways children learn to find happiness ... Learning to build these inner resources for a happier life demands that we endure the hard knocks of the playground – boot camp for the inevitable upsets of everyday relationships. Given how the brain masters social resilience, children need to rehearse for the ups and downs of social life, not experience a steady monotone of delight. When a child gets upset, the value lies in attaining some mastery over that reaction.'
> Daniel Goleman, *Social Intelligence: The New Science of Human Relationships*, 2006

Tips for developing resilience
For all
- Research shows that the most important component of resilience is a solid emotional base for every individual, and knowing that you are loved unconditionally by others. Therefore, it is essential to give your children regular, focused, undivided attention. This, more than anything else, communicates your unconditional love to them. They also need to know that your love for them is not related to their performance, but simply to who they are.

- Resilience emerges out of self-awareness and self-esteem. See the section 'Know yourself' on page 199 for practical tips on developing self-awareness in your children. When they fail or are stressed, help them to understand the link between the situation they are currently facing and their strengths and weaknesses.
- Girls tend to become resilient by building strong, caring relationships. Boys usually bounce back by learning how to problem-solve.

What to say to your children instead of 'Be careful!'
Help your child foster awareness by saying:
- Notice how … these rocks are slippery, that branch is not as strong as you think.
- Do you see … the broken glass, the busy road?
- Try using your … hands, feet, arms, legs.
- Try moving … quickly, strongly, your feet carefully.
- Do you feel … the heat from the fire, the power of the rushing water?
- Can you hear … the wind, the thunder, the silence?
- Are you feeling … scared, excited, tired, safe?

Help your child problem-solve by saying:
- What's your plan … if you climb to the top of the tree, fall into the pool?
- Where will you … put that stick, dig that hole?
- What can you see … to get across, for your adventure?
- How will you … get down, get across, slow down?
- Who will … be with you, help you if …?

For younger children (1–5 years)
- As children get older, start taking them on family walks and slowly progress to hikes. It's good to push them every now and then to break their own personal best. Small children can walk by themselves without being picked up for 15 minutes or so, but they can learn to extend this if they are encouraged.

- Allow children to get dirty and climb trees.
- Obviously keep a watchful eye on your child's antics, but don't always rush over the moment he or she trips or falls. On most occasions, if children think you aren't looking, they will pick themselves up, dust themselves off and carry on as if nothing had happened. They often cry for effect. (Of course, we are *not* encouraging you to be irresponsible parents here!)
- Allow your children to sort out their differences with their siblings with as little interference as possible. Obviously there are times when you must step in, but sibling rivalry is also a way of learning to be socially resilient.

For older children (6–12 years)

- Today's teenagers are more at risk of anxiety and depression than any generation in history, says Andrew Shatte, co-director of the Resiliency Project at the University of Pennsylvania, Philadelphia. 'Yet our ongoing studies for the last 10 years show we can cut the adolescent depression rate in half and make kids more resilient by teaching better thinking skills.' For 12 weeks, the Penn researchers taught children how to tell the difference between productive and self-defeating thinking. They used the story of *The Little Engine That Could* to illustrate the importance of a positive attitude, and of *Chicken Little* to illustrate the pitfalls of catastrophic thinking. Researchers then instructed the children to look at their own fears and ask themselves, 'What's the worst that can happen?' and 'How likely is it that this will pan out?'
- It's never too early to teach children physical and mental relaxation exercises. These include breathing techniques, some forms of meditation, mental imagery and muscle-relaxation exercises. Help your children learn to recognise their own stress triggers and responses, and to identify which relaxation methods work best for them.
- Encourage your children to laugh – read funny stories, watch age-appropriate comedies, laugh at their jokes, play the fool with them sometimes, and find the humour in various people and situations.

- Avoid rushing in to fix what is not working for your children emotionally. Where possible, try to help them to develop coping skills for next time rather than fixing things for them every time.

FLEXIBILITY AND ADAPTABILITY

If the world is going to continue changing as much as we suggest, then a critical skill will be the ability to change and be adaptable. We prefer to think of this as flexibility, because we are not advocating change for the sake of change. Think of a stiff piece of plastic – it is flexible because it can bend into a different shape but, when it is let go, it springs back to its original shape. Our children need the structure of routine as the basis for a consistent and calm life. But they also need to develop an ability to change and be flexible when required.

> 'It means that you stay permanently flexible, because it is only by being so that you can achieve synchronicity with a world that has, itself, entered into a state of permanent flexibility, a world that is being subtly and meaningfully altered every single day. Here's the real secret of successful people and businesses: They are different every day of their lives.'
> Watts Wacker and Jim Taylor, *The 500 Year Delta*, 1998

Tips for developing flexibility and adaptability
For all
- It's important for children (both young and old) to have a routine. However, you can stretch them a bit by following the same routine but in a different environment, such as while away on a holiday or when visiting a friend. This gives you so much more flexibility as a family and ensures that your children learn how to adjust and adapt when situations and circumstances change.
- Develop a trusted circle of friends and family with whom you can leave your children from time to time. Life is a journey to independence and children need to learn such skills from an early age if you want them to be flexible.

- Always have a Plan B in mind. If there is a fairly good chance that you may need to use it, then talk your children through the options before they happen. In this way, they are mentally prepared for change and will not be taken by surprise. For example, if you are going to a meeting that has the potential to run longer than your time schedule allows, resulting in you picking up your child late from school, then warn your child that he or she may receive a message to go to aftercare, and that you will pick him or her up there. Or, you may have a friend who will pick your child up for you if necessary – just make sure that your child knows the plan, if possible. If children feel well prepared and that you are in control, they panic less if situations or circumstances change.
- Remember that some children are more flexible and adaptable than others. Those to whom this does not come naturally need encouragement, but they may also need some time to develop this trait.

For younger children (1–5 years)
- When children start to attend school, they learn to be sociable, to play with each other and to get along. This demands a certain amount of flexibility and adaptability, especially when it comes to sharing.
- Avoid giving in to your children's demands and whines all the time, as this teaches them to try to shape the world around their own wants and desires. Imposing discipline and saying 'no' to your children will help them to develop critical life skills. Focus on the bigger picture next time you feel that it's just easier to give in to a whining child.
- Tell your children stories that emphasise resilience, for example, *She Persisted: 13 American Women Who Changed the World* (2017) and *She Persisted Around the World: 13 Women Who Changed History* (2018) by Chelsea Clinton.

For older children (6–12 years)
- Children can also learn flexibility by adapting their skills and abilities to suit various platforms and different media, such as PlayStations, computers, smartphones, etc.

- Watch from a distance as your children play with siblings and friends. Later, chat to them about their interactions and give positive suggestions and practical examples of what they could have done differently. This is not about discipline or correcting behaviour, but rather a form of training and discussion around options and possibilities.
- Encourage your children to play problem-solving computer games, rather than just 'smash 'n bash' and 'shoot 'em up' games.

PERSISTENCE AND PERSEVERANCE

A 'never give up' attitude is typical of those who are identified as talented. Having said that, however, it is generally true that these individuals are quick to give up things they know they're not good at, and are unbelievably tenacious in those things they want to succeed at.

In a world in which we are spoilt for choice, so, too, are our children. From the multitude of extramural activities on offer from the time that they enter nursery school, to the plethora of games and toys they have to choose from, and the variety of media they have access to, it's easy to see why our children may want to have their cake and eat it, too!

It is essential that parents act as guides and mentors in helping their children make wise choices. This also includes sticking to choices that have been made. For example, if your daughter decides she would like to do ballet but, after the first class, makes up her mind that she dislikes this activity, do you – as a parent – allow her to give it up immediately, or do you insist that she continue for the first full month or the first full term to get a proper feel for it?

Stickability is a wonderful word to associate with persistence and perseverance. Sticking to the task at hand teaches self-discipline and commitment, both highly important qualities for 21st-century living. It usually takes a lot of time and practice to become good at something. Perseverance is a core character trait to possess. It shows grit and determination, which will help a person to succeed alone or as a team player.

Life is rarely straightforward. It will often be unpredictable and will always toss ups and downs at you. It rarely follows a linear path. Therefore, part of any good future-proofing plan involves making sure that your children develop persistence and perseverance.

Tips for developing persistence and perseverance

For all

- Share inspirational stories (tell them, read them, watch movies about them) of people who have persevered in the face of adversity.
- As with all of the aptitudes and skills that we have outlined in this section, it will help enormously to praise your children for the behaviour you are trying to develop in them, especially at times when they are playing games, learning new sports and completing unpopular chores.
- Encourage your children to save up for things they want. Avoid fulfilling all their desires immediately, or they will have little to look forward to, or to strive for.
- Bringing children up with a positive *I can, I am, I will* mentality will assist them greatly in the development of perseverance and persistence. It's all about being committed.

For younger children (1–5 years)

- Don't give up on potty training. Show your enthusiasm and support for your child's efforts.
- Allow your child to become frustrated – it is good for development and pushes him or her to the next level, for example, sitting up and falling over, standing up and falling down, or battling to push shapes into a shape sorter, or a key into a lock.
- Throwing a ball to a child over and over again to help him or her master the skills involved develops persistence and perseverance.
- Praise children when they develop difficult-to-acquire skills that take some time to learn – like riding a bike or playing a musical instrument. Have one of the celebration dinners we talk about elsewhere.

For older children (6–12 years)

- Encourage your children to share their own stories (by telling, writing or drawing them) about times when they did not persevere and the outcomes that resulted, and vice versa.

- Encourage your children to keep a journal. If they wish, it could focus on experiences that have required them to persevere and which have taken place over an extended period of time.
- If, at first, your child does not make a sports or cultural team, encourage him or her to keep trying. Children need to practise to improve.
- We've talked about computer, tablet and smartphone games a few times. Get involved in playing these with your children, and reward them when they reach key difficulty levels in the game.

LEARNING FROM FAILURE

If we develop creative children who are prepared to experiment, then we must expect them to fail. Failure is part of the process of innovation. Obviously we do not reward or encourage failure, but we do reward effort and learning from failure.

This point is linked to 'Experimentation' on page 153, but let's take it a step further. The only way to push our boundaries is to fail along the way. But we should guide our children to 'fail forwards' and not backwards, as the renowned leadership expert John C. Maxwell famously says in Failing Forward (2000).

We must help our children to see that mistakes are stepping stones to success. This is the difference between achievers and average people, and is also linked to persistence and perseverance. One of the most well-known examples of this is Thomas Edison and his invention of the light bulb. Edison and his team tried and failed thousands of times, but he did not give up. Rather, he chose to see each failure as just another way of how *not* to make a light bulb!

We need to help our children to shape their perception of, and response to, failure, and to master their fear of failure. This starts right from the moment they first learn to sit.

Tips for mastering the fear of failure
For all
- Be a positive role model. Let your children see *you* experiencing successes and failures. They will learn how you handle the emotions

that accompany success and failure when they see these in you. Don't hide your disappointment and pain from your children when you experience failure. But also teach them how to be an honourable winner and a gracious loser.
- Celebrate successes to help your children see what they have done well. When children fail, do not try to cover up the failure – allow them to grieve the failure and help them to process it. Too many parents try to pretend that a failure did not happen, or they tend to apportion blame and deflect the failure from the child – 'It wasn't you, darling, it was that silly referee.' Not enough parents acknowledge failure while remaining positive and affirming.
- Provide a structured routine at home. The daily routine can be reassuring for your children after things have not gone well.
- Put your children in situations in which they are bound to fail or mess up in some way, such as playing sport. Everyone makes mistakes; you simply cannot win all the time. This is how you get good at what you do.

> At age 14, Matthew and a schoolmate entered the National Science Olympiad and made pykrete. This is a mix of frozen water and sawdust that should be able to withstand the blast of a bullet. Unfortunately, they forgot to agitate the mixture while it was freezing, much like you would when making ice-cream. The result was that the mixture separated and the sawdust sunk to the bottom. When the pykrete blocks were subjected to the bullet test, they shattered instantly. The experiment was a complete failure. The boys were up until late that night writing up their report and presentation for the next day. Nikki encouraged them to be honest about the failure, to analyse it and report on it, detailing what they had learnt and what they would do differently next time.
>
> Believe it or not, they made it into the top-10 entries in their grade at their school because the teacher said their presentation, and how they had learnt from their failure, was so compelling!

For younger children (1–5 years)
- When your children first learn to sit and then overbalance, or take their first steps and stumble, do not make a fuss when they fail. Have you noticed that when you pretend not to have seen your children take a tumble, they do not cry – they just get up and carry on? However, if they are aware that you have seen them fall, they often produce a spectacular display of tears and really play up the situation. Your response to their failures and mistakes is very important.
- Play games that require taking turns, at both winning and losing.

For older children (6–12 years)
- As children grow older (from five upwards) and make mistakes, you can chat about these. Say things like, 'All of us make mistakes – that's how we learn. So what did you learn from this today? And what will you do differently next time?'
- Play computer and board games to expose children to winning and losing.
- Play team sports in which good sportsmanship must be displayed when winning or losing.
- Role-model good sportsmanship for your children – especially as a parent on the sidelines.
- Watch famous sportspeople and discuss their behaviour, both good and bad.

SELF-DISCIPLINE AND DELAYED GRATIFICATION

Self-discipline is the ability to take action, regardless of your emotional state. Deferred or delayed gratification is the ability to wait in order to obtain something that you want.

In a landmark 1960s Stanford University study by Walter Mischel, four-year-old children were each given a marshmallow and left in a room. They were given the choice of eating it immediately, or waiting 20 minutes, when they were promised an additional marshmallow as a reward for waiting.

In videos of the experiment, you can see the children squirming, kicking, hiding their eyes – desperately trying to exercise self-control in order to get two marshmallows. Some children simply couldn't wait and ate their marshmallow right away. Others waited and received an additional marshmallow. The study's real significance was revealed 14 years later.

The researchers found that the 'grabbers' suffered low self-esteem and were viewed by others as stubborn, prone to envy and easily frustrated. The 'waiters' had better coping skills and were more socially competent and self-assertive, as well as being more trustworthy, dependable and academically successful. This group scored about 210 points higher on average in their SATs (US scholastic aptitude/assessment tests, required to be taken before entering college). For more on this fascinating study, read *Don't Eat the Marshmallow ... Yet!* by Joachim de Posada and Ellen Singer (2005).

Tips for developing self-discipline and an ability to delay gratification
For all

- Practise doing some disagreeable things in daily life. This may be tough to force on your children, but it is worth doing. Your mind and feelings will oppose doing these activities, but nevertheless they should be done. Just as muscles become stronger by resisting the power of weights, so inner strength is attained by overcoming inner resistance. Some mornings brushing teeth can be as disagreeable to a child as tidying up all the toys he or she played with when a friend came to visit and didn't help to tidy up.
- Make sure your children assist you with daily household chores. Don't allow them to procrastinate or grumble about doing them either – chores are part of life.
- Be consistent with the dos and don'ts. By making these rules, you are instilling in your children a lifelong habit of self-discipline, which will help them to develop a strong personality and a positive attitude.

> Nikki's eldest son, Ryan, saved up for an iPod when he was turning 12 and they were still in vogue. A while before his birthday, he and Nikki went shopping to check out the best prices. Ryan had fallen in love with a limited-edition, red iPod – red in support of people living with HIV/AIDS.

> But there were none available in the shops. No problem – Ryan used the internet to source an online supplier based in Cape Town. His birthday was about a week thereafter, so, with a five-day delivery promise, timing was not going to be an issue.
>
> Waiting for delivery is delayed gratification, especially if the item is something you want desperately and you have waited for a long time. The day of Ryan's birthday arrived and Nikki collected the promised parcel from the post office, only to find that only a highly inadequate half a delivery had been made – the parcel contained the speakers and the silicone cover. The iPod itself, in a separate parcel, had been mislaid!
>
> Would you believe that it took another three weeks for the iPod to arrive? Ryan's patience was impressive, and a lot better than that of his parents! There is no chance they will ever use the same supplier again!

- If you're religious, focus on traditions that require self-discipline. Christians, for example, have Lent. For the 40-odd days leading up to Easter every year, many Christians will give up something they really enjoy (such as sugar in their tea, or chocolates, or even a bad habit such as sulking). Muslims similarly fast during Ramadan. Doing this as a family and holding each other accountable builds self-discipline. Different religions and cultures have different practices.
- On Christmas Day, or any other religious festival during which gifts are shared, teach your children not to rip open all the wrappings on their presents immediately, but to savour and enjoy each gift, slowly and patiently. Families have different rituals that can help small children with this process. For example, on 25 December, Christian families may open presents in Christmas stockings before breakfast, go to church, then open family presents around the Christmas tree on their return from church. What is your tradition of giving?

For younger children (1–5 years)
- Let your children make jelly – often. Apart from it being a great science experiment of which they never tire, jelly takes a few hours to

set, which requires waiting and patience. Either make it at lunch time to eat in the evening, or make it the day before you need it. This is an excellent activity for teaching delayed gratification.
- Allow children to keep silkworms. This will require many weeks of picking and gathering leaves, feeding, and waiting for the silkworms to grow and fatten up before they start spinning their cocoons.
- Encourage your children to grow beans. They will have to remember to water them every day, while watching the natural growing process with wonder.
- Take your children to restaurants – proper restaurants, not just fast-food outlets – where they have to sit and wait patiently for their food. Ensure that you find ways to keep your children occupied, distracted and well behaved while waiting for their meal to arrive.
- Teach your children to complete tasks – simple tasks when they are small, and more complicated ones as they get older.
- Extend your children's ability to concentrate by being part of the play experience yourself. The more involved you are in their games, the longer they will be able to play without losing interest or getting bored. Teach your children well, and they will learn how to play by themselves and to concentrate for longer periods.

For older children (6–12 years)
- Create a positive, regular homework habit from Grade 1 – preferably homework at the same time every day in the same place. This regular focus and consistent effort will ensure that your child achieves some rewards and learning will become easier with more practise.
- Place a limit on screen time, especially 30 minutes before bedtime. This is not only extremely healthy, but develops good self-discipline.
- It will become a much bigger issue as your children hit their teen years, but if your child has their own devices, you need to let them monitor, measure and limit their screen time each day. You should start this when they are as young as possible.
- Saving for something special takes a lot of self-discipline, because it takes a long time to save enough for the purchase.

- This point should be obvious – simply do *not* give your children everything they ask for, when they ask for it.

A SENSE OF HUMOUR

By 'sense of humour', we do not mean the ability to tell good jokes. Rather, we believe that the ability to laugh self-deprecatingly at yourself, not to take your own experiments and failures too seriously, and to live life with a lightness of touch is critical to being emotionally resilient and identifiably talented. Every truly successful individual will be able to point back to moments of failure and disappointment.

What makes these individuals successful is how they respond in these moments, and how they pick themselves up and use the failures to develop. We discussed learning from failure earlier, but part of the process is to be able to laugh at yourself and not to take life too seriously.

A good sense of humour is a tool that your children can rely on throughout life to help them:

- deal with failure and disappointment
- see things from many perspectives rather than just the most obvious
- be spontaneous
- grasp unconventional ideas or ways of thinking
- see beyond the surface of things
- connect better with others
- enjoy and participate in the playful and fun aspects of life
- not take themselves too seriously.

The experts agree that our children need a healthy and well-developed sense of humour if they are to manage everyday life happily and successfully. Our children are not born with a sense of humour – it is something they learn, and their ability to find the amusing, the funny, the hilarious is based on what they know. Children with a sense of humour grow up to be adults with a sense of humour. And adults with a sense of humour enjoy life more – their relationships are more successful, they enjoy better health, and they are better able to deal with stress and difficulties.

> One of the young girls in Nikki's lift club spent a whole year in and out of hospital, undergoing chemotherapy for lymphoma. Her mom tells the story of the two duty doctors, whom they nicknamed Dr Yes, Yes, Yes and Dr No, No, No. If they wanted to ask a favour, they always made sure that they asked when Dr Yes, Yes, Yes was on duty because – yep, you got it – he was more likely to say yes! These little labels added a touch of lightness and humour to an otherwise incredibly stressful and serious situation.

Tips for developing a sense of humour

For all

- As with all of the tips throughout these sections, the example you set is probably the best teacher. Don't be scared to laugh at yourself in front of your kids.
- Children love to make jokes, as this is a wonderful, fun way for them to demonstrate new skills and knowledge. They also love to laugh at your jokes. With any luck, the jokes will improve as your child gets older!
- Take your child's humour seriously. Encourage your child's attempts at humour, whether they entail reading (potentially unfunny) jokes from a book, or drawing 'funny' pictures of the family dog. Praise your child for trying to be funny, and be open to surprise – the first time (and the next, and the next …) that your child makes you laugh is one of life's great pleasures.
- Teach children that adults are funny – and that they can be, too. Make humour a part of your day-to-day interactions with your children and encourage them to share amusing observations or reactions, even when you are around other adults.
- Making up stories when travelling in the car can be a good source of instant humour (and an excellent way of passing the time). Someone starts with 'Once upon a time …' and you go round the car in a circle, with each person adding some colourful detail to the story. The story doesn't have to make sense, but it will certainly be fun!

> The children in Nikki's lift club knew that they would always play a word game or two on the way to school. Storytelling is something they all loved to do just before arriving at school, because they would usually end up in hysterics. Children often come up with off-the-wall, sometimes quite bizarre, and frequently hilarious, ideas. One story involved a tall oak tree falling down after being struck by lightning, squashing a hapless squirrel, being hit by a taxi, and having a flying bunny jump out of its branches!

For younger children (1–5 years)
- Create a humour-rich environment and surround your children with funny books. For toddlers and preschoolers, these include picture books or nonsense rhymes.
- Make silly jokes. For example, try calling Daddy 'Mommy' and watch how your three-year-old howls with delight.
- Tickle each other and make funny faces.
- Surprise your child by jumping out from behind the door or doing other nonsense but fun activities.

For older children (6–12 years)
- Older children tend to love joke books and comics. There are also many amusing television shows, hilarious movies and funny websites for all age groups. Some Instagram, TikTok and YouTube accounts are designed for humour – encourage your children to share these with you. Help your children to make good choices, then enjoy them, too.
- Buy your children joke books and make sure that you listen to their jokes. Also teach them how to deliver a good joke, with a pause and a great punchline.
- Use GIFs and funny memes in your family WhatsApp group messages. Don't be put off by their groans at your out-of-date sense of humour – secretly, your children love it.
- Have a family prize for the joke of the week. Write it out and put it up on the fridge.
- Go on family adventures that you can talk and laugh about later.

> Graeme and Hannah have been playing a game since she was about five years old – it is ongoing, and will probably end up being a lifetime thing: they try to scare each other. They lie in wait and then surprise the other, trying to get the hapless victim to jump. Graeme is definitely a master at this. On one legendary occasion, he waited for Hannah to go and brush her teeth. He then snuck into her room and hid in her cupboard. He waited over half an hour while she got ready to go to bed and settle down for the night, and then leapt out of the cupboard. Needless to say, Hannah didn't go to sleep for quite a while afterwards. (Obviously, you need to know your child and how they'll respond before trying it yourself!)

OPTIMISM

> 'Over the last three decades a major cultural shift has taken place in the attitudes of Western societies toward the future. Optimism has given way to a sense of ambiguity ... [which] threatens to stifle hope at a personal as well as a social level.'
> Miroslav Volf and William H. Katerberg, *The Future of Hope: Christian Tradition Amid Modernity and Postmodernity*, 2004

Optimism means being able to expect the best from life's experiences. It means nurturing hope, and having confidence and a strong belief in your ability to deal with any situation. It is about thinking positively. Being able to look on the bright side helps all of us to surmount challenges and manage life's difficulties. Optimism is not about being foolish or unrealistic.

Without optimism, we often become a victim of life's circumstances. We simply react to what is, rather than take part in shaping our own reality. Complaining about how tough life is does nothing to help our children grow up with a sense that their destiny lies in their own hands, and that they have the power to choose and shape their lives. Living in an Age of Possibility means it is essential that we empower our children from a young age. They must learn early on that all choices come with responsibility and consequences.

If we don't have optimism for the future, our children are in danger of growing up with a sense of hopelessness. This is easy when you take into account the staggering amount of negative press that surrounds them in every country of the world. It is our involvement with, and influence on, our children that can transform this negative into a positive.

Tips for developing optimism
For all
- When dealing with success, focus on what traits in your child made the success possible, and examine other successes that might stem from these traits. In this way, you keep a future focus and can link it to a success that your child has just achieved.
- Don't praise indiscriminately. Telling children that everything they do is great, rather than helping them to experience real successes and persist in the face of reasonable obstacles, puts them at a disadvantage. It creates an overly strong self-focus and often makes them more vulnerable to depression. So, validate success, but also acknowledge when your children's efforts are not successful. Children learn to recognise empty praise.
- Help your child to see that there is good and bad in most situations. Make a game of looking for the silver linings in seemingly negative situations. For example, if your child can't play outside because it's raining, look at the positives of indoor play, or highlight the advantages of having extra time to study. Even a broken leg can bring the fun of having friends sign the plaster cast! The game can get silly, but that's okay – it's a good habit to form.
- Rephrase what your child says in order to accentuate the positive. Use different words to make more positive sense out of a situation. For example, your child might say: 'I never have anyone to play with.' You, as parent, might reply: 'Sometimes it's hard to find a friend, but last week you had a good time with Mary.'
- Tell your own stories of overcoming hardships: 'When I was a child, I thought ... but then I realised ...'
- Use stories or movies to inspire conversation.

For younger children (1–5 years)
- Play with your children as often as possible. It creates that 'feel-good' sense for both of you and increases their happiness quotient.
- Involve your children in household chores – from making beds to cooking. This is a way of giving them positive strokes because they feel included, useful, capable and part of the exercise. It engenders an 'I can', positive feeling, which is also good for building their self-esteem.

> **'Hope is that thing inside us that insists, despite all evidence to the contrary, that something better awaits us if we have the courage to reach for it, and to work for it, and to fight for it.'**
> Barack Obama, *The Audacity of Hope: Thoughts on Reclaiming the American Dream*, 2008

For older children (6–12 years)
- Optimistic thinking does not mean downplaying your child's responsibility where failure is concerned. It is perfectly acceptable – and certainly instils optimism – to look at external circumstances that may have contributed to things going awry. But it's also important to assess where your child went wrong and to ensure that he or she takes responsibility for the error or failure. Instead of a self-blame session for your child, however, it's affirming – and optimistic – to discuss what your child can personally do in the future to improve next time. See this as a 'looking for opportunities to do better' approach.
- The ways in which adults *think* and *express themselves* about a child's experiences are very powerful in shaping the child's beliefs about the reasons for success or failure. For example, an optimist might say: 'It seems to me that you usually get good results when you give yourself enough time and really try hard with your maths homework.'
A negative person, who fails to boost his or her child's self-esteem, is more likely to say: 'You see! You *never* allow yourself enough time and you just don't try hard enough with your maths homework.'

SELF-CONFIDENCE

> 'So if you want a person to achieve his utmost and to persist in the face of resistance, reinforce his belief in his strengths, even overemphasize these strengths, give him an almost unreasonable confidence that he has what it takes to succeed ... And if this person succeeds, should you praise him for his hard work or for his unique strengths? Always the latter. Tell him he succeeded because his strengths carried the day ... It doesn't matter if this assessment is, in part, an illusion because it is an illusion that will serve to create a better reality. It will reinforce the self-assurance he needs to be resolute and persistent when taking on the next challenge, and the next.'
> Marcus Buckingham, *The One Thing You Need to Know*, 2005

Self-confidence usually grows out of mastery. Young children learn to master skills through repetition. Whether it's learning to walk, talk, match shapes, identify colours or play a sport, practise and plenty of failure lead to learning and, ultimately, success. And, of course, the better you get at something, the more confident you become in your ability and in yourself.

Self-confidence in one aspect of your child's life can easily transfer to other aspects. There can be a positive knock-on effect.

It seems that some children are just born plain confident, while others acquire confidence over time. There is plenty that parents can do to help build their child's self-confidence, which is a highly desirable trait to possess during the child's school years and in later life. Self-confidence does not manifest itself in arrogance or boastfulness. It is a secure sense of self, a sense that 'I am able' and 'I am worth it'.

Tips for developing self-confidence
For all
- Encourage your children to ask for what they want assertively and clearly, pointing out that there is no guarantee that they will always get it. Acknowledge them for asking, and avoid anticipating their desires. (This is different to anticipating and fulfilling their basic needs for food, water, sleep, stimulation and appropriate attention.)

- Teach children to change their demands to preferences. Point out to children that it is not possible or good for them to get everything they want, and it is pointless to display anger in this regard. Encourage them to work against anger by setting a good example. Reinforce their behaviour when they display appropriate irritation rather than anger.
- Teach your children life skills, such as how to swim, how to cross the road safely, how to build a fire and light it, how to make a sandwich, and how to answer the telephone or make calls themselves. (These are just a few ideas among a plethora of possibilities.)
- Encourage other significant adults in your circle to play social sport with your children, and even family board games and apps. Children's self-confidence gains an additional boost when other adults show interest and confidence in their abilities.
- Celebrate and acknowledge your children's achievements and strengths. For example, acquire or make a family celebration plate that is brought out at dinner time for a particular family member to eat from on any day when he or she has won a race, been especially compassionate towards a friend in need, been extraordinarily helpful, etc. Remember to celebrate not just achievements or birthdays – the 'what' – but, more importantly, anything that comprises the good inner nature of your child – the 'who'. And Mom and Dad get to use the plate, too!
- Always have a Plan B up your sleeve just in case you need it, and teach your children about this important secret to success, too. Knowing there is another plan to fall back on certainly provides a modicum of self-confidence.
- Stick to your promises. If your children have confidence in you, they also develop self-confidence.

For younger children (1–5 years)
- Show your belief in your children's capabilities by giving them responsibilities, such as feeding the goldfish each morning, setting the table, helping you to maintain the garden, or assisting you with preparation for meals.

- Arrange play dates for your children. When they are small, you will need to 'play and stay' instead of 'drop and run' to role-model for your child how play dates work and to build their confidence in this area. The older they get, the more confident they will become when you drop them off to play with a friend.
- Attending playgroup and preschool builds social skills and self-confidence.
- Play perceptual games, simple card games and basic board games with your children. As they learn 'how', they develop confidence.

For older children (6–12 years)
- From the age of six, allow your children to walk to their classroom by themselves from the school gate. Children are on a pathway to independence from the time they are born. When we let them go, little by little, we are showing our confidence in them.
- Together with your child, work out the study method that suits him or her best. When you hit the correct button here, your child's self-confidence improves, as well as his or her marks.
- Help your child to know him- or herself – see 'Building a Talent Profile' on page 251.

HEALTH

The biggest asset you have is yourself. It follows then that the more care you take of that asset, the easier living and learning will be. Physical health is becoming increasingly important as we live longer than people in ages past, and we need our bodies to function effectively for many more years than previous generations did. At the same time, food has become less healthy and nutritious, poorly affected by mass farming techniques and relentless refining and processing.

Of course, health is holistic. It's not just about keeping your body healthy, but your mind, emotions and spirit, too. Stress, anxiety and strong emotional reactions can all interfere with our ability to learn, to absorb and process information, and to use it efficiently and sensibly. Teach your children to honour their bodies. And teach them to get in touch and in tune with themselves, to know when they need to take a break, and when enough is enough.

Health is so important that it will be taken into account when your children negotiate a work contract in the future. We are also well aware that overuse of devices and screens can negatively impact our eyesight, sleep patterns, muscle tone, and mental and emotional health.

Tips for keeping your children healthy

It is not our intention to provide you with comprehensive information on health and nutrition – that would be a book in itself. We recommend that you read various books on the physical development of children, as well as on child health and nutrition, to assist you in understanding what is happening (and what is *supposed* to happen) within your child's body during the first decade of his or her life. In addition, do not hesitate to seek expert professional advice about anything that concerns you, for example, from occupational therapists and developmental specialists.

For all

- Good nutrition optimises the way your mind and body works. A well-functioning mind and a healthy body increases self-esteem and resilience.
- Buy a good water filter and guide your children into a habit of water being the drink of choice to quench their thirst. Educate your children about the health consequences of drinking cool drinks and energy sports drinks that are high in sugar. The first organ to dehydrate when the body needs water is the brain, which will make your children irritable. They will also find it difficult to concentrate, which will interfere with their performance and ability to learn.
- Make exercise and recreation a family affair. If your children see you exercise, they are more likely to take it up themselves and develop a lifelong positive habit.
- Bring your children up with some form of spiritual life. We are multidimensional beings and spirituality is part of who we are. This will enable your children to make decisions about their beliefs

and meaningful sources of spiritual nourishment when they are older and better informed. Encourage tolerance of all faiths and creeds.
- Teach your children to honour the planet and take care of the environment. This is the world they will inherit. Good habits start young, such as sorting the household refuse into recyclables, glass, plastic, cans and garden waste. As in many other families these days, it is their children who have pushed the Codringtons to recycle, reduce meat consumption and consider the planet in the commercial decisions they make. Listen to your children on these issues – they do seem to know what we must do to protect our planet.

For younger children (1–5 years)
- Teach your children healthy media habits from a young age. This will help them to protect their minds from 'media pollution' and their bodies from radiation from one screen or electronic device or another.
- Part of a good routine is that there is a time to eat and a time to sleep.
- As far as possible, have set mealtimes and try to eat at least one meal a day together as a family.

For older children (6–12 years)
- Inform and educate your children about drugs and their effects from an early age by having frank and honest conversations and discussions with them.
- Teach children to 'read' their own bodies so that they can tell you when they have a headache, need a doctor or physiotherapist, feel down, etc.
- Do not overschedule your children so that their days are literally spent going from one organised activity to another. Bear in mind that while extramural activities are an essential part of your children's lives, they still need time to play, socialise and 'chill'. They need downtime to simply 'be'.

Digital detox

In Nikki's book *Tech-Savvy Parenting* (2014), written with Arthur Goldstuck, they discuss the impact of gaming and social media usage on the brain. Moderation is better than bingeing. Incorporating technology into your children's lives includes setting boundaries. Everyone should be off screens for at least an hour before bedtime to allow brain chemicals to normalise, including the sleep hormone melatonin, which is affected by the blue rays of screens. Children should not be going to sleep with their devices. Apart from the fact that they keep them awake because they can continue connecting and gaming, they also disrupt sleep well into the night as alerts keep coming in on social media apps. Smartphones emit radiation, and the majority of tweens and teens in Nikki's digital-safety workshops admit to falling asleep with their cellphones next to their heads as they listen to music. Have a charging station where all devices go at bedtime – including yours.

3. LEARNING

In a world in which information is being generated at an unprecedented rate, it is absolutely essential to continue to learn throughout your life. A love of learning, in addition to the skills and competencies you *have* to learn, will be among the most important characteristics we can instil in our children to ensure that they remain continually relevant – as well as continually intrigued and engaged by life. Regardless of what life throws at our children, if they are willing and eager to learn, they will be able to work out how to cope. We need to stop trying to educate and overwhelm our children with a whole lot of information they may only *possibly* need. Instead, we need to start instilling in them an ability and desire to learn what they need to learn, when they need to learn it.

CURIOSITY

This remains the 'best toy in the store'. It's about exploring and searching for new ways, ideas or approaches to accomplish things. Asking 'why' is an innate human drive that we need to protect and encourage. Accepting the status quo today does not signify progress. We need to support our children's quest to explore and discover their world.

'Encouraging kids to explore their ideas – no matter how unusual or strange those ideas might seem – is within the power of all parents. The key here is creating a relationship and an environment in which questioning becomes second nature,' comments eminent psychologist Roger Schank in *Coloring Outside the Lines* (2001), which we highly recommend you read.

> A friend of Nikki's overheard her six-year-old daughter, Claudia, and a friend discussing why big people have children. This is how the conversation went:
>
> So that big people can play [with the children].
> So that big people can love.
> So that trees are climbed.
> So that big people can go out and work to earn money for the little people.
> So that big people can have big houses.
>
> Out of the mouths of babes!

Why forms the basis for all human enquiry. It indicates a passion for life, a quest for knowledge and understanding, and fuels all learning. If you have a preschooler, you will be all too familiar with the constant stream of 'why' questions. It's fascinating to listen to what young children ask about, but it can sometimes become rather irritating because they ask so many questions so often.

According to neurophysiologist and educator Carla Hannaford, once speech is in place, the child will process thought verbally until about the age of seven. This stream-of-consciousness speech (as they think it, they say it) acts as a problem-solving tool for four- to six-year-olds. 'Why' is the generator of that process.

In her book *Smart Moves* (2005), Hannaford comments: 'This stream of consciousness speech, in varying degrees, is essential to language and thought development. Inner speech development (when children think before they speak) doesn't normally occur until around age seven, so children literally think aloud. I'm sure children of this age wonder if adults ever think because we are so quiet!'

So next time your child asks another 'why' question, know that it is a vitally important part of his or her intellectual development.

Tips for developing curiosity
For all
- Take your children to visit places of interest, such as the planetarium, museums, zoos, game reserves, etc. These places provide a variety of contexts for the 'why' questions, as well as opportunities to connect information between experiences.
- Go on holiday to different places so that your children can start to compare their holiday experiences.
- Most children are curious about where their parents disappear to each day when they go to work. If you work away from home in an office, then make sure you take your child to your place of work for a visit. When your child is old enough – from around age six – let him or her sit in with you for half a day to see you in action.
- As mentioned previously, do not always provide your children with answers to their questions. Rather help them to discover the answers for themselves. Psychologist Roger Schank has a great deal to say on this subject:

> 'When children ask questions, they're expressing interest in a subject and setting the stage for a true teachable moment. Most children (and most people in general) don't ask questions to receive answers. They ask them because they're intrigued, puzzled, and provoked. They want the chance to bounce ideas off an expert, to get some guidance so they can find the answer themselves. This is especially true when children ask open-ended questions ("Why do we die?", "Why do birds have wings and we don't?"), but it's also true when they ask factual questions.'
> Roger Schank, *Coloring Outside the Lines*, 2001

So, engage your children in discussions. Ask them questions in return, such as, 'What do you think?', 'What do you know about birds?', 'Why would they need wings?', etc.

> On National Women's Day in 2007, Matthew was seven years old, and he asked Nikki why it was a public holiday in South Africa. When she answered that it was Women's Day, he said, 'Does that mean we need to buy you something?' She said no, and he countered with, 'Don't you think we should at least buy you a bunch of flowers?' Very dear.
>
> Later in the day, both her boys wanted to know why there was a Women's Day and not a Men's Day. Instead of answering, Nikki asked them why they felt women were important in the world. Matthew jumped in by saying that if there weren't any women, then there wouldn't be any babies, and if there weren't any babies, then eventually no people would be left on Earth!
>
> This topic can — and indeed it did — lead to a long discussion on many issues related to women, for instance, the courage of the women who marched in protest against carrying passes in apartheid South Africa; the fact that not long ago women were not permitted to vote and many were expected to do menial labour; the fact that, even today, comparatively few women hold leadership positions in politics, commerce and industry, although that has started to change.

- When your children come home from school, ask them some additional questions. For example, what did they find interesting in the classroom that day, or did anything bother them or seem unclear about what they learnt, or did they ask any interesting questions?
- Use books, television or videos as a springboard for thinking. You can encourage an enquiring mind by asking children interesting questions about characters in books or on TV, such as 'I wonder why that person did or thought that?', and wait for their answers.
- Don't be judgemental about your children's questions. If you tell them that their questions are silly, then they may lose confidence and

avoid asking more questions. In the same vein, don't be critical about their answers. If needs be, ask a follow-up question, such as, 'Why do you think that?'
- Don't be afraid to say, 'I don't know' – you can't have all the answers! But do follow up your 'I don't know' with an expression of curiosity and interest, such as, 'When we get home, let's check on the internet or in the dictionary,' or 'Let's ask your aunt, because she's interested in this topic and is sure to know.' Encourage the process of enquiry to find the answer rather than dead-ending the thought process. This will develop a love of learning and an insatiable curiosity.

For younger children (1–5 years)
- Allow your children to explore their environment – the house and garden – instead of sitting them down in front of the TV.
- Play hide-and-seek with your children, or hide objects around the house for them to find.
- Play peek-a-boo with a baby.
- Do not do everything for your children, or teach them everything. Let them learn through exploration – make time for this.

For older children (6–12 years)
- Remember that the best learning experiences for children under the age of 12 are real, concrete experiences (with people, toys and equipment, and through their own body movements and senses, etc.) and not virtual ones. Concrete learning enables children to create meaning and real understanding about the world around them.
- Show an interest in the YouTube, Instagram and other social channels your children follow. Ask them to show you their favourite clips and ask them engaging questions about these.
- Make a conversation jar (or basket). This works well with older children, say, from the age of seven upwards. Whenever a family member has a question or an interesting thought, he or she can write it on a piece of paper and put it into the jar. From time to time, the conversation jar can be brought to the dinner table. Each person has

a chance to pick a piece of paper out of the jar and to answer the question. Then everyone else at the table can add to the answer, person by person, going around the table. Questions could be about anything, for example, 'What makes us hiccup?', 'Who is God?', 'If you weren't yourself, who would you like to be?', 'What happens when you die?' A conversation jar creates interesting discussions, shows that the family values curiosity, enables different members of the family to share their knowledge, and encourages them to find out more about the things that interest them.
- Watch TED videos and documentary and informational YouTube channels with your children, and then discuss the content afterwards.

INFORMATION PROCESSING AND FILTERING

Google the phrase 'internet minute' with the current year. The most recent of these overviews was for 2018, as we wrote this book. This is what happened online in just ONE MINUTE (actually, in EVERY MINUTE) of 2018:

- 973 000 Facebook log-ins
- 18 million text messages
- 3.7 million Google searches
- 4.3 million YouTube videos watched
- 187 million emails sent
- three new print books were published, while 30 ebooks were published and over one million blogs were updated
- 266 000 hours of Netflix videos watched
- over two million people were using Skype
- 300 hours of video uploaded to YouTube (just think about this one, and ask yourself how you will ever keep up with the information overload).

Clearly our children are growing up digital, and they appear to be extremely comfortable navigating the world with technology. They will live with constant information overload, and much of that information will be changing and becoming outdated as quickly as it arrives. Sadly, we now also have to deal with the deluge of 'fake news' that constantly assails us. It is important to know that at least some of the information we consume is deliberately designed to manipulate and misinform us. When faced with this inundation of information, in a world that is online 24/7, millennial children need strong traditional reading, writing and spelling skills, as well as good, old-fashioned comprehension skills. To be able to make sense – quickly – of so much information, solid foundations in all these disciplines will be essential.

The development of all these skills can only be achieved effectively if there is a solid foundation of school-readiness skills. The building blocks of preschool learning are shape, colour and quantity. As far as possible, a child should experience these concepts in concrete, real-life form through the medium of play. Reading, writing, spelling and maths are semi-concrete and abstract principles, which are built on seemingly unrelated perceptual skills.

Parents of preschoolers would do well to improve their knowledge in this regard. Preschool learning is a miraculous process that unequivocally demonstrates the powerful and almost magical connection between the brain and the body. The body is quite literally the architect of the brain, adding weight to the importance of balancing a child's real and virtual play experiences. (See Chapter 2, page 36 for more detail.)

> Graeme remembers buying a new smart TV a few years ago, and struggling to install it. One of his daughters did a quick YouTube search of the make and model number and quickly found a few tutorial videos that had the TV set up in a flash. Forget Google, YouTube is the most-used search website (and app) these days.

Tips for developing information-processing abilities
For all
- Talk your children clever. Language is the way in which we communicate with the world. Children need to learn this from you.
- If possible, teach your children more than one language.
- Develop a love for books and reading in your child.

- When you have finished reading your child a story, ask him or her questions about the story you read together. You could also ask your child about the set work the class is reading at school, just to test his or her comprehension skills. These are of vital importance in a world of information overload.
- Play with your children often to improve their concentration skills. Children need to be able to concentrate in order to read, write, spell and do maths. A child naturally only has about a minute's concentration for each year of his or her life, so it is up to parents to increase this by engaging their children in fun and stimulating activities.

> Even children who struggle to read can develop a love for books. Graeme's youngest daughter, Rebecca, has autism, and by the age of 13 has not yet learnt to read. But she loves books. She loves having books read to her. She loves taking books with well-known stories and pretending to 'read' these to her own toys as she retells her favourite fairy tales. For Rebecca, the best Graeme can do is help her recognise that books are a key tool for learning in her life, and hope that she will one day be able to read for herself.

For younger children (1–5 years)
- When your children are small, keep them socially active with other children whom you would like your children to spend time with. Children learn and gain a great deal from face-to-face socialising, including language development, which is the foundation for information processing. What children learn face to face, they cannot acquire from on-screen activities. At this age, choose friends for your children whose parents have a similar outlook to yours. Obviously, as children become older, they will make and choose their own friends. But gently continue to guide them, and keep an eye on whether or not they are choosing friends with similar value systems.
- Ensure that your child moves a lot and has opportunities to play outdoors on jungle gyms, with balls, and also with other children. Movement not only strengthens the body, which will help a child to

sit comfortably in a chair at school for lengthy periods of time, but it also stimulates and strengthens the visual system, which is so important for reading and writing activities.

For older children (6–12 years)
- Choosing friends with similar value systems becomes even more important the older your child gets, and the more he or she interacts with technology. In other words, do you know whether or not your child is playing on-screen activities when visiting his or her friends? Do you know what type of TV programmes, movies, games and apps your child is being exposed to at friends' homes?
- Create family rules about emails, messages, social media, screen time, etc. As your children become older, they will spend more and more time interacting with on-screen media. This time will need to be managed. In order for your family rules to be effective, however, you, as parents, will have to adhere to them, too. Create device-free zones or times, especially mealtimes and the hour before bedtime.
- Encourage your children to play with games that stimulate their intellect, thinking skills, reasoning and problem-solving. Encourage them to 'fact-check' TV programmes that interest them by accessing the internet to do follow-up learning. And develop your own ability to spot fake news and misinformation.
- Before computers, we researched topics by starting with the general and working towards the specific. We would find a general encyclopaedia entry and work our way towards more detailed information. Today, however, if we tried to start with the general in a Google search, there might be over one million websites to consider! As a result, the new approach to research today is to be as specific as possible in an online search request. In this way, we generally find the specific information we are looking for. The downside, however, is that we often end up with loads of interesting facts, but no context for that information. In addition, not all the information that we find in these searches is necessarily factually correct or sound – in fact, some information is deliberately false.

- Speed-reading and touch-typing are excellent skills for greater efficiency in life. Being able to operate and navigate technology confidently – from smartphones to computers to the internet and other electronic gadgets – will enable learners to acquire, manipulate and disseminate information quickly. Competence in this area will assist with time management and enhance communication and presentation skills. You will find that your children are far more intuitive about these things than you are. Allow them to teach you to be technologically literate, too.
- Work out your children's preferred learning style so that they learn in the best way for them. This means that taking in, storing and retrieving information for later use will be easier and more effective, yielding positive results and increasing confidence. Putting in focus and effort will make far more sense if learning is not a constant battle.
- Discover your children's interests and passions. Create projects for them in this area and, when they are older, allow them to develop their own projects. Support these with enthusiasm and watch how easy it is for them to invest their attention and effort. If they experience the rewards of their commitment, they will be more willing to focus on and put effort into things about which they are less enthusiastic, because they will have worked out that there is always a return. Help your children to develop some real and meaningful goals based on their strengths, interests and passions. Often, goals set in the school environment are fairly artificial and don't relate to real life. You may need to look at non-academic activities here, such as photography, building model aeroplanes, scrapbooking, etc.

I saw it on the internet

Sadly, we need to teach our children a lot of discernment a lot earlier than in our day. They need to know that they can't trust everything they read on the internet, and they need to be taught skills to discern good from bad information, and good from malicious sources. This includes teaching them to stand up to adults in their lives, and ask probing – but respectful – questions.

A recent survey of who was more likely to spread fake news online indicated that the biggest culprits were teenagers and people over the age of 60. Hoaxes are commonplace and garner a lot of publicity, and they spread like wildfire online (like Blue Whale and the Momo Challenge). If you want to check whether something is true or just an urban legend, visit https://www.snopes.com before you embarrass yourself.

It is beyond the scope of our book to provide the details of how to develop this discernment in your children, but it begins with helping them develop the basics of logical analysis, theory testing, critical thinking and questioning. As with so many other things we talk about in this book, they will learn this best if they see you modelling it for them.

Don't believe everything you read online. Before you share some 'can you believe it?' information, do a fact-check and, most importantly, ask three simple questions: is it right (as in factually correct), is it good (as in wholesome and edifying) and does it add value to society?

MASTERY OF TECHNOLOGY

It probably goes without saying that it is critically important to be confident with and skilled in technology in today's world, otherwise you will simply be left behind.

This doesn't mean giving your children free rein with devices. It is essential that you put firm rules in place, with consequences if these are broken. In addition, spend time connecting and communicating with your children. Invest your time in them to develop their values, their moral compass, their passions and good media habits to prevent technology from filling a void and being abused.

But equally, don't be scared of technology. Your children must have access to it and learn how to use it appropriately and skilfully.

Tech-Savvy Parenting (2014) by Nikki Bush and Arthur Goldstuck is a must-read in this regard. We do not live in an 'either or' world, but a 'both and' world, when it comes to technology. It is part of every facet of our lives, but as parents we must find a middle ground with technology in order to enable our children to adopt a balanced approach to it. It should not consume them or negatively affect their relationship with their parents.

Tips for developing a mastery of technology
For all
- Very young children under the age of two do not need to watch TV or screens. Far better stimulation can be obtained through play, exploration of their world, and interaction with their parents and other people.
- As they get older (between the ages of four and five), allow your children to play on the computer and on your phone and to experiment. This generation is naturally wired and interacts intuitively with technology.
- From time to time, play digital games *with* your children so that you know what they are being exposed to. This will also enable you to better appreciate the attraction of these programs.
- There is absolutely no reason why parents cannot master the technologies available. Most parents get left behind, not because of lack of ability, but rather from a conscious decision that this is all too much. Such an attitude is not good for your children – keep up, stay in the loop, and they will reap the benefits!

For younger children (1–5 years)
- Limit TV viewing and computer access.
- Be vigilant about the content that your children watch on TV and the games they play on computers. There is some really good stuff out there, but also some pretty meaningless, and even harmful, content.
- Children love repetition, which is how they master something. Your child will want to watch the same DVD over and over again, as well as play the same computer games repeatedly. You will need to gauge when your child is ready for something new and more challenging, which is one of the reasons why you need to watch or play with your child from time to time.

- Teach your children to ask permission to switch on the TV or a computer. It's a good habit for them to acquire and is also part of setting boundaries.

For older children (6–12 years)
- Find out your children's school curriculum regarding the subject of computers or Information Technology (IT). Some schools teach children how to use specific computer programs, such as Word and Excel, while others teach digital skills by allowing children to use computers or tablets for various academic subjects or extension activities.
- Encourage the use of different platforms, but also instil in your children the need to be responsible in terms of their media usage. They must understand that learning to be a discerning user of media will ultimately protect them.
- Allow your children to teach you about technology.
- Send your children on relevant training courses if possible.

'When should my child get a cellphone?' is a question we often get asked. If children are under the age of 13, they really only need a cellphone to make emergency calls and for you to be able to communicate with them. They therefore only require a basic feature phone or a kiddie phone, not a smartphone. They can play games and use apps and WhatsApp, etc., on your cellphone, which means that you can see what they are doing and coach them to do it well.

Bear in mind that a smartphone gives your child access to all the world's information, and also gives the world access to them, which can be both a good and a bad thing. Your children need to have the maturity to deal with the potentially destructive side of social media and instant messaging before you give them free rein with digital devices. After the age of 13, it is social currency to have a smartphone.

In addition, much of their learning will require use of, and access to, the internet. Once again, you need to keep your finger on the pulse of things. Teens are natural risk-takers, so it stands to reason that an agreement that governs usage should be reached. You will find a comprehensive Tween and Teen Cellphone Contract for download on https://nikkibush.com. It makes for a really good conversation with your child.

ONLINE SECURITY

Just as we teach our children about stranger danger and not to touch or expose themselves to someone else's blood, so we must instil in our children the need for online security for their own protection.

Tips to ensure the online security of children
For all
- Ensure that your family computer is placed in a public space, with the screen facing the room. This will enable you to keep an eye on what your children are accessing. However, the smaller the device, the more impractical this rule becomes. You might want to have a rule that your children can't use devices in their bedrooms.
- Activate the filters that are available on your search engines. As your children get older, invest in software that will protect them from inappropriate content.
- Do not put a TV or computer in your pre-teen's bedroom.
- When purchasing games and apps, take note of the age restrictions and, if possible, ask for a demonstration of the game.
- Teach your children to honour, value and protect their own minds. You can teach them that inappropriate content is much like pollution. Instead of polluting the planet, however, it pollutes their hearts and minds. Disturbing content is also very difficult – if not impossible – to erase, particularly in children under the age of seven, who have not yet developed filters to protect themselves.
- Keep the lines of communication open; keep talking. This should ensure that your children will feel comfortable to come to you with any problems they experience online.

For younger children (1–5 years)
- Always sit with your preschool children when they are using devices, especially if they are online.
- Be aware of what your children are doing in other people's homes. When they go for play dates, are they playing with toys and children, or are they playing on-screen activities? Get to know the parents of the children with whom your children are friendly to gain a sense of their values and to enable you to have open discussions with them.

For older children (6–12 years)
- Teach your children *never* to give out their personal details via their phone, the internet or email to strangers or marketers without checking with your first. Teach your children not to put too much information on their profile on any social-networking sites.
- Young children should not use chat rooms – the dangers are too great. As children get older, make sure that they use well-monitored kids' chat rooms. Encourage even your teenagers to use monitored chat rooms.
- Teach your children not to trust a digital persona by telling them to:
  - always treat digital friends as strangers
  - always keep in mind that photos can be created and altered.
- Do not overreact and 'blanket-censor' access to the internet. This will not benefit your child and is likely to encourage deception.
- Remember that you provide the access, so you also set the boundaries.
- Install filters and software to monitor usage on your home computers.
- Discuss the need for online protection with your children.
- Limit 'screen time' to a certain number of hours per day. This includes all screens – phones, TV, computer, internet, etc. There should be no phoning after a certain time, and phones should be switched off or ignored at certain times, such as family meals. Remember that this must apply to everyone!
- When your children are young, they should share the family email address rather than have an address of their own. As they get older, you can ask your internet service provider to set up a separate email

address for them, but your children's mail can still be processed through your account.
- If all your precautions fail and your child does meet an online predator, don't blame him or her. The offender must always bear full responsibility. Take decisive action to stop your child from any further contact with this person.

4. KNOW YOURSELF

Self-awareness refers to knowing your internal states, preferences, resources and intuitions. Jonathan Cook, a psychologist at the Gordon Institute of Business Science, identifies three important components of self-awareness:
- **Emotional awareness:** Recognising your emotions and their effects.
- **Accurate self-assessment:** Knowing your strengths and limits.
- **Self-confidence:** Having a strong sense of your self-worth and capabilities.

These days, most people know that there are multiple intelligences. The school system measures mainly language and mathematical skills, as do IQ tests, with a slight emphasis on logical analysis. The problem is that these types of intelligence are no guarantee of success in most of life's arenas. Analyses of successful people show that, in addition to being 'clever', they are intelligent in other ways. As Howard Gardner's research shows, one of the critical abilities in exceptional people is the ability to know yourself. This involves knowing – and accepting – your strengths and weaknesses.

> A fascinating thing about having more than one child is seeing and experiencing just how different each child is. Nikki's youngest son, Matthew, had to prepare for a verbal Afrikaans test. They spent a considerable amount of time learning the names of fruit and vegetables. Matthew really knew the work and was excited about the test.
> However, he was less than enthusiastic about his result, because he didn't achieve a merit. The thing is that Matthew is a visual learner, not an auditory one, and so of course he will do better in written rather

than verbal tests. It is so important that Matthew understands that he is not stupid – his natural strength lies in what he sees and not what he hears, and that's okay. He will pick up the marks in written work that he loses in oral tests.

Nikki's eldest son, Ryan, however, is an auditory learner. He finds oral tests far easier than written ones. He has had to work hard over the years to adapt his dominance profile to an education system that still favours written work. But he is winning, because he understands where his strengths lie and that his weaker areas do not indicate that he is stupid.

The person who did his profile at the age of eight asked Ryan if people had ever told him he was slow or stupid. He nodded his head (and Mom almost burst into tears!). What the profilogist said next was the best thing to happen to Ryan in his three years of primary school: 'Ryan, let me tell you something. You have the brain profile of Einstein. Do you know that he was one of the cleverest people who ever lived? So don't ever believe anyone who tells you that you are stupid! Sometimes you just take longer to get out the information than others. You are a very clever boy! Always remember that.'

A few weeks later, a full IQ test revealed that Ryan does indeed have a high IQ. It needs to be nurtured and understood by his parents and teachers, and especially by himself. This information made it far easier to make the decision about which school would be best for him.

KNOW YOUR STRENGTHS (AND WEAKNESSES)

'Your job is not to provide him with a realistic picture of the limits of strengths and the liability of his weaknesses ... Your job is to get him to perform. Stated more bluntly, your job is to build his self-assurance, not his self-awareness ... In short, the state of mind you should try to create in him is one where he has a fully realistic assessment of the difficulty of the challenge ahead of him and, at the same time, an unrealistically optimistic belief in his ability to overcome it.'
Marcus Buckingham, *The One Thing You Need to Know*, 2005

Who am I? Where have I been? Where am I going? The answers to these questions will determine our capability to chart our own destiny and realise our potential. Self-awareness includes understanding our personality and recognising our strengths and weaknesses, and our likes and dislikes. Developing self-awareness can help us to realise when we are stressed or under pressure. It is also a prerequisite for effective communication and interpersonal relationships. In addition, it is important in developing empathy for others.

In his book *Now Discover Your Strengths* (2001), Marcus Buckingham strongly suggests that many of us have an incorrect view of personal development. Ever since we brought home our own report cards from school, we had it drummed into us that our developmental focus should be on our areas of weakness. Remember that moment your parents read your report card? It may have displayed a few As, a B or a C, but if there was one F on it, what did your parents focus on? The F, right?

Buckingham suggests that we should instead focus on developing our strengths, and simply ensure that our weaknesses are not big enough to hold us back materially. No one can be good at everything, so why focus on bringing your weak areas up to 'acceptable' levels; that is, merely average? Why not focus on developing your strengths into world-class assets?

> 'Don't waste time trying to put in what was left out.
> Try to draw out what was left in.'
> Gordon Dryden and Jeanette Vos, *The New Learning Revolution*, 2005

Children today are being encouraged in the area of self-assessment in the school system, too, often being asked to evaluate themselves and keep track of their own progress.

It is our job to help our children to develop an accurate and fair assessment of themselves.

Just as people are different physically (some are short, some are tall, some are fast, some are slow), so, too, are our brains different. Each of us has a unique range of abilities in relation to our different intelligences. The most successful people in life seem to have at least one category of intelligence that is significantly more developed than normal, but they also have fair to good use of most, if not all, of the other intelligence categories as well.

Our task as parents is, firstly, to identify the built-in abilities of our children. Secondly, we must help them to develop their strengths, building their best intelligences into truly world-class capabilities. And thirdly, we need to help them raise the status of their other intelligences so that they have a fully rounded base.

At some stage in the future, there may be drugs to assist in this development, just as there are drugs to enhance physical performance. We may or may not want our children to use these artificial stimulants. Imagine a world in which the top students at a school were randomly drug-tested in the way that athletes are today? But, in the absence of these 'short-cut' routes to intelligence, there are many things we can do as parents to develop the various intelligences that our children have – and need. We should start with getting to know our children.

Tips for developing self-awareness of strengths and weaknesses
For all
- Start with obvious and non-emotional areas of assessment in which a certain characteristic holds no distinct advantage or disadvantage. Help your children to understand the difference between an introvert and extrovert, or an expressive or receptive person. Many people misunderstand these labels, thinking they are about confidence, loudness or being outgoing. They are actually about the sources from which an individual draws his or her energy. If you gain your energy from being alone and are drained by being with people, then you are an introvert. If you gain your energy from being with people and cannot spend long periods of time alone without feeling drained, you are an extrovert. Help your children to understand these differences. Where you have a mix of introverts and extroverts in your home, teach them to respect the needs of other family members for space and for interaction.

> After Graeme's daughter Amy's second birthday party, she was sitting on the floor surrounded by her presents. The afternoon had been a whirlwind of friends, clowns and activity. Now, her grandparents were trying to engage her and to spend some quality time with her. But Amy had reached her 'people interaction limit'. She said simply and clearly, 'Granny, go home now!' Graeme didn't need a psychological profile test to know that his eldest daughter is an introvert.

- Your children cannot know what they are good at and what they are not good at just by thinking about it, or even based on their feelings. They should be encouraged to try as many activities as possible. They may surprise themselves by having an aptitude for something unexpected. In their pre-teen years, especially, we should be encouraging our children to engage in as wide a variety of pursuits as possible. Even if you spot an aptitude early, be careful not to pigeonhole your child and fixate on this one area of strength too early.
- We must realise that even some of the most successful or gifted people in the world were not brilliant the first time they tried something. The greatest pianists in the world (apart from Mozart!) still had to spend a few years banging away fairly tunelessly at a keyboard. The greatest artists probably started by smearing finger paints on scraps of paper. Every successful person spends years of hard work learning the basics required for success. As parents, we sometimes need to push our children when they want to give up to help them get over 'the hump' as they develop from good to great.

For younger children (1–5 years)
- When your children complain that they are not very good at something, take the opportunity to point out their strengths and to emphasise that everyone is different. They can be a good friend and a great helper, among many other examples.
- Grandparents have a particularly important role to play in helping children feel good about a variety of different strengths they might

possess. As you watch from whatever vantage point you might have, work hard as a grandparent to look for the unexpected and unusual characteristics that you can praise and nurture.

For older children (6–12 years)

- If your children consistently display a flair, an aptitude or a passion for an activity, where possible and if you can afford it, you should involve them in some specialised coaching and tuition so that their natural ability can be nurtured and assessed by a professional in that area. However, involvement in too much of one thing could cause an imbalance. Also remember that children in this age bracket still need time to play.
- Allow your children to take part in cultural events that encourage participation and offer constructive feedback, such as the national Eisteddfod competition. In such a competition, all talent is recognised with certificates for different levels achieved. The adjudication is usually highly constructive, pointing out a child's areas of strength and weakness, with practical advice on how to improve.

Around Eisteddfod time in 2005, Ryan was entered for the prepared reading competition. Nikki had been extremely busy with her business and had not spent much time helping Ryan to practise his three pages from Roald Dahl's *James and the Giant Peach*. He assured her, however, that things were going well. Three days prior to his performance, Nikki finally sat down to listen to him read and was inwardly horrified at his poor delivery. There was no fluency, a lack of expression, and the entire reading passage was running over time. Drastic action was required. Working from her knowledge of Ryan's auditory strength, Nikki came up with a solution that has since become the blueprint for Ryan's study skills, because it really works for him. She read the extract to him while he had his eyes closed, and then he read it back to her. They did this three times, and the improvement was dramatic. They did this exercise twice more before D-day, and Ryan received a gold certificate for his performance. Things happen more

> quickly, easily and confidently when you can harness your child's natural strengths. By using the same technique for studying subjects such as Geography and History, Ryan is more confident of doing well in his tests.

This aspect is discussed in far more detail later on in Chapter 7 under 'Building a Talent Profile' (see page 251).

EMOTIONAL INTELLIGENCE

Emotional intelligence is the measure of an individual's self-awareness (*intra*personal) and their ability to relate to others (*inter*personal).

Children will need to be socially and emotionally mature to build and maintain the relationships that they will require to succeed in the 21st century. Academic qualifications are simply not enough to ensure success in life. Emotions and feelings play an important role in our lives, as they drive our behaviour and influence our values. Emotional intelligence (EQ – emotional quotient) is the ability to recognise, understand and manage our own feelings, as well as be aware of the feelings of others. It is the ability to show understanding and empathy, as well as to see things from others' point of view.

Emotionally intelligent people learn to control their emotions and to moderate their emotional reactions to situations. They listen effectively and are able to give constructive feedback about themselves and others, and are able to set goals and devise plans for achieving those goals. People with EQ see problems as opportunities. They are also able to communicate clearly and effectively, which helps them to deal efficiently with conflict and group situations.

Tips for developing emotional intelligence
For all
- Praise less and encourage more. Praise focuses on the outcome (winning, or the end product). Encouragement focuses on the process, or the effort involved in reaching a goal (winning is not everything, especially at any price).

- Use what is called *descriptive praise* to let your children know when they are doing something well. Of course, you will need to get into the habit of looking for situations in which your child is doing a good job or displaying a talent. When your child completes a task or chore, you could say: 'I really like the way you tidied your room. You found a place for everything and put each thing where it belongs.' When you observe your child showing a talent, you might say: 'That last piece you played sounded so good. You really have a lot of musical talent.' Don't be afraid to give praise often, even in front of family or friends. Also, use praise to point out positive character traits. For instance, 'You are a very kind person.' Or, 'I like the way you stick with things you try, even when they seem hard to do.' You can even praise a child for something he or she did not do, such as: 'I really liked how you accepted my answer of "no" and didn't lose your temper.' Teach children that all emotions are okay, but it's their response to them that is important.

> One of Graeme's friends had a feisty six-year-old daughter who had inherited her dad's quick temper. In addition to disciplining her when she lost her temper, her smart parents got her to manage her rage. When she felt angry, she had to walk calmly to the bathroom, close the door, and stand there and scream and howl all she liked. She then had to emerge calmly from the bathroom. It was not a long-term solution, but it really helped her to work through a stage in her life, to accept her emotions and manage them appropriately.

- Children will copy you. You are their role model. It is a 'do as I do' world. Children will no longer swallow 'do as I say', especially if what you say does not match your behaviour! This has huge implications for parents who must 'walk their talk' or lose credibility. Children only want to engage with you if you offer them something authentic, which means being consistent.
- Choose caregivers well, and 'co-parent' consistently with your spouse, ex-spouse, life partner, step-parents, grandparents, caregivers and

other significant adults in your children's lives. It is so important that all parties agree and stand together on everything from issues like watching TV, screen time, use of devices, to diet, homework time and getting gifts, among many other things. Consistency and a united front leave no room for children to manipulate the situation, which they are quick to do if they spot a gap or a weakness.

- Do not be afraid to apologise to your children when you have made a mistake. In fact, look for opportunities to talk to your children about why you do what you do, and help them to see your own self-awareness. For example, if – like most people – you get short and snappy when tired, explain this to your children. If you're going through a busy patch at work, pre-empt it with your children by asking them to point out when you are being unpleasant or somewhat irritable. You can even make it a game, awarding 'prizes' when they point out that you are not acting your normal self during a busy time.
- Teach your children how to listen well by being a good listener yourself. Teach them the importance of eye contact and face-to-face communication. It is through verbal communication in the presence of others that we best learn how our words and actions impact upon people. We see their reactions and realise that they, too, have feelings and emotions. In today's world of electronic and text communication, much of this learning is being missed or bypassed. We cannot gauge how we make others feel. Today's young people thrive on sending text messages to each other. This needs to be balanced with face-to-face communication experiences.
- Make a determined effort to be really present when you are with your children. It is so easy to be distracted, and children know instantly whether or not they have your attention. Failure to attend to your children will often lead to attention-seeking behaviour, which is frequently misread as playing up or being naughty. Yet generally the only remediation required is for us to learn how to bring our attention to the present moment, instead of allowing our minds to wander off to the unfinished work on our desk, the unpaid accounts or tomorrow's meeting.

- Be consistent with your communication, your behaviour, and the boundaries and limits you set for your children. It helps them to feel safer and makes life more predictable. They will also respect you more.
- Allow your children to experience the consequences of their actions. Do not overprotect them from the mistakes they make. Be especially careful at school. When your children report on issues that took place at school, it is unwise to assume automatically that your children's teachers or friends are wrong and your precious child is right.
- Teach children that good relationships bring satisfaction and fulfil emotional needs much more than material possessions or screens. This is a rather tricky issue to navigate when children are being bought 'things' for doing well in tests and exams, and when a lost smartphone is replaced with a new one within a couple of days.
- Recognise appropriate behaviour as often as possible. Remember that whatever you focus your attention on tends to expand and develop.
- Eat together and play together. By playing games with your children, you demonstrate appropriate winning and losing behaviour, turn-taking, playing by the rules and sharing. You also show your children that you enjoy their company and like to spend time with them.
- Work out the love languages of each person in your family and then express love in ways they understand. In Gary Chapman's bestselling book, *The Five Love Languages* (1997), he lists the love languages as words of affirmation, acts of service, physical touch, quality time and gift-giving. For example, if the primary love language of your first child is words of affirmation, then this child feels loved when you spend time talking with him or her, and affirming him or her with words. But if your second child's love language is quality time, then he or she really feels loved when you spend quality time with him or her without distraction. As your children get older, share this information with them so that they understand both themselves and their parents better. By understanding your family's love languages, you will keep your emotional tanks full and be able to respond in ways that are appropriate to each person. This will deepen your relationship by improving the quality of your communication.

- When you talk about your feelings, be sure to label them so that your children understand. A great game to play around the dinner table or while driving in the car is the Sweets and Sours game.

The Sweets and Sours game

This game is ideally played at the dinner table or in the car, when the whole family is together. It enables you to hear about everyone's day and teaches your children how to acknowledge and label feelings – an important step in the journey towards emotional intelligence.

Round 1:
Each person gets a chance to share a 'sour' ('the worst thing that happened in your day'). Mention what it is and how it made you feel. For example, 'By mistake I left my takkies (sneakers) at home so I couldn't play tennis. I was very cross with myself because I really wanted to play.'

Round 2:
Each person gets to share a 'sweet' ('the best thing that happened in your day'). Mention what it is and how it made you feel. For example, 'Robyn came to play with me this afternoon and we had fun. It made me happy.'

During the process, no family member may interrupt another. It is a game about listening and sharing.

> Nikki's youngest son was three and a half when her family started playing the game. Nikki thought Matthew would be too young to participate, but was taken by surprise, as he actually led the process from the first session, and still does today. Nikki also found her husband's reaction very interesting. At first, he would just tell the family what happened and Nikki would have to follow up by asking, 'And how did that make you feel?' Men, in particular, are not used to discussing and labelling their feelings, so this is a good exercise for them, too! The family still plays this game today.

For younger children (1–5 years)
- Use empathic listening techniques to help children to label their feelings. For example, when you pick up your daughter from school and she is not talking but rather giving off emotional vibes, you can say something along these lines to acknowledge her feelings, which may even open the door to a conversation: 'I can see you are very upset about something,' or 'I can tell you're excited. What happened?'

For older children (6–12 years)
- Help your children to work out the difference between a need and a want, and to use money appropriately in fulfilling these needs.
- Teach children about delayed gratification by encouraging them to save up over a period of time to buy something.

> When Amy was about to turn seven, she asked for an iPod for her birthday. Graeme said that she needed to save up because she was too young for such an expensive item. Amy saved some of her pocket money, worked for money and requested cash instead of Christmas presents. By her eighth birthday, she had saved nearly R1 000. What is more impressive is that she had worked at it for more than a year. Children of this age can be taught about long-term thinking and setting goals.

- Teach your children to understand another person's point of view. This is best achieved by conversations about how different people view the world. You can use movies and TV shows to start these conversations. After watching a movie, have discussions about key scenes or dramatic or touching moments in the movie. Ask your children what they think the different characters were thinking at the time. Emphasise how and why different characters would have different views of the same event.

> Nikki took her children to see the movie *SpongeBob SquarePants* the year Matthew turned six. It was billed as a suitable movie for children from four upwards. It still stands out in Nikki's mind as highly unsuitable for young children, but it provided a very educational moment. After the movie, Nikki raised the issue of the despotic king who, as a law unto himself, condemned innocent characters to death without trial. The king was never punished for his injustice and unfair, immoral conduct. Throughout the movie, poor behaviour was neither punished nor rectified. What were children to think and learn? Nikki asked her children what they thought of the king. They immediately said that he was horrible, unfair and ugly. Then she asked them how they thought kings, presidents, prime ministers and leaders should behave. They were quick to tell her that they should be fair, just and, of course, kind. They were incensed that the king had failed to listen to anyone who had tried to tell him he was wrong. Despite feeling that she had watched an animated version of the American War on Terror, Nikki found that this dreadful movie did, in fact, provide a good lesson in emotional intelligence, or the lack thereof.

FUTURE-FOCUSED

> 'There is a restlessness about talented people. They are not always clear about where they want to be going, but they know that they want to be on the move.'
> Alan Robertson and Graham Abbey, *Managing Talented People*, 2003

Talented people are never satisfied with the status quo – good enough is never good enough. Their restlessness is focused on the future – on a world that they can visualise in their heads, and then try to turn into reality. Being future-focused involves imagination, creativity, hard work and resilience, with a specific focus on what could be, and how we get there.

Tips for developing future focus
For all
- Speak to your children about the future. Create a strong interest in new inventions, in the changing world and in the future itself. Generate excitement and a belief in their ability to create a great life for themselves further down the track as they become part of the solution for the challenges facing the planet.

> Because of Graeme's work as a futurist, he is naturally exposed to new technologies and ideas on a regular basis. He has made a point of bringing many of these new technologies home with him. From software-controlled LEGO® robots and home-automation devices to 3D printers and Amazon's Echo, Graeme's home is a laboratory from the future. You might not be able to do as much as Graeme has done, but make a point of budgeting for new, experimental gadgets. You might even get the family involved in deciding what tech you should all buy next, and then work towards it, and have fun unpacking and playing with it when it arrives. Graeme's children certainly have.

For younger children (1–5 years)
- When your children are at the fantasy stage and they say, 'One day I want to be …', or 'When I'm big, I want to be …', it can be the start of some wonderful conversations. Note how these discussions change and evolve as your child discovers more and more about him- or herself and about life.
- Tell your child the same story for five days in a row. But, every day, make the ending different and explain to him or her that the same events can have different outcomes.
- Plan far ahead, and give your children the sense that they're always working towards and anticipating many future events. For example, you could start planning *next* year's Christmas holidays now – or at least the high-level decision about where to go and who to go with.

In fact, plan all of next year's breaks and holidays and weekends away this year, and put a calendar up on the fridge to highlight the dates. Let your children live in the future as much as possible.

For older children (6–12 years)
- Encourage your children to read science-fiction books and watch sci-fi movies. Discuss the content with them, and chat about the likelihood of some of the scenarios. Get them to imagine what careers they could pursue to be involved in these futurist visions.
- Focus your children's attention on various kinds of jobs and careers as they are growing and developing. We are so used to hearing about the traditional trades or professions, yet most people find employment in other spheres. As we have already discussed in Chapter 3, this will increasingly be the case.
- Discuss current affairs with your children. They hear about these on the news and you should contextualise these issues for them. Current affairs can form the basis for good conversations about various industries in which your children could find a niche for themselves in the future.
- Ask your children how they would solve some of the problems of the world, such as traffic congestion, global warming and littering. Their solutions will range from the simple to the complex and might even be quite profound for their age. They need to know that we value their opinions and want to hear what they are thinking.

5. RELATE TO OTHERS

Daniel Goleman refers to 'social intelligence', Howard Gardner to 'interpersonal intelligence' and David Livermore to 'cultural intelligence' in labelling the competencies that determine how we handle relationships with others. Each of these researchers stresses two overarching categories of social competence:
- **Empathy:** This is an awareness of others' feelings, needs and concerns. Empathy requires an understanding of others, as well as the ability to sense, anticipate and meet others' needs; the ability to be comfortable

with diversity and to leverage it; and a 'political' ability to read a group's emotional currents and power relationships and to respond appropriately.
- **Social skills:** These require an ability to induce desirable responses in others; to persuade others and influence them; to communicate, manage conflict, show leadership and be a catalyst for change. Social skills also involve the desire to cultivate relationships with and between others; to collaborate and cooperate with them; and to foster group synergies in the pursuit of shared goals. Many of these skills are developed as children play and live in community with others. If you have more than one child, you need to observe and listen in on their interactions. You may need to intervene to assist them in becoming good friends. Speak to them about the value of friendship and interactions. Don't just tell them to sort their problems out – they need to learn the skills of negotiation, compromise and discussion. You need to teach your children these skills and to talk about options with them. In addition to these things, there are two further specific areas of expertise that you should work on: communication, and teamwork and collaboration.

Tips for teaching children to relate to others
For all
- Make sure your children socialise with others from an early age. Do your best to ensure you select groups that are deliberately diverse in their make-up. Remember that diversity is not just about race and gender, but also about personality profiles, language, socio-economics, religion, physical ability/disability and many other factors. Be intentional about exposing your children to people who are 'different'.
- Play dates are an important way of helping your children to learn how to relate to others.
- Let your children see you in social situations. It is not always advisable to drop off your child at a friend and disappear. Sometimes parents need to 'stay and play', too, to show children how to behave in social situations.

- By allowing your children to attend school, you are providing them with an opportunity to relate to others, to socialise and interact.
- Playing sport gives your children an opportunity to relate to others through teamwork or in a competitive situation.
- Eat dinner together as a family.

COMMUNICATION

There is no doubt that the most successful people in the business world are those who are able to communicate effectively. This includes public speaking, debating and negotiating abilities, written communication skills and, increasingly, multimedia-based emotive 'edutainment' communications.

The variety of media and on-screen activities available to children today put them at risk of mainly watching and listening rather than talking. Roger Schank (*Coloring Outside the Lines*, 2001) comments: 'Let's assume that you have a reasonably bright child possessing a mind teeming with original thoughts. If, however, your child never learns how to express those thoughts, teachers, prospective employers, and bosses will assume him to be ordinary at best and dumb at worst. Verbal ability, therefore, is what people require to show their intelligence to the world.'

In school, your child is just one of many. This means that, as a parent, you have a great deal more opportunity to develop your child's communication skills than his or her teachers do.

Tips for developing communication skills
For all
- Engage your children in conversation from the day they are born. 'Talk them clever' and model good speech through ongoing conversations.
- Help your children to verbalise their thinking and reasoning skills by playing word games in the car.
- Eat dinner around a table, face to face, as often as possible. This is where children learn the art of conversation, and about listening, taking turns and debating. As long as everyone puts their devices away, of course.

- Don't criticise or lecture your children on their verbal mistakes. Correct them as you speak back to them. They will absorb good language usage from you.
- Model good listening skills. When your children talk to you, don't always do other things at the same time. Stay still, make eye contact, and focus on them to let them know that you are really listening.
- If you have more than one child, it is important to spend time alone with each one from time to time so that the more natural communicator doesn't overshadow the less expressive child.
- More than anything, show interest in your child's thoughts and ideas. You can also get any child to talk and communicate on subjects that he or she feels passionate about.
- Provide your children with interesting life experiences that they can talk about.
- Watch television or a movie with your children from time to time and chat to them afterwards about the characters, plot, etc.

For younger children (1–5 years)
- Speak to your children as intelligent human beings. Don't talk down to them or use 'motherese'. Talk to them like adults. If you tell a child that this is a 'choo-choo', that is the word they will associate with their toy. Then, a few years later, you change it and tell them it is a 'train'. You can understand why this would be confusing to a young mind. Use the correct words, speak in complete sentences and actively develop your child's vocabulary.
- Handle speech impediments with a speech therapist early on. Good, clear speech is a gift.
- Give your children opportunities to tell you stories. You can start by letting them finish your stories, but go further and let them tell you their own stories.

For older children (6–12 years)
- Play fun word games such as *30 Seconds*, *Pictionary*, *Bananagrams* and *Cranium* to exercise verbal skills in an entertaining and humorous way.

- Get your children to read out loud to you.
- Support your children's speech-making efforts at school. Encourage them to take part in cultural activities such as drama and debating, and to gain confidence and practise through competitions such as Chatterbox and the Eisteddfod.

TEAMWORK AND COLLABORATION

We live in a world in which more and more interaction and collaboration are required. Leaders are not those who are technically superior to their peers, but rather those who are able to coordinate, inspire and mobilise their peers to operate as a cohesive unit.

Tips for developing teamwork and collaboration
For all

Nobel prizes in scientific fields have been awarded for over a century now. In the early years, it was typical for individuals to be awarded these prizes. Possibly once or twice in a decade, a team would receive the award. In the last few decades, this trend has been reversed, with individuals only rarely receiving Nobel prizes in medicine, physics, chemistry and even economics. The implication is clear – teamwork is now required for important breakthroughs in science. See the lists of laureates at https://www.nobelprize.org.

- Teach one of your children how to do a task or activity, then ask this child to teach his or her siblings later. Reward all your children when they have achieved this goal successfully.

Nikki watched her sons play various online computer games together. She was amazed at the amount of collaboration and teamwork that existed between them; first, to teach Nikki's younger son the tricks of the game and, second, to beat the computer. Ryan and Matthew really helped each other to achieve the best possible outcome. It was delightful for

Nikki to listen to the mutual encouragement and excitement that emanated from their collaboration. Of course, this was not always the case. At times, Nikki's eldest wished to play individual games without his younger brother, or simply didn't feel like assisting him at that particular time. Nikki then had to step in to facilitate the situation.

- The evening meal is a good time for teamwork and collaboration. Children can assist with the preparation of food, from topping and tailing beans to grating cheese. And they can lay the table while you cook. As they get older, they can light candles and pour water into glasses, too. By the time you sit down to dinner, everyone can have played his or her part in putting the meal together and preparing the eating space. Then it's back to teamwork to clear the table after dinner, stack and wash dishes or load the dishwasher, and tidy up.
- If you have a dishwasher, then emptying it the next morning also creates an opportunity for teamwork. Even three-year-olds can help. Give them the cutlery to sort into categories of knives, forks and spoons. Then ask them to thread these items onto the hanging cutlery holder or to place them back into the cutlery drawer. Children love being part of a team and being allowed to help. This is an opportunity to convey your belief in their capabilities and to show them that they are a welcome part of the team.
- The same can be done when handling an item or facility that requires regular maintenance, for example, the family swimming pool. One person can clear the leaf trap, another can test the water, and someone else can brush the sides of the pool. Then everyone can put the safety net back on the pool together, because this just makes the task so much quicker and easier.

In certain American First Nation traditions, when young warriors participated in competitive sports, the winner of each competition was required to congratulate all those who had competed against him. The reason was that he only did his or her best because he was pushed to do so by the other competitors. As we encourage our children to become involved in competitive pursuits, this may be a great story to tell. Good sportsmanship is an excellent example to follow.

For younger children (1–5 years)
- Young children love doing chores around the house *with you*. For example, let them wash the car and bicycles with you. Of course, they won't do a great job when they are toddlers, but enjoy teaching them to do it with you. It won't be too long before they get really good at it. In addition, they are spending quality time with you while you teach them the valuable life skill of looking after possessions.
- Let younger children assist with the care of family pets.

For older children (6–12 years)
- Almost anyone who works in a corporate environment has been on some kind of team-building activity. These range from the dangerous (such as river-rafting, fire-walking and abseiling) to the strenuous (such as carrying people over an obstacle course, or pushing them through a spider's web of ropes) to the inane (such as building paper aeroplanes and composing team songs). These activities proved to be fairly corny when you had to do them at youth camps during your teenage years, and even more corny in the business world. But why not get some use out of them by tackling a variety with your children? They will love these activities, especially if they get to do them with you.
- Encourage your children to play at least one team sport. It's good for them. Even if – or maybe, especially if – they are not in the first team.

> Nikki's children played in a round-robin tennis tournament towards the end of primary school, with both children playing singles and doubles matches. For the first time, it became really obvious to them that a big difference existed between the two games. Ryan, the eldest, reckoned it was far more difficult playing doubles, because he never knew what his

> partner was going to do (not being in a regular doubles partnership). This made it difficult to develop teamwork and collaboration. Of course, Ryan recognised that the better the teamwork and collaboration, the greater the chance of winning the match. A good (but frustrating) life lesson.

- Encourage involvement in cultural activities that require teamwork – in an orchestra, in school plays, etc.

COMFORT IN DIVERSITY

In addition to working in teams, our children will increasingly work in diverse environments. Diversity does not just relate to gender, skin colour or age. It relates specifically to world views. Television, the movies, social networks, the internet as well as the global mobility of people ensure that our children interact with others who have very different value sets, religious backgrounds and world views.

We need to raise our children to understand who they are and what they stand for. At the same time, they should accept that not everyone is the same or does things in the same way they do. In the past, your family friends raised their children the same way as you did – they generally had similar values, probably went to the same church, etc. Today, this is no longer the case. In fact, you can no longer even rely on your own family members having the same values as you!

This is one of the 'side effects' of globalisation. Our children have been exposed to a great deal of diversity and are far more accepting of people of different races, colours and nationalities than we ever were as children – mainly because this exposure was alien to us. The increase in mobile international families has developed a whole subculture of children with a broad life experience at a young age. To these children, we really are living in a global village.

'Twenty-first-century leaders will become more multiskilled than their twentieth-century predecessors. Knowledge of languages, cultures, and a wide range of subjects will be vital to achieve success …

> One of the most important characteristics of a multiskilled leader is the ability to encourage diversity ... The true challenge facing the organizational world is not geographic distance but cultural distance.'
> Subir Chowdhury, *Management 21C*, 2000

Tips for developing comfort with diversity
For all
- Parents must first reflect on their own biases and explore their own feelings about diversity. They need to understand these before they can truly help their children to confront their own. For many, this may involve difficult memories of the prejudiced and confusing messages they received about different kinds of people.
- Provide your children with as many positive experiences of diversity as possible. Seek out friendships with families from other cultures.
- Encourage your children to learn about different cultures, languages and ethnicities. A well-informed child is more likely to understand and respect other people's values. If you have friends from different cultures or religions, it is highly educational and enriching to be invited to share in some of their rituals.
- Help your children to be proud of their own distinctive traits – their race, culture, gender, etc. The more they know about *why* your family does what it does, the more they will understand why some families do not do things in the same way.
- As the cliché goes, there is nothing like travel to broaden the mind. Try to travel to places with different cultures, and deliberately expose yourself and your children to these different cultures.
- Learn another language.
- Create an environment in which children can see positive images of diverse groups. Comment when you see any stereotypes on TV or in movies. Let children know that it's unfair to label people.
- As a family, you could sponsor a child from another country through a feeding programme.

In South Africa and elsewhere around the world, an increasing number of families are adopting children cross-culturally. This should help to create a wonderful new world as mixed families and people of 'mixed race' become increasingly common in the world.

> Graeme and his daughters were walking through a shopping centre recently when one of his daughters drew his attention to 'the black man' ahead of them. Graeme was concerned, as he felt that he and his wife had tried hard to ensure their children did not notice or mention skin colour when referring to people. He asked his daughter to repeat what she had said, and she explained, 'Look at that black man, next to the green woman.' It turned out that Hannah was referring to the colour of the couple's T-shirts. Often, we impose our issues on our children, rather than seeing the world through their (innocent) eyes.

For younger children (1–5 years)
- Use some of the beautifully illustrated books available in bookshops and libraries about children around the world to teach your children about diversity. These books discuss how children from different countries dress, what they eat, their particular customs and festivals, etc.

For older children (6–12 years)
- The media often reports on events and happenings in other countries that may be different to how things are done in your own country. Focus your children's attention on these stories and use them as the basis of discussion. Keep a map of the world handy (either an atlas or a globe) to enable you to point out where in the world this particular story is happening. Context helps children to visualise things.
- Involve your family in community service.
- Take your children to eat in different restaurants. It's an easy way to introduce them to a variety of cuisines and foreign tastes, some of which they will like and some that they will dislike.
- Speak about diversity issues, e.g. personality, regularly.

There are many other ways to do what we have suggested and many things that you can do to develop the X-factors in your children. We encourage you to not just do what we have said, but to find your own way and carve your own path. Any ideas you have that we haven't mentioned, please contact us and share them. We would be delighted to hear from you.

Chapter 6

What can school do for your child?

'So what should we be teaching? Many pedagogical experts
argue that schools should switch to teaching 'the four Cs'— critical
thinking, communication, collaboration, and creativity. More broadly,
they believe, schools should downplay technical skills and emphasize
general-purpose life skills. Most important of all will be the ability
to deal with change, learn new things, and preserve your
mental balance in unfamiliar situations.'
Yuval Noah Harari, *21 Lessons for the 21st Century*, 2018

If all the world's information is at the end of our children's fingertips, and they can bypass even adults and libraries and go straight to Google, why on earth do we still need to send our children to school? What does education today mean, and how are schools changing to adapt to a fast-changing world? Are schools so far behind that a formal education is not even a requirement any more?

We think these are very important questions to ask, and we hope, in this chapter, to help you reframe your view of education, schools and the learning process. We know that many of you are thinking that the school system is old, slow, broken and irrelevant. In fact, in the first edition of this book we were very critical of schools and how slow they are to evolve and adapt. However, in the past 10 years we have seen many schools make enormous strides (though not all, unfortunately) in adapting and reinventing themselves for these primary reasons:

- To bring education in line with how children are naturally wired to learn – something that was completely disregarded when school was first invented. It was not about the child; it was about shaping and moulding workers for production lines who could all to the same things, such as writing legibly, reading fluently, being punctual, taking orders and being obedient.
- To take advantage of a host of technological advances aimed at the education sector (often called EdTech), many of which are offered for free to public schools.
- To create an educational environment that is more reflective of the world 'out there'.
- To prepare our children for the changing world of work, in which the jobs they do and what they sell – products and services – will be constantly changing (as we have indicated in previous chapters).

Education is currently experiencing significant flux and change, incorporating many experimental approaches and an almost overwhelming number of options and choices. Even 'traditional' schools, with decades, and even centuries, of history, are changing at a rapid pace. This can be stressful for parents, as most of us have don't have much more than our own memories of school to guide us in deciding on what school should be like now.

So let's start with a very important fact: if what we've said in this book so far resonates with you, it should be obvious that our children's schools should *not* look or feel like the schools we attended. Parents will have to learn to engage in new ways with the schools of the 2020s, and be confident in the education partners they choose for their children. And they will need to learn to be comfortable with some experimentation along the way.

> Graeme remembers that his matric-year group was one of the first to use calculators in their final maths exams. His grandfather, who was a maths genius of note, was most upset about what he saw as a huge downgrade in the standard of maths being taught. Of course, the

> opposite was true: using calculators allowed the curriculum to shift to more advanced calculus, in particular. Graeme was surprised to see a repeat of his grandfather's attitude when Hannah's school introduced compulsory iPad usage just a few years after Apple's tablet device was launched. Some parents complained that: 'We don't pay school fees so that our children can sit and stare at a screen all day – we want teachers to teach, not use devices to do their jobs for them.' It is lost on these parents that they themselves spend hours every day staring at screens at work.

School does not need to be perfect in order to benefit our children. After all, children never did, and never will, leave school perfect in every way. In actual fact, a school that experiments, experiences some failures and struggles, and forces children and parents to be more resilient, creative, empathetic, etc., will actually better develop the X-factors we discussed in the previous chapter than a school that just hums along without challenging itself or its learners.

Together, parents and schools must focus on the end goal, which is to produce children who are as future-fit as possible. Don't get lost in the details, seeking perfection and pushing back against innovation and change. The big picture is quite simple, really. Our children need to receive a solid, broad-based grounding to ensure that they are literate and numerate.

This will allow them to:
- create connections and draw conclusions
- develop a rich vocabulary and use language confidently
- build strong reading and comprehension skills to deal with information overload
- develop discernment to figure out what is real and what is fake
- foster a curious and enquiring mind that can think critically and ask good questions
- establish the confidence to express their ideas and try them out, even at the risk of failure.

These qualities are nurtured at home, in that solid base of home learning that we spoke of in Chapter 2, and they are further developed at school, as a critical component in our children's progress.

Schools still have an important place in society today for another reason. Let's get real for a minute. While we have a wide variety of options to choose from, including home-schooling, cottage schools, boutique educational institutions, government schools, private schools and online education, to name but a few, only a small minority of parents stay at home with their children today.

Nikki often surveys the parents who attend her talks and has concluded that those who work full time are parenting for only two to three hours per day. And most of that time is not spent doing quality activities with their children, but getting through whatever tasks must be accomplished in the day.

This means that while schools provide learners with an education, they are also caring for children, who can constructively utilise their time while their parents are at work. Teachers have become an extension of the family. Most people reading this book will either be single parents, full-time workers or double-income households. Those parents who stay at home with their children are likely to be self-employed, and are thus also not focusing on their children 24/7. With this in mind, we need to choose our children's school carefully, as it is 'co-parenting' with us. And once we've made our choice, we need to support that institution.

Schools are an important microcosm of society; it is where your children have to find their place and learn to sink or swim; it is where they discover their strengths and weaknesses, their interests and talents. Social learning is part of being at a school. Your children get to learn in the company of their peers, with an adult to guide and encourage them.

While children can learn a lot on computers and laptops – there are amazing educational programs available, and Google can dish up facts and figures at the press of a button – the flame of curiosity doesn't burn brightly in a vacuum. It is usually sparked and spurred on by human interaction. Even for children undergoing a blended learning experience, one where they can largely drive the pace of their own learning because it is computer-based, a human will carefully guide them.

School is about much more than content shared in classrooms. There is a 'hidden curriculum' that shapes our children in profound ways. Think for a moment about your favourite teacher from school: how much of what he or she actually taught you (the content of their subject) do you remember? Probably very little. It is more likely that you remember that teacher because of the life lessons and intangible values you learnt from him or her, rather than the curriculum he or she taught.

For this reason, we need to help our children take responsibility for their development at school – and especially this 'hidden curriculum' – as early as possible. Whether you are home-schooling your child or sending them to formal school, here is some advice to help make the educational marathon meaningful, which will add value for the rest of their lives:

- Help them to delight and find pleasure in their own learning from the earliest age.
- Encourage active participation, research and experimentation, and allow for failure.
- Encourage effort and hard work in areas and subjects they enjoy, as well as those they don't.
- Understand that the learning journey doesn't always have to be easy, but it does need to be interesting.
- Encourage a growth mindset versus a fixed mindset.
- Provide them with feedback from people both at home and at school: humans learn better in social settings.
- Teach them that reading, comprehension and research are the portals to knowledge.
- Help them to discover that actually 'doing' – putting knowledge to work in real and tangible ways – is the ultimate form of learning. Otherwise, knowledge is just information.
- Tell them that learning how to follow instructions is a life skill.
- Encourage them to present their thoughts and ideas with clarity and enthusiasm – it's a skill that will take them far.

We also need to constantly remind ourselves to give our children the gift of time. Much like Rome wasn't built in a day, education is a lifelong process. Children develop their competencies at different rates, and as parents we need to be on the lookout for those magical moments when things come together. This is where you start appreciating how incredible the learning and development process really is. Be observant. Be watchful. Be a good cheerleader.

And remember that, while a report card still allows for access to a tertiary education, your children need to leave school with more than just a set of marks. The character traits they have developed during their formative years will determine whether or not they are equipped for life and the process of lifelong learning. Education, learning and development happen both at home and at school. And none of it happens in an instant. Parents and children all need to learn how to enjoy the ride.

> **'Schools, parents and teachers remain at risk of implementing quick-fix approaches to bridging the gap in the education space, often without the necessary understanding of the bigger picture. In many schools today, technology is being used as a band-aid rather than a real solution. While the presence of technology allows schools to claim that they are on the right track and that they are able to prepare children for the 21st century, in truth, many of these interventions are simply IT supporting traditional learning, reinforcing what was needed 50 years ago.'**
> Nikki Bush and Arthur Goldstuck, *Tech-Savvy Parenting*, 2014

HARNESSING CHILDREN'S CURIOSITY
The Hole-in-the-Wall project

Dr Sugata Mitra, professor of educational technology at Newcastle University in the UK, devised the now famous Hole-in-the-Wall project in India in 1999. He was fascinated by the fact that rich people seemed to produce intelligent children, and he wondered if it was related to their exposure to mediums that fostered learning and education, which poorer children were unable to access.

In New Delhi, Dr Mitra's team carved a hole in the wall that separated the NIIT premises, where he worked, from the adjoining slum of Kalkaji, and installed a computer with high-speed internet and a touch pad for use by the children 'next door', but with no instructions whatsoever. The computer was simply left there, and Dr Mitra and his team observed the children's behaviour with the machine.

These were Indian children who could not speak any English, and the computer was American. What ended up happening was that the children learnt to use the computer by watching and copying each other, and experimenting and teaching each other – all in a very short space of time.

The conclusions drawn from this experiment, which continued for some years in many different places in India, were the following:

- That 6–13-year-olds can self-instruct in a connected environment and if they are in a social group. The ideal size of a learning group is four or five, although in the slums there were often much larger groups interacting at the same time around one computer. (Google 'Hole in the Wall' to see the amazing footage and to watch some of Dr Mitra's insightful TED talks.)
- If you allow the educational process to self-organise, the learning will come; it's not about *making* it happen, it's about *letting* it happen. The teacher sets the process in motion and watches as the learning unfolds.
- What is necessary for IT-enabled learning is a reliable broadband connection, collaboration, encouragement and admiration.
- That a curriculum of big questions had to be created to encourage children's curiosity about how the world works. Instead of teaching them specifically about tangent angles, for example, a question could be posed about the possibility of a meteorite hitting the Earth, leading to the magical concept of tangent angles through self-discovery, not instruction. Teachers need to raise the question and then stand back and allow the answers to come.
- Punishment and exams exist only to make children perform; children perceive them as a threat. And threats make our children's brains shut down. Children should learn for pleasure, not because they feel threatened.

Dr Mitra has co-opted British grannies, many of whom have had previous teaching experience, to be the learners' cheerleaders. The grannies provide encouragement remotely, via platforms such as Skype, to the children who are part of Dr Mitra's ongoing experiments. Technology in education is therefore making a huge difference in underprivileged areas. Dr Mitra believes that it can be used very effectively in underperforming areas where schools don't exist or are substandard, or where teachers are not available or are substandard.

What Sugata Mitra highlights in the Hole-in-the-Wall project is children's innate curiosity to learn. Babies are born explorers of their environment, whether they are putting dirt in their mouths, checking out what's behind the couch when they are crawling, or pointing to things before they can speak, non-verbally asking the question, 'What is that?' Their pointing is not just foraging for information, but is linked to language acquisition and building their vocabulary. Supporting their sense of curiosity is the central role of any parent, even when they start asking the exhausting 'why' questions, which begin at around age three.

A child's curiosity needs to be encouraged in a positive way. They have a constant desire for new information, sensations, experiences and challenges, and seek us out in a quest to gather information about, and knowledge and understanding of, the world in which they live.

Children are interested in their world, and we should be interested enough in their thought processes to play a game of 'serve and return'. In a helpful analogy of the to-and-fro communication between a parent and child, think of a tennis ball crossing the net between two players. The child serves the ball to us by asking a question, and we return service by either giving them an answer or, more ideally, by asking them another question. The longer the ball is kept in motion, the deeper and more interesting the learning becomes. This 'game' carries on for the entire time that our children are in our care.

Paul Harris, professor of education at Harvard, says that children between the ages of two and five years ask an average of about 40 000 questions that require an explanatory answer. This is very important in learning how to think. As children realise there are things they don't know, they ask more answers. 'They also discover there are invisible worlds of knowledge that they have never visited, and that other people are the source of information ... language transfers information,' says Ian Leslie in his excellent book, *Curious* (2014).

Leslie likens children to investigative reporters pumping adults for information. Questions bring knowledge. Even if they don't use that information immediately, it might be useful in making connections in the future.

Curiosity is rarely goal-orientated; it can simply be curiosity for curiosity's sake. There is often serendipitous and surprise learning when we have enquiring minds that are allowed to wander and ask why; it is also how the dots get connected between disparate and seemingly unrelated bits of information. Curiosity is also an antidote to boredom, because you can be curious about anything and everything. Even a passing interest can be transformed into a lifelong passion, or could lead to an innovative thought that could be an industry game-changer.

As authors and researchers ourselves, we can attest to the value of reading widely and interviewing people from a range of disciplines. In this way we can cross-pollinate bits of information and discover hidden connections. It adds a richness and freshness to our thinking and our ability to impart knowledge and understanding to others. This is how we innovate in our industry, and it provides a thrill and quiet sense of satisfaction.

In the quote below, Leslie puts forward the case for knowledge acquisition:

> Knowledge, even shallow knowledge – knowing a little about a lot – widens your cognitive bandwidth. It means you get *more* out of a trip to the theatre or a museum, or from a novel, a poem or a history book. It means you can glance at the first few paragraphs of a story in *The Economist*, grasp its essentials, and discuss them later (with enough stored knowledge, you can connect the dots without reading the entire article – you can fill in the gaps). It means you can engage with the

person next to you at lunch on a broader range of topics, contribute meaningfully to more meetings, be more sceptical of dubious claims, and ask better questions of everyone you encounter. Whoever you are and whatever start you get in life, *knowing stuff* makes the world more abundant with possibility and gleams of light more likely to illuminate the darkness. It opens the universe a little.

His explanation about the importance of 'knowing stuff' makes a lot of sense. Nikki often tells young people in her audience who are about to leave school to study further, or who are just about to enter the world of work, that they need to be interested in other people and be interesting themselves. 'If you don't make a point of knowledge acquisition, and you have to keep excusing yourself to check things up on Google to appear intelligent and be able to contribute to the conversation, you will not appear interested or interesting, but rather dumb, unintelligent and disinterested in the world around you. It is still important to know stuff!'

Put another way, knowledge is the bedrock of curiosity and innovation, and companies will pay a premium for it. Make sure you add a good whack of knowledge into the base of your child's triangle. We believe that these two elements are key to good schools: building a bedrock of knowledge, and fuelling the curiosity children naturally have so that they want to discover more about the world around them and more about themselves in the world.

While we share three drives with other primates — the need for food, shelter and sex — there is one key differentiator, and that is a human being's ability to wonder why and ask questions. Around the time our children turn three and start speaking properly, they can send us round the bend with their endless 'why' questions. This, though, lies at the heart of developing their curiosity — an essential part of deep knowledge acquisition, which, in turn, leads to innovative thinking.

There are three parts to the skill of asking questions in both children and adults:

1. You discover that you know that you don't know (essentially acknowledging your ignorance and that you have information gaps – curious people put their ego aside when they acknowledge their own ignorance).
2. You are able to imagine different competing possibilities/answers/solutions.
3. You understand that you can learn from others by asking questions.

The interesting thing is that questions lead to more questions – if the answers a person receives are valuable. In the case of children, the response they get to their repeated and probing questions is extremely important to keep their sense of curiosity alive. Curiosity is a feedback loop based on asking questions. When feedback stops, questions stop coming. This is not to say you should provide answers to all of your child's questions, immediately. In fact, the opposite is true. You should frame your responses with further questions to push them to dig deeper for themselves, for example: 'That's a really interesting question. Where do you think you could find more information about this?'

Curious learners go deep and wide. When children have to make an effort to find answers, the learning deepens, moving information from the working memory to the long-term memory.

When children mull information over and find meaning in it, they turn it into knowledge. Contrary to popular thinking, children really do need to develop a rich bank of knowledge in their *own brains* instead of relying on Google, which acts as an 'external brain'. Without an internal knowledge bank, children will have difficulty discovering connections and having innovative ideas as they develop.

'Machines are for answers and humans are for questions,' says Leslie in *Curious* (2014). 'All innovation starts first with a question. Google can help you discover some dots (facts), but it can't tell you what you ought to be asking. An incurious person may not even question the first thing that comes up on Google!

'The truly curious will be increasingly in demand. Employers are looking for people who can do more than follow procedures competently or respond to requests; who have a strong, intrinsic desire to learn, solve problems and ask penetrating questions.'

Leslie goes on to explain that the world needs billions of enquiring minds to solve global issues, and that enquiring minds will be an organisation's most valuable asset.

So, keep those questions coming!

CHOOSING A SCHOOL

Now that we have the big picture of why school is important, and what we should be expecting from a school experience beyond the curriculum and exit examination, let's look at a checklist for choosing a school for your children.

Few areas of parenthood create more anxiety than the selection of the right school for our children. In our parents' day, we were either sent to the government school in our area, if our parents could afford it, or we attended a private school, of which there were only a handful to choose from. Today's parents are faced with an entirely different scenario. We are not necessarily limited to the government school in our area, and a plethora of private schools now exist to choose from, all offering a variety of teaching approaches, value systems and facilities.

While we revel in the wide selection, it is the responsibility of us as parents to investigate all the available options. This can be both a time-consuming and confusing exercise, but it is one that will really make you ponder your own beliefs and values. What is important to you? Where are you going as a family? What do you want for your children? What preparation do your children need to survive and thrive in the future world of work?

Remember that success in life is not necessarily determined by academic success. Today, the focus is on developing your child's social and emotional skills. Emotional intelligence and the ability to relate to – and manage – people effectively are greater indicators of success than any other factors. Your child is a whole being and you need to find an education system that takes this into account.

Remember, your children will attend school for the better part of a decade, so you need to consider whether the school of your choice is prepared to change as the world around us changes. And, of course, keeping in mind that our children are not being prepared for the world right now, but for the world of the future. So, what kind of future does your children's prospective school think it is preparing its learners for? It is essential to consider this question, as it is vitally important for your child's future.

If you are in the fortunate position where you are able to choose a school for your child, here is a discussion guide for you to consider when choosing which school is best suited to you and your child (and remember, as we said, there is no such thing as a 'perfect' school):

DISCUSSION GUIDE FOR THE PARENT WHO IS SHOPPING FOR ANY SCHOOL

Know your child

Every child is unique; each child has his or her own strengths and weaknesses and unique combination of characteristics. Use the preschool years to track these traits. When shopping for a school, you need to bear these traits in mind. The school you select for your child should be one in which he or she will thrive. Your child's playgroup and preschool teachers may be a source of good advice.

Also, if it becomes clear that your child is not thriving in the school you have chosen – and you have done everything you can to fix this – you shouldn't hesitate to move your child to another school. (However, if you're contemplating a third or fourth such move, maybe there are some deeper issues that you need to identify and deal with!)

Know your values

Is it important to you that the school you choose will develop your child as an individual, or that it produces children in a particular mould? This is an important question, because the answer will differ depending on your outlook. Some people really value the type of child turned out by particular schools.

Ask schools what values they promote and see if they match those you are trying to instil in your child. What is the religious or educational approach at the school? Make sure it is in line with your thinking, or the way in which you are raising your child. The school might be affiliated to a particular faith, or it may follow a traditional, Montessori, Waldorf or Reggio Emilia approach.

Know your lifestyle

Do you work full time, part time or not at all? Are you a single parent or a two-parent family? Where do you live or work? How far away is the school from your home or place of work? Choosing a school that is perfect for your child but far out of your way can make life difficult. School needs to fit as comfortably into your routine as possible so that your child can arrive on time every day and you can participate fully in your child's school activities. Is the school family-friendly or totally school-focused? Does it consider the requirements of working parents? Is it emotionally supportive within the classroom of children who come from difficult family circumstances?

Know your budget

It is pointless sending your children to an expensive private school if this demands that both parents have to work themselves to a standstill to afford it and therefore can't spend quality time with their children. Remember that a good education is no substitute for quality time spent as a family. School fees should not be such a drain on the family budget that you are unable to afford going out for a treat now and then, or giving your children other rich life experiences outside of the school environment.

Also, make sure you appreciate all the 'extras' that schools require when setting your budget – these can range from school uniforms and sports equipment to technology requirements and school trips, and can add up very quickly. Ask the school about the typical total annual cost of a student, not just the published fees.

Ask about the philosophy of learning

What are the theoretical underpinnings of the school's approach to teaching and learning? Do they have a good understanding of how children learn? This is a vital issue to consider, as there are many different approaches to education, some of which are quite experimental.

Interestingly, we are seeing how education is being reshaped around how children *actually* learn and not how we *think* they should be taught. This does not mean that there should be no structure or rules in the classroom, but finding the intersections between how children are wired to learn naturally, and what will be required of them in the future world of work, is a critical shift that leads to the development of new approaches and new curricula.

There is a groundswell of interest in more child-directed learning, based on the premise that teachers should not get in the way of a child's innate love of discovery. There is also a re-emphasis of 'learning by doing', and so we are seeing a resurgence of interest in the Montessori, Waldorf, Jenaplan and Reggio Emilia philosophies, among others.

Schools are also mixing it up, piecing things together to create unique or adapted approaches to education. Thinking Schools, Future Nation Schools, Microsoft Schools of the Future, Square Peg and project-based learning are examples of this around the world. Make sure you ask about and understand the approach of the schools you are considering.

Investigate the curriculum

It is important to look for a balanced programme that is child-centred and play-directed. The programme should stimulate your child's social, emotional, motor, perceptual, mental and physical development. Is the learning programme geared towards the development of the child as a whole? Activities should be developmentally appropriate for the age and stage of the child. This can vary vastly, especially in the preschool years.

In preschool and junior-primary environments, ask to see a checklist of the daily activities. The daily programme should consist of routines (toilet time, snack time, rest time, etc.), creative artwork, free play, gross-motor-development work, manipulative play (problem-solving, for example, construction toys and puzzles), and fine-motor work, such as threading and pegging. Preschool children require a structured day with short 'activity rings' and ample time for free play. Through the routine of the programme, children become familiar with what is going to happen next. This makes them more secure in their preschool experience, which forms part of their journey to independence.

When you visit the school, pay attention to the artwork on the walls. Look for large pieces of paper using many different mediums and varied subject matter. Every child's work should be different, which shows that individuality and creativity are encouraged. Be wary if you see lots of photocopied, coloured-in pictures on the walls.

Look at the learning spaces

Purpose-built schools and schools undergoing radical shifts to update themselves may have new-look, reconfigurable learning spaces. Ask how these work. If they have old-fashioned classrooms, you may want to ask how they are adapting these contained learning spaces for any new approach to education that may have been mentioned.

Check the layout of the classrooms. This is particularly important in the preschool environment, as it provides children with structure. Are there areas demarcated for different activities, such as fantasy play, a construction corner, a book corner and interest tables?

Check the cleanliness of the grounds, classrooms and toilet facilities. This shows that the staff care and are careful.

Technology usage

Technology is being used more and more to market schools, but parents need to scratch beneath the surface to see how deeply a school can adapt to change. It's great that the school has Smart Boards, iPad labs or bring-your-own device policies, but what is actually being *done* with the technology in the classroom?

What type of courses are teachers enrolling in, and how are they integrating this new learning into the curriculum or in the way they teach? What is the underlying philosophy of the school with regard to how children learn? What is the difference between children interacting with technology at home versus what they do with technology at school?

Learning to talk the language of machines so that you can teach them to do stuff is called programming or coding. As our children will be working alongside machines in the future, this is an important skill to acquire, and it can start as early as preschool. (By the way, the early stages of coding do not have to be done with any kind of technology at all – there are plenty of multisensory games that provide basic foundations for what children will do with a bot next, because coding is actually just a series of steps in the right order.)

Find out how the school is incorporating coding, programming and robotics into their curriculum. Some schools will have it as part of the school day, and others will offer it as an extracurricular activity.

STEM stands for science, engineering, maths and technology, and extends to and is incorporated in games and toys. At toy fairs and innovation conferences around the world, more and more distributors are adding bots to their ranges. LEGO® is no exception, with LEGO® Robotics. It organises two international competitions each year that extend the value of their products and robotics outside of schools:
- WRO (World Robot Olympiad)
- FLL (First LEGO® League)

This allows learners to test their robotics skills in a competitive environment and generates recognition of their abilities. These competitions are run provincially, nationally and internationally. Interschool robotics challenges encourage students to interact with their peers, apply their knowledge of programming and robotics, and allow parents to witness the growth of their child's abilities.

Robotics makes thinking visible
- With robotics, and programming in general, becoming an increasingly ubiquitous part of our lives, it is essential that future members of society at least have an understanding of the value, operation and limitations of programming and robotics, even if they do not pursue a career in these fields.

- Robotics is the 3D manifestation of 2D programming and, as such, it is easier for students to conceptualise and understand what they are learning when they see the coding in action.
- Robotics is built on the principles of Six Simple Machines, the technology and engineering principles that govern all forms of machines in the world. Being able to comprehend and recognise these principles, as well as being able to manipulate them in the safety of a robust product, allows students to have an appreciable knowledge of the machines in their daily lives.

Innovation and change

Ask what the most recent experiments in curriculum design, school systems and educational techniques have been at the school. Ask for examples of experiments that have worked, and those that have not worked and have been abandoned. You're looking for evidence that the school understands and embraces true innovation values, and is prepared to try things, and adapt and learn quickly in their educational approach.

Extracurricular activities and opportunities

School, as we discussed, is about a lot more than what happens in the classroom with the formal curriculum. Much of the 'hidden curriculum' happens during activities outside of the classroom, including during sports and cultural activities. The school should have a wide range of these activities available, or at least should support the children in doing extracurricular activities at or away from the school. Ask which of these activities, if any, are compulsory. Learning to work as part of a team, being part of a community, learning to persevere, and learning how to win or lose while pursuing both individual and common goals are only some of the many benefits of extracurricular activities.

Professional qualifications of the teachers

Is the person in charge a qualified educator in the specific age category of your child? There is a world of difference between pre-primary and senior-primary education. Do not be afraid to ask about staff qualifications.

You should also ask about the teacher-to-child ratio. The younger the children, the lower the ratio should be. In some schools in which there are larger numbers of children, the teacher may have one or two assistants.

Continued professional development for teachers

Enquire about what sort of courses the staff go on to keep abreast of changes and developments in education. You are entitled to ask about staff qualifications and the staff's professional development.

Assessment and feedback

How will your child's development be monitored and assessed? Are there formal assessments? What feedback will you receive, and when? Regular formal evaluation is essential in identifying and addressing possible problems at an early stage, but note that the types of tests and examinations you used to write are not the only way to assess your child's progress. This is one of the important reasons for having qualified staff at a school.

Security and access control

What kind of security and access-control measures are in place? Check if teachers have playground duties. The playground must be supervised at all times.

For pre-primary and junior-primary schools especially, look around the playground and check out the equipment. Is there sufficient equipment and is it well maintained and safe? Ensure that there are swings, jungle gyms or other climbing apparatus. A sandpit and bike track for scooters are also necessary.

Check for grassed areas. Ensure that there is no concrete under jungle gyms, etc. Is the sandpit covered at night to keep pets out, and is it covered to provide shade for children during the day? Are swimming pools, ponds and water features fenced or netted?

Aftercare facilities

Check the aftercare facilities. Who runs the programme and what does it consist of? You do not want your child watching TV all afternoon or being left alone unsupervised on the playground.

Follow your instinct
When you have looked into all measurable aspects of a school, such as facilities, fees, etc., it is important to take a bit of quiet time to assess what your gut feel is telling you about the school. Ask yourself about your first impression of the school. Look at the intangibles. Was the human touch evident? How did the teachers speak to the children? How did the children speak to – and about – the other children? You are probably going to look at many schools, and that can become quite confusing when they all have similar facilities and profess to have similar values. Talk to other parents whom you trust and who know your child. It is always valuable to listen to other points of view.

Remember that school selection can be a highly charged issue and everyone has a very personal, and even an emotional, view. Think carefully about the people you choose to speak to.

Know that this is a journey
Getting your child school ready is a journey that starts from birth, and the next stage of your child's education is no different. It's a constantly evolving process that will need to be fine-tuned from time to time, perhaps with a visit to the teacher, or some extra lessons, a pair of glasses, extension activities, or even a change of school if necessary.

There is a kind of evolution that takes place within your child as he or she grows and develops. Today we are not faced with a one-school-fits-all scenario. If you feel that corrections to the course you are pursuing are required (by you or your child), then these are perfectly acceptable and necessary. Children are more resilient than you think. As long as they feel loved and secure, they will adjust to new situations.

Be aware of shopping distractions
- Where are most of your friends sending their children?
- Where are most of the children in the preschool going?
- Where did you and your spouse or partner and the children's grandparents go to school?
- What is the distance from home to school, or from school to your place of work?

These distractions can heavily influence your choice of school instead of allowing the child's needs and the family's values to drive the school-selection process. Obviously, you should not ignore the practical implications of choosing a school that is convenient for you, but you need to find the best balance possible.

GETTING THE MOST OUT OF YOUR CHILD'S SCHOOL

Once you have decided on a school and your child is settled there, you need to get the most out of that school. The secret to this is that parents must be involved. Not as defenders of their children and critics of the teachers, which is a very destructive current trend that can destroy the teacher-child relationship irrevocably, but as active partners in the education of their children. It's the only way that our children will be prepared for the realities of the world of work in the 2020s and beyond.

Schools and teachers cannot do it alone – not even the best ones. The need for teamwork in education has never been more critical – for the sake of our children. We need to combine the best of what schools have to offer with the best of what parents have to offer to achieve a meaningful result.

Understandably, many parents are under huge time and financial pressure, which keeps them away from their children and limits their involvement in their educational journey. However, we need to bear in mind that studies have proven that children whose parents show an interest in their child's development and who get involved with school life do better at school academically, stay in the school system for longer, and are less likely to do drugs, abuse alcohol or fall into bad company.

Being involved means helping out at school events, being on committees, attending the school play or sports fixtures, and making the time to chat to your child about school, homework, projects, etc. You might not be able to do all of the above, but get involved as much as you possibly can. If you feel strongly that schools need to change, or if you are not happy with a fundamental aspect of the school, the best place to effect change is from within.

So, get involved in some way. It's also the best way to meet people and to create a real social network. This will create a sense of belonging and togetherness, as well as a network you can fall back on. Your child will also feel more secure knowing that there are layers of known support.

PARENT-TEACHER MEETINGS

A word on parent-teacher meetings, which take place a few times a year to enable you to keep tabs on your children's progress and have face-to-face feedback from your child's educators. Some parents love them, others hate them. Regardless, they can be invaluable to both parties. Parent-teacher meetings provide an opportunity to:

- discover more about your child's progress and how they operate in a classroom setting, which can be very different from how they act at home with you
- resolve social and learning challenges
- share information. Teachers need to know what is happening at home, such as the arrival of a new sibling, an illness or death in the family, a divorce, moving house or trauma, etc. All of these can affect your child's performance, behaviour and development.)

Of course, this does not mean that we will always be in agreement with the teacher, and conflict can arise due to different viewpoints. However, it must be remembered by both parties that the best interests of the child are at the heart of this process, and practical, helpful solutions need to be found.

Here are some tips for more productive and less stressful parent-teacher meetings from Michael Grose, a former teacher and Australia's number-one parenting educator:

1. **Work from a fresh slate.** Sometimes meetings can be marred before they start, as negative past experiences can carry residual resentment. Every new meeting offers a fresh opportunity to create better outcomes for your child.
2. **Prepare well.** Before a meeting or conference, list any questions that you want to raise. Keep the questions short and to the point. Similarly, it may be useful to list some of your child's strengths and areas of improvement that you've seen at home. Writing information down

in advance ensures that your point of view is expressed and that critical information is covered. Similarly, make sure you take notes during the meeting so that vital information isn't missed.
3. **Listen first.** Give the teacher a chance to make an assessment of your child's progress or behaviour. This may sound obvious, but some meetings never get off the ground because an enthusiastic parent takes over.
4. **Ask what you can do.** Show your commitment to producing better results by asking for exercises that you can do at home to develop skills. It may be a good opportunity to ask for recommendations for outside resources to help you and your child. Often teachers know about camps, extension activities, organisations and therapists that can encourage educational and social growth.

Using Michael's guidelines will ensure that you go into the meeting with a positive attitude, an approachable demeanour and a willingness to work collaboratively. And one final word of advice: we don't always know how our children operate in the school environment, because we are not there. It can be quite different to how they act in the home/family setting, because at school they are finding their feet in a much larger group, and dealing with the stresses, challenges and joys that come with academic learning. Listen carefully to the teacher for these insights.

In Nikki's and Graeme's regular interactions with school principals and educators, the most common complaints are the following:
- Children lack the skill of independence because their parents are micro-managing them and doing everything for them. Many children are growing up in a state of learned helplessness.
- Parents undermine the teacher in front of the child and behind their backs at home. This is breaking down respect and trust and making the job of the teacher that much harder; ultimately, it gets in the way of a child's learning experience in the classroom.
- Parents do not trust the teachers and schools to make appropriate decisions as professional educators.

DON'T UNDERMINE YOUR CHILD'S TEACHERS

While we don't always agree with our children's teachers, those disagreements must be dealt with in private and not within earshot of our children. If we don't, we are doing our children a disservice. We risk raising children who are egocentric and give up too quickly when things get a little hard, and who are quick to blame others for their lack of happiness or success.

In Blair King's article in *The Huffington Post*, dated 14 March 2016, he shares four very solid pieces of advice for parents, which we agree with completely:

1. **Parents, you are not your child's best friend, you are their parent.** This is a common trap that some parents fall into today in an effort to keep everyone smiling and happy. Be your child's best friend at your peril – soon they will be pulling all the strings and calling the shots, with you and everyone else. When you have raised them to adulthood, then you can be best friends.

2. **Parents, learned helplessness is your fault, not your child's.** When we are constantly clearing and smoothing the path for our children, they are at risk of becoming helpless and lacking in resourcefulness. They also know that if they tell a parent they can't do something, or that something is too difficult, their parent is likely to step in and complete the task for them. This leaves children incapable, ill-equipped and unwilling to try to figure out how to accomplish tasks for themselves.

3. **Parents, you must advocate for your kids, but you must also support your child's teacher.** We are not in the classroom with our child, and they can behave quite differently in class than they do at home. Blair, who is married to a teacher with 15 years' experience, says that parents often forget that teachers are trained professionals and don't treat them with the respect they deserve.

    If you question your child's teacher in front of your child, you are telling your child that the teacher's authority is not to be respected.

When a teacher tells you something, don't turn to your child and ask if what their teacher is saying is true. You may think you are involving your child in the discussion, but what you have actually done is to question that teacher's reliability to their face. Think of it from the teacher's perspective. You have essentially told them that you won't believe what they just told you until your child confirms it.

4. **Parents, your child's teacher cannot replace your role in your child's education.** As parents pay more for their children's education and spend more time at work, they expect teachers to pick up the slack and fill in for them, by instilling manners, good behaviour and values in their children, for example. This is our job as parents; teachers simply don't have enough hours in the day to take on these tasks. Of course, they will supplement what we teach our children at home and build on our foundations, *but we must take responsibility for building those foundations.*

School alone cannot prepare your child for the future, and nor can you. It is going to take a strong partnership between home, school, teacher and learner, and this needs to be based on mutual respect.

Parents provide many canvases on which their children can express, explore and discover themselves. Home is one; sporting and cultural arenas are another; school is a major one; and there are more.

In closing off this chapter, let's take a look at the school canvas. Have you ever thought of school as a place that belongs to your child? It is a space where they are able to exist without you, with some independence, where they can try out and practise what you have taught them. It is a space that you have chosen for them that is filled with other people, both pint-size and adult-size, and they will also add their own colours to your child's palette. School is filled with new experiences that will colour their world.

While we love to be in control of most aspects of our lives, as well as those of our children, there are times when we need to let go and trust that we have chosen the perfect place for our child to be, right now. It is *their* place, and we need to let them own it, as well as all the experiences that come with it, both positive and negative. Every experience, formal and informal, is a teachable moment in some way, shape or form.

Artists get to choose their own colours and their own media – water colours, oils, pastels, charcoal, etc. – as well as their own subject matter and which feelings to express, based on their interactions with life. To empower our children to paint their own canvas, we must allow them to experience life for themselves.

Even if we set the value system for our children and they tend to see the world through our eyes (certainly in the early years), they need exposure to other people in a variety of environments in order for their value system and point of view to have any meaning at all.

Children need to be part of their own learning process. They need to co-create and experience it to own it. While you might be paying the school fees, the school experience belongs to your child. It's not about you. It's largely about their journey and the unique canvas they are creating. It's their world. It's their place. Honour and support it, and watch your child thrive and grow.

Chapter 7

Building a Talent Profile

'An unexamined life is not worth living.'
Socrates

We live in disruptive times, and organisations will be looking for more than just our kids' report cards when they apply for jobs. Yes, they will want young people who have a school-leaver's certificate and appropriate tertiary qualifications, but that's just the start. Increasingly, companies are, and will be, looking for the X-factors for success – those things that can't be taught or quantified, including creativity/innovation, resilience, commitment to continuous learning, self-knowledge and the ability to work in a team.

A current mantra in human resources is that you hire for attitude and train for skills. This makes sense when you look at the amount of continuous disruption facing the workplace. Many of the jobs your children will be employed to do in future may not continue to exist after they'd done them for a year or two, which means your children will need to be highly flexible and adaptable. As organisations become increasingly innovative, cutting-edge and flexible in order to thrive, they will look for those characteristics in their employees, too.

With this in mind, young people should focus on providing a Talent Profile that will not only contain all the information that would normally be included in a written CV, but will showcase their unique, in-demand X-factors for success.

And note that this is not something you do only when you're looking for a job. Believe it or not, this process can start from around the age of eight!

WHAT IS A TALENT PROFILE AND WHAT DOES IT DO?

A Talent Profile is a living document that gets constantly updated. Think of a sort of multimedia timeline much like Facebook, rather than a traditional, written CV (curriculum vitae or résumé). Think about a potential employer who says, 'Tell me about a situation where you displayed creative problem-solving/innovative ideas/resourcefulness/teamwork/leadership/your effective presentation skills/knowledge of technology,' etc. A Talent Profile will ultimately consist of some, or all, of the following to provide the person reading it with an interesting window into who your child is and what they can do, including:

- written sections with the usual CV-type information
- sections that profile talents, skills and character attributes, with examples
- multimedia items such as videos, podcasts and photographs, or links to these
- links to personal websites and blogs
- links to social media profiles
- links to projects or endeavours if they exist online
- multimedia referrals from people (teachers, clients, employers, friends, family, etc.).

A Talent Profile showcases your child's:
- uniqueness/essence
- self-knowledge and self-awareness
- interests and passions that may not be directly linked to the work they are applying for
- innovative and creative way of marketing themselves
- background and provides context for who they are
- personality and character.

The aim of a Talent Profile isn't just to get a person a job or a position; it is to ensure that the job on offer is what he or she really wants. Think of the concept of ikigai mentioned in Chapter 3 – to live a fulfilled life requires not just doing what you are good at or what someone will pay you to do, but also to do what you love and what will make a difference in the world.

EXPAND YOUR VIEW OF TALENT

We need to expand our view of what talent is. We are conditioned to see talent in the narrow context of children being mathematically, linguistically, athletically or culturally orientated. But talent is more than that; it's about digging deep to discover the essence of who your child is. What is that core 'something' that makes them unique? It's that essence that they will take with them wherever they go and be able to apply in any situation.

> Take us, for example: we are both speakers and authors – that is what we do, it is how we express ourselves, but it is not *who* we are. Who we are is 'sense-makers'. We make sense of big volumes of complex stuff so that it is accessible to other people. We do so in creative ways, via our talks and books and online resources. That is the essence of who we are; it's what gets us up in the morning. We find value in bringing this to the world, and we can apply this essence wherever we find ourselves.
>
> We see our own children's essences, too. Looking beyond their report cards, we can see that Amy is a storyteller, able to quickly recognise the crux of every situation and make sense of it in images, movies and words; Hannah is a social-justice warrior who stands by her principles and is able to cut through complexity to see right and wrong with laser focus; Rebecca has the most remarkable memory for movies and music, using them not only to make sense of her autistic world, but to connect and communicate with those around her; Ryan is driven by the need to care and by discovering how things work and by fixing them; and Matthew's talent lies in his visual spatial skills.
>
> We are not describing traditional skills or jobs when we think about the 'talents' of our children. What we are describing is the essence of

> who they are, and what engages them. When our kids are operating in these talent zones, they are fully absorbed. And as long as they put these core strengths to good use, in any context, they will be making a contribution, and are likely to experience a sense of personal satisfaction and success. The concept of ikigai, of creating a life of meaning, becomes a reality.

WHY IS A TALENT PROFILE IMPORTANT IN PRIMARY AND HIGH SCHOOL?

CVs have always been documents relating to adults, but Talent Profiles are for everyone from primary school up. Your child's Talent Profile is a highly practical and concrete exercise in self-awareness and self-discovery. It helps them to create a marketing tool to help them in times when they might need to be noticed (which can be as early as when they are 10 to 12 years old). It can be used in the following situations:

- In applications for leadership positions at school, such as school counsellors, or team and house captains.
- For obtaining a place on a team or a committee, or as part of a recreational group.
- For involvement in environmental groups or community service organisations.
- In applications for school- or youth-exchange programmes.
- In applications for admission to high schools, or to apply for bursaries and scholarships.
- In applications for tertiary studies.
- In applications for student jobs.
- In applications for full-time employment.
- In entrepreneurial endeavours, for example, when looking for partners and funding.

A Talent Profile will raise your child's awareness of their own unique, special qualities, and they will be creating their own track record every day. Good self-knowledge developed over time will give them self-confidence when they want to take advantage of future opportunities.

A Talent Profile can also help a child learn how to make discerning choices about how they spend their time. They become selective about the activities they choose to be involved in, which leads to a balanced life, as they are prioritising based on their own self-awareness. This eliminates overscheduling, overstimulation and stress in general.

A Talent Profile gives a child hope for the future, as they start believing that they will be able to create a satisfying life *for themselves*. And that they are talented and unique by virtue of *who they are*, backed up by their life experiences.

EXAMPLES OF WHAT CAN BE SHOWCASED IN A TALENT PROFILE OF YOUNG CHILDREN

Here are some common examples that will showcase your child's special qualities. This can be presented in writing, with pictures and videos added for additional impact:

- You have a new puppy and your 10-year-old daughter does puppy-socialisation classes with you. This showcases her ability to care for others, leadership, discipline (she shows up for all the sessions) and commitment to learning new skills.
- You have an 8-year-old son who likes to make extra money. Once a month, he sells popcorn and candy floss outside your home from a little stall he has designed. He uses your cellphone to WhatsApp the people on the residents' list in your area and uses family labour to make all his wares. This showcases entrepreneurship, initiative and resourcefulness.
- Your 9-year-old builds and programs a LEGO® robot to perform a few basic tasks. This showcases design skills, technical ability, coding, problem-solving and project management.
- Your 11-year-old likes to volunteer to walk and wash dogs at the local animal rescue centre. This showcases community service, selflessness, consistency and generosity.
- Your 12-year-old makes it into the school's debating competition, which showcases communication skills, critical thinking, creativity, powers of persuasion and teamwork.

- Your 10-year-old loves cooking and selling his creations, which showcases his creativity, ability to follow instructions and entrepreneurial talents.
- Your 8-year-old creates unusual art or fantastic constructions that no one else gets to see but you. Although the child might not become an artist in future, it does showcase her creative and visual talents, as well as innovation, self-direction and making thinking visible (ideation).
- Your 12-year-old has taken three years to progress from the C-team to the A-team, which shows perseverance, commitment and a bit of strategic thinking. If you get them to break down how they achieved their goal, it can be a great exercise in self-awareness. And get a video testimonial from the team coach.
- A child suffered illness and/or loss for over a year, but bounced back to physical and mental health – this is worth documenting, as it showcases resilience, perseverance, resourcefulness and mental resolve.

From these examples, you can see that there is much of value that is not acknowledged by the system, or in public, but which contributes to the essence of your child. This is why school is just *one way* by which to measure or judge a child. Your child has many more layers to discover and explore; these are what make them interesting and unique individuals. We need to help them find and spot those qualities.

The Industrial Era celebrated people's similarities and sameness, while the Age of Possibility seeks points of difference that set people apart from one another. What makes your child stand out from the crowd? Are you closely observing, and will you spot it?

ADDITIONAL BENEFITS OF CREATING A TALENT PROFILE
Children can:
- discover their strengths and weaknesses
- discover what interests them and what does not
- set realistic goals for themselves, for example, they might want to progress from the C-team to the B-team, and they have to work out what must be done to make that happen.

The benefits for parents are the following:
- You will discover more about your child, including what goes on beneath the surface. You will discover the way in which they express their interests and passions.
- It can lead to interesting conversations, which can build a bridge between parent and child. For example, if your daughter says, 'I'm very good at tennis,' you should discuss this with her. Clearly she enjoys the game and would like to continue improving at it. 'You are in the C-team now. Are you happy to stay in that team, or do you think there is room for improvement?' And, 'If you want to improve, then what do you think you need to do to make the B-team?'; 'Is there anything you would like me to do to help you to achieve that goal?'; 'What do we need to put in place to help you – more coaching, more practise time?'; 'How will you know if you have been successful?' This is a way to help your children to set their own goals and assess themselves accurately.

HELPING YOUR PRIMARY SCHOOL CHILD WITH THEIR TALENT PROFILE

When your child is in preschool, do take note of their natural interests and abilities. Keep personal notes for later use in their Talent Profile file. It's easy to forget things when you live in an era of information overload and busyness. From the age of eight years, you and your child can start working on their Talent Profile together. We recommend that you do this by involving them in The Mirror Game©.

This won't happen all at once, but bit by bit. In the process, they will be creating a little booklet about themselves that they own. It's a story about them – they are the central character. You can call this *Project Me*, which relates to the concept of MeInc., mentioned in Chapter 4 (about jobs of the future). The children who piloted The Mirror Game© enjoyed it so much that they did not want to stop. Well, it was all about them, after all, and adding colour and pictures just contributed to the fascination.

Although it is neither a test nor a deep psychological assessment, The Mirror Game© should provide you with valuable information about your child and help you to discover more about them. It should also be fun:

'Come, let's play The Mirror Game© to find out more about what a hugely special person you are!'

Your children may get stuck from time to time and say something like, 'I don't know what to write down.' You need to be encouraging without necessarily giving them all the answers. Remember, how you see your children and how they see themselves could be very different. The various steps in the game give them the opportunity to write down how they see themselves, and how they think you, their friends and teachers see them.

By bringing both internal and external perceptions together in one document, the children gain a very interesting picture of themselves, which could lead to some really interesting discussions.

The Mirror Game©

Step 1: My physical mirror (what I look like and how I see myself)

- On a clean page or piece of paper, write the heading: 'My physical mirror'.
- Write down your name and age.
- Draw a rectangle in the middle of the page. Draw a picture of yourself in this 'mirror' – face, body, arms, legs, etc. It can be as creative or as comical as you like.
- Now create a mind map around the mirror, filling in at least 10 words that describe you physically, for example:
    - tall
    - strong
    - brown hair
    - blue eyes
    - freckly nose
    - pretty mouth
    - dainty fingers
    - smiley eyes.

Note to parents: *Try to encourage positive attributes where possible.*

Step 2: My emotional mirror
- On a new page or piece of paper, write the heading: 'My emotional mirror'.
- Draw another mirror on this page. (It does not have to be rectangular; it can be circular or oval, for example.)
- Now draw a picture of how you think your heart looks or feels.

Note to parents: *Give your child creative licence here to draw a Valentine's heart or a real biological heart. It doesn't matter what it looks like. Do not judge the picture. You can make comments such as, 'That's a really interesting heart', or 'I love your heart.' There is no right or wrong.*

- Now create a mind map around the mirror with 10 or more words that describe how you feel about yourself and your life at the moment, for example:
  - happy
  - sad
  - angry
  - hurt
  - hopeful
  - excited
  - left out
  - friendly
  - victimised
  - bullied
  - worried.

> When Nikki's son Matthew was completing this section of The Mirror Game© at age nine, he asked if it was possible to be happy and sad at the same time. He had conflicting feelings that day – he was happy because he loves most things in his life, but sad because his beloved teacher had announced she would be leaving at the end of the term to live in another country.

Step 3: My family mirror
- On a clean page or piece of paper, write the heading: 'My family mirror'.
- Draw another mirror on this page. You can choose any shape.
- Now draw a picture of your family, including yourself.
- Create a mind map around the mirror, with five or more words that describe your family, for example:
  - fun
  - loving
  - adventurous
  - boring
  - talkative
  - supportive
  - big/small
  - busy
  - rushed, etc.
- Under your mirror, at the bottom of the page:
  - Write the word 'Mom', followed by two words that describe her.
  - Write the word 'Dad', followed by two words that describe him.
  - Write down the names of your brothers and sisters (if you have any) and two words that describe each of them.

Note to parents: *If there is a primary caregiver who spends a lot of time looking after your child in your absence, such as a grandparent or an au pair, then include them in this list.*

This is a very interesting section, as we rarely ask our children these questions. It will reveal information to you about your family brand, which may or may not be what you expect to hear. Do not show any response if your child says something unexpected or negative. File it away in your head for processing at a later stage or, if appropriate, use it to open up a really interesting conversation with your child once he or she has completed the game.

You do not want your child to feel bad for having written down an observation that takes you by surprise. If you have an obvious negative reaction, you will battle to get an honest answer out of your child in future. This document should not be a 'parent-pleaser', but an honest exercise in self-awareness.

For example, a colleague once asked her 11-year-old twins to describe her in one word. The children said 'rushed'. She was fairly horrified at their perception, because it was not how she wanted them to view her. But she saw it as constructive feedback and set about amending how she ran her life. Within a year, she had managed to radically alter her children's perception.

Step 4: My friendship mirror
- On a clean page or piece of paper, write the heading: 'My friendship mirror'.
- Draw another mirror on this page.
- Now draw a picture of yourself with a favourite friend or friends. Name the people.
- Down one side of the mirror, write a mind map of all the people you consider to be your friends.
- On the other side of the mirror, write a mind map of some words that describe how you think your friends see you, for example:
  – loyal
  – trustworthy
  – honest
  – kind
  – supportive.

Note to parents: *At this point, you can ask your child: 'Why do you think that your friends say/feel these things?'*

- At the bottom of the page, make a list of words that describe what you think makes a good friend.

Note to parents: *Ask your child: 'Do you think you are a good friend to other people? Why?'*

Step 5: My school mirror
- On a clean page or piece of paper, write the heading: 'My school mirror'.
- Write down the name of your school.
- Draw another mirror on this page. Inside it, draw a picture of your school or some aspect of your school. It can be anything that comes to mind (the building, a sports field, a big tree, a teacher, the school badge, etc.).
- Now write down five words in a mind map on one side of the mirror that physically describes your school.
- Next, write down five words on the other side of the mirror about how you feel about your school emotionally, for example:
  - happy
  - scared
  - hopeful
  - fun
  - challenging
  - easy.
- Under the mirror, write down the following:
  - My best subject:

  Note to parents: *Ask your child why this is their favourite subject.*
  - My best teacher:

  Note to parents: *Ask your child why this is their favourite teacher.*
- On a new page, write down the first of two headings: 'Academic goals for the year', and beneath this heading, write down what you want to achieve academically.

Note to parents: *Discuss what your child needs to do to achieve these goals and what you need to do to help make them a reality. In 6 to 12 months' time, when your child redoes The Mirror Game©, you will both be able to assess whether or not he or she is on track, and why. Ensure that these commitments are written down on this page.*

- The second heading is: 'Extramural goals for the year', and beneath this heading, write down what you want to achieve extramurally.

Note to parents: This is the ideal time to discuss which sports and cultural activities your child would like to do, and how many of these he or she should be involved in to allow enough time for work and play. Discuss what your child needs to do to achieve his or her goals, and what you need to do to help make them a reality. Ensure that these commitments are written down on this page.

The 'Five Why' process

When Nikki's son Ryan was 12 and completing this section of The Mirror Game©, he commented that Mrs van Eck was his favourite teacher. Nikki asked Ryan the following five 'why?' questions, and found his answers to be quite revealing about what is important to him in a learning situation:

1. Why is Mrs van Eck your favourite teacher?
   Because she is on the ball. When something happens in the news, she uses it in the lesson the next day. (A recent example he cited was of a political cartoon from the newspaper about xenophobia, which was used in the English lesson.)
2. Why is it important for you that your teachers use events that are happening right now in their lessons?
   Because it makes learning real. It's not just about something that happened long ago; we can relate to it. It means the teachers know what's going on in the world – they are sharp and together.
3. Why should learning be real?
   Because then it's more interesting.
4. Why should lessons be interesting?
   Because then I pay better attention in class.
5. Why is paying attention that important?
   Because then I remember the work more easily and I get better marks in my tests and exams.

The 'Five Why' process helps you to reach the core of the issue and to find out what the child's true value is. This process can be applied to just about anything, and it will help the person doing it to align him- or herself to their highest values. It's a technique often used in management. At the

> end of the five whys, when the employee has voiced his or her core value, then the manager can ask, 'So how can I help you to achieve/reach that?'
>
> In the example with Ryan, Nikki could have gone one step further and asked why it was important to him to get good marks in his tests and exams, which may have opened up a wonderful discussion about his future. Nikki could have ended the conversation by asking, 'How can I help you to achieve that?'

Step 6: Mirror, mirror on the wall ...
This is the final section of The Mirror Game©.
- At the top of a new page, write down the heading: 'Mirror, mirror on the wall'.
- Then answer the following questions:
  1. What's your favourite colour?
  2. What's your favourite number?
  3. What's your favourite animal?
  4. What's your favourite meal/food?
  5. What's your favourite chocolate/sweet?
  6. What's your favourite holiday destination?
  7. What's your favourite space at home?
  8. What's your favourite game?
  9. What's your favourite sport?
  10. What's your favourite activity with your mom?
  11. What's your favourite activity with your dad?
  12. What's your favourite activity with your sibling/s?
  13. What would you like to do for your birthday this year?
  14. What would you like for your birthday?
  15. What would you like to be when you grow up?
  16. What makes you laugh?
  17. What makes you cry?
  18. What do you like about yourself?
  19. What don't you like about yourself?
  20. What are you not so good at?
  21. What are you really good at?

22. Is there anything special that you would like to do after school that you are not doing now?
23. Who would you really like to play with/spend more time with at school?
24. Who would you like to help you with your homework (if anyone)?
25. Who in your family would you like to spend more time with than you currently do?
26. Who is your hero (who inspires you, or who do you look up to)?
27. If you could change anything in the world, what would it be?
28. If you could change anything in your life, what would it be?
29. What do your teachers/coaches say about you (how do they describe you)?
30. What do your parents say about you (how do they describe you)?
31. What makes you special (one of a kind, unique)? How would you describe yourself in no more than five words?

Note to parents: *This last question should reveal how your child views him- or herself. In a nutshell, this is your child's personal brand – at this time of his or her life.*

Some other information you might like to keep aside for future use includes:
- love languages
- temperament
- personality
- brain-dominance profiles
- learning styles.

THE REPORT CARD OF LIFE

As mentioned previously, Talent Profiles need to be 'kept warm', or constantly updated from the word go. Even in primary school, children are required to write letters of motivation if they want to become involved in particular areas of responsibility within the school structure. Ultimately, the Talent Profile will become your child's ticket to a tertiary educational institution or a possible job. More than this future goal, however, it becomes your child's 'report card of life'; these are the X-factors that schools do not test for or formally report on.

The idea behind developing a Talent Profile is not to create a tool of judgement or assessment as such, but rather to create a document that will help children to get to know themselves and how they operate in the world. It should be a document of which they feel particularly proud, as it acknowledges them as human beings and celebrates who they are. Your children should appreciate all their strengths and weaknesses, since it is these traits that make them unique.

A Talent Profile will also give your children something to look forward to and goals to aim for. Maintaining the current academic average, or improving by just a few per cent, or keeping your place in the team are all goals. The object of a Talent Profile is not to make your children overly competitive or boastful. Rather, it encourages them to engage in a dialogue with themselves. By putting together a concrete record of their life that tells their own story, they build their self-awareness, self-confidence and a large dose of emotional intelligence, qualities that are essential for a bright future. They are the hero in their own story, and kids just love that.

A CV is normally updated if and when required, and not as a matter of course. The Talent Profile is quite different and should be kept 'warm' and be updated at least every six months or so (for children). For yourself, it could be updated on a monthly basis, so that you remain flexible, nimble and ready to move if opportunities arise to change jobs, apply for promotions, pitch for new business, etc.

Keeping your Talent Profile constantly updated is a fabulous exercise in self-awareness and an ongoing reminder that you are responsible for your own talent. Whether or not you are employed, self-employed or temporarily unemployed, you remain your own managing director, brand manager, marketing manager, sales manager, human resources manager, etc.

The Talent Profile allows each of those portfolios to go to work – on you! As Tom Peters (*Brand You 50*, 1999) states: 'View yourself as the boss of your own show, even if that show happens to be playing just now at Citigroup or General Electric or ExxonMobil. In other words: Distinct or Extinct.'

TALENT PROFILES ARE A REFLECTIVE TOOL

Can you see how developing a Talent Profile with your child gives you the opportunity to connect with him or her by having interesting conversations? These will help them to ultimately make good choices for themselves, thanks to the self-knowledge they will gain through the process. It is part of their journey to self-discovery, and affords them ownership, responsibility and accountability. As a parent, your child's Talent Profile will help you to:

- hold interesting and revealing conversations with your children
- discuss important choices with them that may help them discover who they are and where they are going
- discuss responsibility, accountability and values with your children
- connect and engage with your children about their uniqueness.

This is a wonderfully affirming opportunity. It will also initiate training your children to develop their own framework for stability in an uncertain future – making a conscious connection with themselves. Self-reflection is a powerful contributor to personal success. It's a great trait to cultivate.

Building their own Talent Profiles will highlight similarities between family members, while also helping each person to carve out their unique niche – what sets them apart. A reminder, once again, that your children are not you, and that their future will not follow yours. Instead of moulding them, rather facilitate their evolution. And this happens within the context of family life and against the backdrop of the family brand you create.

Creating your own Talent Profile

If you are convinced of, or at least intrigued by, the possibilities of a Talent Profile for yourself, then follow the steps below to create your own. This is an adult version of The Mirror Game©.

By doing this exercise, you will gain a complete picture of yourself as you are today. It will help you to either get to know yourself better, or to package yourself more appropriately for the job on offer. After completing the process, take some time to edit the information into a document you can present to a prospective employer. Keep it warm by revisiting it and updating it from time to time.

The Mirror Game© for adults

Step 1: My personality mirror (who I think I am, what I think or believe about myself)
- List your personality traits, for example:
    - introvert/extrovert
    - optimist/pessimist
    - spontaneous/controlled
    - like to follow/like to lead
    - able to influence others
    - problem-spotter
    - problem-solver
    - fussy
    - headstrong
    - anxious
    - hard to please
    - intolerant
    - sociable
    - funny
    - popular
    - sensitive
    - confident
    - loyal
    - perfectionist
    - consistent
    - diplomatic.

You may have gathered much of this information via various profiling techniques over the years, for example, from DiSC Profiles, Enneagram, Myers-Briggs, dominance profiling, etc. A good resource is Florence Littauer's book, *Personality Plus* (2005).

Step 2: My skills mirror (what I am good at)
- List your strengths, followed by a list of your weaknesses.

Step 3: My growth mirror (where do I see myself going?)
- Detail your growth opportunities as you see them for yourself:
  - over the next one to two years
  - over the next three to five years.

Step 4: My dream mirror (my personal vision)
- Detail what you believe your purpose is at this point in time.
- Then detail your vision for yourself in the future.

Step 5: The 'What I do' mirror (the value I add)
- This is not a description of your current job and responsibilities. It is more a summary of the value you believe you add to your company or prospective employer; for example, a data capturer could redefine her role as: 'I'm the underwire bra of the organisation.' In other words, without her there would be no data with which to underpin the organisation's activities!
- Think creatively about what it is you actually do, for example, 'I ensure cash flow', 'I manage labour resources', 'I come up with ideas', 'I'm a hotshot problem-solver'.

Step 6: My personal best mirror (my best work so far)
- Draw up a list of your best work so far.
- Then draw up a list of areas in which you think you do your best work.
- Also list areas of your work that give you the most enjoyment and satisfaction.

Step 7: My testimonial mirror (what others say about me)
- Detail what colleagues and employers say about you – the positive and the negative.

Step 8: My networking mirror (who I know – my connections)
- This is more important than ever before. List your social networks (virtual), as well as your real-life networks. With some job applications, your networks can determine your worth.

- If you have any social-networking websites, include the URL addresses. These would include LinkedIn, Facebook, Twitter, Instagram, etc. Bear in mind that sharp employers will do a Google search for your name anyway, and today they employ the services of companies that will do an online risk assessment of you. Make sure you do that search first and see what comes up. Be careful about your digital footprint – it might work against you when applying for jobs. What seems amusing to you and your friends on social media might not be so clever when viewed by a potential boss!

Step 9: *My work experience mirror (work I have done)*
- Include a portfolio of work experience or projects completed. Be detailed and provide a short list of responsibilities for each position held. Include specific comments from colleagues or superiors if relevant. Give contact details if appropriate.

Step 10: *My education mirror (my education history)*
- List your qualifications and years of study, as well as your academic and curricular responsibilities.

Step 11: *My biographical mirror (my name, address, etc.)*
- This is all the mundane but essential details about you that need to be mentioned – from your age to your address, home language, driver's licence and any other details that are important but won't necessarily 'sell' you. If the interviewer is interested, he or she can read the biographical stuff later.

Step 12: *Your company mirror (about the prospective employer)*
- What I know about the company.

Step 13: *Your industry mirror (about the industry your prospective employer operates in)*
- What I know about the industry.

Step 14: The position being offered mirror (about the prospective position)
- Write a paragraph on 'What I believe about the position being offered'.

Step 15: The 'Do I fit?' mirror (do I fit the job?)
This is the interesting part of the process. At this point, having done some soul-searching and having documented your thoughts, it should be clear to you whether or not you actually want this job.
- Detail your reasons for applying for this job/position. Do you believe you would be a good fit with the prospective employer, and why?
- Link relevant experience that is directly or indirectly connected to the job on offer. You may think you would be a good fit precisely because you have no experience in that area, and therefore would bring a fresh eye and some useful skills into the equation.

This is a superb exercise to have done prior to attending an interview, as you will have considered and answered many of the questions you are going to be asked. In fact, you may have given yourself a distinct advantage over other candidates being interviewed for the same job.

Above all, be honest. Smart employers understand that you do not intend to join the company for the rest of your life, so don't make any false promises or statements in this regard. If all you want is three years of experience, then say so. This will establish the correct relationship right from the start. Taking full responsibility for promoting your own talent is the best example you can give your child. You can now walk your own talk.

Chapter 8

Build a values-based family brand

*'You are the storyteller of your own life.
You can create your own legend or not.'*
Isabel Allende

The world is filled with brands, whether they are celebrities who are their own brands or commercial entities, and they all clamour for our attention and that of our children. Similarly, technology, as much as it has the power to connect us, also has the power to distract us from each other. We need to make sure that our family sounds a strong and clear note in the midst of that noise. We like to think of family as one of the 'brands' in our children's lives: hopefully the most powerful and influential brand with which they associate.

Time and attention are the currencies that run between us and our children. We trade those currencies between us – between parent and child. We are the most time-starved generation of parents ever, and we are raising the most connected generation. An article in *The Economist* (March 2019) reported on how the young people of today are the most depressed, anxious and lonely generation. It is something we hear often from other parents, and educators and therapists. So, warning bells are sounding. The situation is, potentially, a recipe for disaster. But it doesn't have to be. There is hope.

In the first edition of this book, we said that the family is where hope lives. We still stand by this. Family, no matter how it is made up, is the building block of society as the creator of fundamental human values. We can no longer rely on governments, religions or communities to determine the values, morals and traditions to which a family wishes to subscribe. That's the way the world used to work. But, we now know that governments are flawed, religious fundamentalism is dangerous, and that even some of our friends and our children's teachers don't necessarily share the same beliefs and values as we do.

We live in a world of increasing shades of grey, rather than black and white. As a family, we need to choose our shade of grey – our own values and world view. It is against this that your children will measure other value offerings in the future. As a parent, you have to provide some kind of basis for them so that they can make discerning choices when they interact with brands, or other people, or organisations, via technology. Something is always going to be on offer.

Brands are spending billions of dollars researching our kids and their wants and needs, because they want a share of their hearts and minds – and money from our wallets. The following five key insights should always be kept in mind in your quest to build a strong family brand:

1. Your kids want a real and authentic relationship with you. This is one of your children's highest values. As their parents, you are still the brightest crayon in the box. While you may often be absent, your children still need you, and no one can replace you. So regular face-to-face family time is important, even in bite-size chunks. Spending quality time with your kids is the biggest advantage you have over commercial brands. Are you using that advantage?

2. Their deepest desire is for a sense of belonging and togetherness. This is a basic human desire: to belong to a community. Family is your child's first community. They may try to replace it with social media and instant-messaging communities, but nothing replaces the warmth and emotion of real human connection. It raises their happiness quotient in a way that a virtual connect can't, and never will. If your kids can't find a sense of belonging and togetherness in your family, they will look for it elsewhere and, today, elsewhere is a very big place, both online and offline. And not everyone offering them attention and a sense of belonging has their best interests in mind.

3. 'Give me an experience and only then will I promise you a relationship' is the mantra of this generation of young people. Your children are stimulated by action and experiences, not just by words and platitudes. This is largely because they are multisensory human beings, just like adults. Big commercial brands focus on this human need by offering interactive experiences in stores, or via concerts, etc. To counteract their influence, make time for family adventures and travels, and institute seasonal and celebratory traditions. These experiences will become increasingly valuable. Further on in this chapter, we will suggest some traditions and rituals to add colour to your family life, which will anchor your children to your value system and create shared memories. Many of these cost nothing.

4. Do you see me? Do you hear me? Am I important to you? These are the three very important questions children non-verbally and subconsciously ask of their parents every single day. And they need an overwhelmingly positive 'yes' answer in order to feel validated and acknowledged. Children need attention, and if they can't get positive attention, then, sadly, even negative attention will do. Children (like adults) have negative attention-seeking strategies that they use when they are feeling 'invisible', and these can be destructive. Make sure you keep their emotional cups filled and teach them how to fill their own, so that they are not susceptible to unscrupulous marketers. It is easy for children to fall for false promises of love, attention and acceptance in their desire to belong (this is actually no different for adults).

5. Family is the value-creator of today's society. This is very important, which is why we have already mentioned it twice in this chapter. If your child is to grow up with discerning and critical thinking capabilities, which will empower them to make good choices as they progress through life, this has to be learnt at home, within the family unit. Even if they ultimately create their own set of values and forge their own world view, they've got to start from somewhere.

The pressure on kids today to own 'stuff' in order to be popular with their peers can cause untold damage between parent and child. Brands offer promises with values attached to them: 'Buy this, and your friends will love you.' So, how can your family brand compete with this? Are you building a strong enough family brand to withstand these temptations? Are you making family *your* most important value? If you were the CEO of a company, you would know your competition in the market; we are suggesting that, as the CEO of your family, you should know it, too.

Interestingly, the *Sunday Times Generation Next Survey 2018* of youth aged 8 to 21 confirmed yet again that family, religion and education are still our kids' top-three values. They are the three things kids do not want to do without. This is very good news for us as parents, but it also means that to retain that position in their hearts and minds, we need to work proactively on our family brand.

What is a world view, and can we change it?

A 'world view' is a set of beliefs that helps us make sense of the world as we experience it. Our world view helps us to decide what is right and wrong, good and bad, normal and weird. One of the easiest things to say, but one of the toughest to implement, is that our world views need to change. If the world is changing as much as we suggest it is, then we can't possibly imagine that the world view we grew up with is going to be adequate in the future. As we update this book, people all over the world are struggling to adjust their world views. In the US, there is deep division over the Trump presidency; in the UK, Brexit is dividing the nation; and there are riots and protests taking place from France to the Philippines, Brazil and Russia.

We are at a moment in history where many of the 'rules' that helped us to make sense of the world no longer apply. One example that relates to parenting is the debate about whether physical punishment is good or bad for children. Who do we trust to best inform us on whether smacking children is a good form of discipline or not: our religious leaders, our parents, our own experience, or psychologists or teachers? When the various experts we rely on to help us decide what is right or wrong disagree with each other, our world view is called into question. And when we question one aspect of our world view, it can sometimes feel as if our entire foundation is being shaken. It's one of the reasons why some people so strongly defend their traditional views. Others, again, overreact and abandon everything they've ever believed in.

This, then, is the challenge we face in the 2020s and 30s: which parts of our world views will stand the test of time? Which will remain largely unchanged and lay a foundation for the future, and which parts need to be updated, adapted, challenged and changed? There is no simple answer to this question, and each of us, and the communities of which we are a part, has to navigate this for ourselves. However, we all need to accept that at least some parts of our world view will need to be revised. That is the starting point for all of us: to accept that our world view needs to change. Once we've accepted that, we will have to be constantly alert to those parts that must change, and those that must stay the same. And we will have to evaluate very carefully why we make the decisions we do, and who and what we accept as authorities in this regard, and why.

This will not be an easy task, but the 21st-century parent cannot afford to let their children get stuck in an outdated world view. Instead, they must help their children develop into optimistic, open-minded individuals who are also discerning thinkers and can make good value judgements.

YOU ARE THE FAMILY BRAND MANAGER

As a parent, you are the CEO and brand manager of your family. Here are some questions for you and your family to consider:
- What does it mean to be a Smith, a Naidoo, a Van Niekerk, or a Mandela (insert your own surname here)?

- How does it feel right now to be a member of your family?
- How would you like it to feel to be a member of your family?
- How do your children perceive you?
- How do you want to be perceived by your children?
- What's important to your family?
- What are your values and beliefs?
- What do you stand for?
- What are your family traditions?
- Do you know where you are going? Do you have a plan, or are you just trundling along?
- When your family is mentioned in conversation, what do people immediately associate with you? What qualities do they mention? (We can think of families for whom the following descriptors immediately come to mind: adventurous, charitable, fun, social, sporty, generous, competitive, etc. Other people describe your family in very specific words, whether you are aware of it or not.)

Brands must always add value, whether they are commercial brands such as Nike, Tesla, Coca-Cola or Samsung, or 'people brands' such as Nelson Mandela, Elon Musk or Michelle Obama.

WHY CREATE BRAND FAMILY?
Building a family brand needs to be done consciously and consistently, as with any good commercial brand. Consider these various important reasons why you should actively create Brand Family:
- To deliver your message, beliefs and values to your customers (your children) via a combination of communication and experiences.
- Because we are all in sales, whether we like it or not: we are continually selling ideas, values and beliefs to our children, even if subconsciously.
- To differentiate yourselves from others.
- To help your children to develop their own identity, which is critical between the ages of 8 and 18.
- To invest in, and build, strong relationships.
- To empower children with values and beliefs to make them more discerning.

- To beat the marketers at their own game.
- To compete with your children's peers as they enter their teenage years.

BRAND-BUILDING IS A PROCESS

We are not advocating that parents head for the family boardroom and put together a clinical business plan. Building Brand Family is more about raising awareness of the beliefs, values and attitudes you are conveying to your children, and deciding whether or not these qualities will be your children's best preparation for the 21st century. We need to take responsibility for how we design our lives.

Since every family is different, each family brand will be unique. However, we would like to suggest three basic pillars on which family brands should be built: *values, togetherness* and *structure*. These pillars are not prescriptive, but simply provide you with a creative and flexible framework within which you can make your family brand distinctive. They offer all family members a platform to develop Brand You.

We believe this exercise to be imperative and not optional. And everyone can do it. Fortunately, as parents, we have some distinct advantages over marketers who spend billions trying to connect with us and our children:

- We do not have to prebook media space.
- We can change our strategy and tactics by the day, or by the hour, if needs be, in order to retain our children's attention, hearts and minds.
- We know exactly how our children operate, so we can tailor our communication and ideas to meet their specific needs. We can personalise our message, which is what kids today seem to want.
- Just like the context or landscape can change, so we can change our tactics.
- We love our children unconditionally and certainly not because of what they are going to buy.

The question is, are we using our face-to-face advantage in this noisy, cluttered world – or not?

Since we would like our children to remain loyal to their values and become discerning, open-minded thinkers over time – for their own self-protection, particularly when they are slightly out of our sphere of influence as teenagers – we need to start thinking like marketers, and build on those three pillars.

PILLARS OF BRAND FAMILY
Values

What is your moral compass? What is your moral centre, and why? These are important questions for 21st-century parents to answer. Values refer to our principles or standards, which are unique to each family. We all have our own blueprint (Brand You) and 'family print' (Brand Family), and both of these are influenced by our values.

Today, diversity surrounds us; it is the new status quo, and it is up to us to respond to it and make the right choices. If your children see you as accepting of everything and questioning nothing, they will not learn the skill of discernment that is vital to their survival in the future. To learn to be discerning, children need an internalised set of values against which to measure other value offerings in life. If we fail to assist our children to develop values, they may just adopt the values of the most attractive brands on offer. Now that's a scary thought!

It is a fact that many parents are no longer leaving their children an inheritance because they are living longer and spending their wealth on health care or an exciting retirement. However, all children are left a legacy of values. As adults, and particularly as parents, we need to consider the values we have retained from our own upbringing and decide whether these are still applicable to the family we are creating today in the context of the 21st century. We get to choose. Sometimes we add or take away from our values menu, based on personal experiences or what we have seen or heard. Shaping our values and attitudes is a continuous process of learning, unlearning and relearning.

How to instil values and attitudes

1. **Role-modelling**
   - Children do as you *do*, not as you say.
   - They need to see you in action.

- If children respect you and feel safe, they are more likely to buy into your values. For this generation, respect is not a given – we have to earn their respect.

2. Teachable moments

This refers to those moments that just 'happen' and which provide a good opportunity for explanation or teaching. Your child asks a question, you reflect on what is going on verbally, or you actively demonstrate your response to a situation. For example:
- A motorist has broken down. You may stop to help if you feel this would not be a threat to your physical well-being, or you may call the emergency services for assistance. You are demonstrating kindness, helpfulness and compassion.
- A friend has just had a baby or is ill and you deliver a meal to her home to provide some relief from everyday responsibilities. This shows thoughtfulness, kindness and compassion.
- You help out in the school library with the covering of books. This shows your support for your child's school and demonstrates helpfulness.
- You contribute to various charities on a monthly basis, as well as give toys to orphanages at the end of each year. This demonstrates generosity, kindness and compassion.
- You submit your tax return each year. This demonstrates integrity, honesty and responsibility.
- Your children clean the car with you and wash their bicycles. They learn to value and respect property.

3. Conversation

- Children overhear adult conversations all the time. You convey your values about things through what they hear. You are often unaware of what they have heard.
- By answering your children's questions, or helping them to find the answers for themselves, you convey values and attitudes.
- You can show your children that it is a positive quality to be a good listener. We were born with two ears and one mouth, so we should

listen twice as much as we speak. By listening to what they have to say, we show our children that we value their input and opinion.
- Today, children are exposed to many inappropriate things from an early age. Be prepared to have discussions about them. This is an easy way to convey your values, or to develop a family approach to a variety of topics or situations.

4. Doing everyday stuff together

There are many things that can be done together around the family home, such as gardening, cooking, tidying up, watching TV, playing or doing homework. These activities provide interaction opportunities and informal banter. Values are passed on subconsciously, often without direct discussion.

Always bear in mind that you are the role model. Your children will do as you do, and not as you say. Choose caregivers well and co-parent consistently with your spouse, ex-spouse, step-parents and caregivers. Inconsistency causes value confusion. Your window of opportunity to form strong relationships and really influence your children's values is shrinking because they are growing up more quickly and entering adolescence earlier. Never give up. Values will make you children safer and more resilient in an ocean of constant change.

Clearly there is going to be no free ride in the future. But there is also no free ride now. You are going to have to make good choices so that your children can develop a strong moral compass that will make them discerning individuals, capable of standing up for their own values and beliefs. The time when they will have to do so will arrive sooner than you think. Once your child is prepubescent, around 9 or 10 years of age, he or she will already be under serious pressure to conform to their peer group – to be cool or be left out. Will your child have a strong set of values so that they can safely navigate that minefield? And will he or she have an established, trust-based relationship with you so that the communication lines remain open?

Some moral issues our children will possibly face in the next few years:

- **Cloning:** When we learn how to clone human beings, will they have a soul? This may sound like a spiritual question, but it isn't. If clones do not have a soul, then they are simply biological robots. They could be sent to war as cannon fodder, or as biotechnical machines. How would the military use them? Would the use of chemicals in war be an issue then? Could clones sue the government if they contracted strange illnesses or developed cancer? Would this be relevant? Some people believe there is no such thing as a soulless person, which is why spiritual and emotional intelligence is so important. What will the implications be of such 'machines' running the world? The ultimate question would be: Are clones real human beings or not?
- **Environmentalism:** The overuse of the planet's resources is a chilling legacy that our children will inherit. We are the first generation of adults who know how we could end the world. From overfishing and deforestation, to pollution and dwindling water supplies, all overshadowed by the spectre of global warming, we know the world is in crisis. We are also the first generation of adults with the wealth, resources, technology and global networks to actually solve these problems. But we need to make a concerted effort. It is our children who will inherit our mistakes and our inaction, but also our resolve and vision to create a sustainable world to live in. We need to help our children to develop a mindset of sustainability, which includes changing how we live in our homes today.
- **Bioethics:** This is an area riddled with moral complexity, and could place enormous pressure on your children's value systems in the future.
    - A good example of bioethics is the stem-cell debate. Is it acceptable (or even palatable) to fall pregnant, and then abort the foetus, to provide stem cells so that your living children can effectively fight the diseases they have? Should we interfere with nature? What are the implications of continually bypassing nature?
    - A mother may have the choice in future to 'house' her baby outside her body in an artificial uterus halfway through her pregnancy. This technology already exists. What implications does this hold for the emotional and developmental aspects of the child, or for mother-child bonding?

- Our children will be able to make choices about the type of child they want. They will be able to alter the gene structure of the embryo by taking out unwanted disease genes such as Alzheimer's. But if they remove that gene, then they must choose what to put in its place. So your grandchild may not get Alzheimer's, but he or she may be short, for example. In addition, if you spent $100 000 to remove an unwanted gene (for breast cancer or Alzheimer's, for example) from your in utero daughter because of your family's health history, would you allow your daughter to one day marry a person who carries the very gene you had removed?

Togetherness

The pillar of togetherness is about creating opportunities for connection; it is to spend time in each other's company, skin to skin or face to face. Because we are so busy, we need to make a conscious choice to be together, whether by enjoying a family adventure away from home, building a treehouse together, playing rough and tumble on the bed, or by simply sharing a meal together around a table.

Focused time is when parents and children spend time purposefully together. It can include everyday, mundane activities like feeding young children, or driving a child to or from an after-school leisure activity. At these times of daily interaction, parents can tune in to their children's needs by empathic listening and by reading the cues and clues that they give about how they are feeling. These are relationship-strengthening times, which offer parents the opportunity to guide and influence their children.

After you have shared experiences together, you can create a family story about them, for example: 'Remember when Dad jumped out from behind the bathroom door and Mom nearly died of fright?' or 'Remember when the elephant started to charge us in the game reserve and Dad couldn't get the car into reverse?' This is the stuff of which memories are made, because shared experiences are rich in imagery and emotions. Memories create a tapestry that we can claim as our own work of art.

And, within this tapestry, family members are the heroes in the very personal stories they have helped to create, which gives them a reason to buy into the family brand.

How to promote togetherness

Children today are surrounded by digital devices that offer them instant entertainment with a wide variety of choice and flexibility. However, on-screen media do not meet the togetherness objective that we have in mind for the development of Brand Family. While choosing to play a screen-based game with your child, or to communicate with him or her via a digital device, is relevant in the connection equation, in this section we focus on togetherness activities that foster face-to-face human contact and a connection in a real, rather than a virtual, way.

In order to compete with the attraction of on-screen media, you will need to follow these guidelines to share time and space with your children:

- Do not place a TV set in a child's bedroom.
- You decide when they are allowed to be on screens.
- You decide where they are allowed to be when they are on a device (in their room or in a public space).
- Be selective about programme content (TV, internet and gaming), and choose programmes together.
- Limit their – and your – screen time.
- Play real games together.
- Eat together as a family as often as possible.
- Stay and play instead of drop and run in the early years of play dates with friends.
- Create family adventures and holidays together.
- Find reasons to celebrate, honour and acknowledge each other.
- Talk and stay connected.
- Model good listening skills. Don't talk through walls.
- Make eye contact.
- Be interested in your child's world.
- Know your child's love languages.

- Hug and say 'I love you' – often.
- Read bedtime stories (and not the one-minute variety!).
- Spend time together – children want you.

In Chapter 5, we provided you with many practical ideas for developing the X-factors for success in your children. Many of these can also be used to create 'togetherness' experiences. Get creative! By wanting to spend time together, you are conveying many important non-verbal messages to your children, which can really boost their self-esteem. For example:

- I want to be with *you* right now.
- I like being with you.
- I'm not going to let anything interrupt our time together or get in the way of our relationship right now.
- I don't want to be doing anything else right now.
- I believe in you.
- I love you.

Structure

By now, you have probably realised that we are rather keen on frameworks and structure. Some of the most successful families we know have developed some form of structure and various family routines that provide a road map for progressing forward. Some of these families are unaware that they have achieved this, but by observing how their family operates, one detects a clear framework that provides security. And, within that framework, there is also freedom, creativity and flexibility.

> We've mentioned this before, but Graeme's family has learnt the value of following set routines in order to help Rebecca deal with anxiety and confusion. As much as structure and routine are essential for her, it is also important and valuable to everyone else in the family. It doesn't have to be boring or predictable, though. You can plan spontaneity, and grab it when it comes. But the confidence, calm and security that comes with structure and routine are invaluable.

Natural rhythms and routines

Natural rhythms need to be honoured and respected right from the start, even though we have the ability to override or ignore them. From babyhood, children need to learn that there is a time to sleep, to wake up to eat, and to play or work. They are trained into these routines by their parents. It is a myth that there is no flexibility within routine. In fact, children who have to follow a set routine are, in general, easier to take out and about, whether to restaurants or on holidays.

Babies and young children with set routines are easier to 'read', and thus have their needs met appropriately without too much fuss on either the child's or the parent's part. This is the first step in providing boundaries for the child; they also learn to tolerate frustration, and acquire self-discipline and self-regulation skills.

Here are some ways to teach children about natural rhythms and routine:

- Go camping. Wake up with the sunrise and go to sleep just after sunset.
- Listen to the birds, insects and wildlife at different times of the day.
- Gaze at the stars.
- Watch the clouds altering shape and position during the day.
- Work out on which side of the house the sun rises and sets each day.
- Keep pets. Children will learn that pets need regular feeding at specific times of the day, just as humans do. They also need care and attention.
- Allow children to help with household activities from around three years of age. Certain activities usually take place at the same time every day, which teaches them about structure and routine, for example, making the beds, laying the table, cooking dinner, putting dirty clothes in the laundry basket.
- Stick to a routine of cleaning teeth, going to the toilet and reading a story before bedtime.
- Have seasonal celebrations. For instance, go out for a spring picnic at a local park, or hold a last dinner under the stars as summer changes to autumn and the leaves start falling from the trees.

Routines can turn into family rituals – 'experiences' that anchor our children into our value system – while also helping them to find their own identity and moral compass.

Family rituals and traditions

Rituals or family traditions contribute to all three pillars of Brand Family: they convey our *values*, provide *structure*, and create a feeling of *togetherness* and *belonging*. They provide a sense of 'we are in this thing called life together'.

Rituals are concrete experiences that have a greater effect on children than a parental lecture on family values. Children learn best through real experiences in which they are personally involved. The experience ultimately becomes the message, so to speak. The 'doing' leads to 'being'.

Rituals are memorable things we do over and over again; they become part of who we are and how we operate in the world. It might be how you celebrate birthdays, or spend your holidays, or eat your meals. Regardless of what they are, rituals should become an integral part of the fabric of family life, and part of our family brand.

We believe rituals are an important part of:
- creating shared memories
- bonding as members of a family
- creating emotional anchors to the family beliefs and value system
- creating rites of passage
- creating a unique family brand.

Lots of different things make families unique, from the size of the family, to its values, religion, favourite holiday places, etc. A family is a space in which its members are acknowledged and honoured. It is where they can celebrate their successes and achievements in life and share their failures. Different families do these things differently. Some relate to particular occasions, such as Christmas, Eid, Pesach, etc., but all form part of a family's identity – 'the way things are done around here'.

Make a conscious choice to actively use rituals and celebrations to create family memories, to highlight developmental milestones and to celebrate the rites of passage of your children. Rites of passage, other than religious ones such as bar mitzvahs and christenings, for example, have mostly fallen away in Western society.

Research tells us that children are losing hope in the future from a very young age. Some school principals say this is happening from as early as the senior-primary phase. 'Why bother? What for? Who cares?' are regular refrains from children in early adolescence. Children are giving up, because they think there is nothing to look forward to any more. Do they really want to lead the stressful lives their parents lead?

We believe that finding ways to celebrate and honour children as they progress from one life stage to another can be of enormous help in validating their worth and uniqueness, and in giving them things to look forward to.

Types of rituals and celebrations
There are so many different types of rituals, for different reasons.

Daily rituals:
- Eating around the dinner table.
- Playing the Sweets and Sours or Roses and Thorns game at mealtimes. (Everyone gets to share something horrible that happened to them during the day, and in the second round they share something good that happened – all the time connecting what they say with feelings by labelling them: X happened and it made me feel like Y.)
- Having a family celebration plate, which is used to acknowledge a family member or visitor to your table for doing something special.
- Lighting candles at the dinner table every night, not just on special occasions.

Bedtime rituals:
- Telling a bedtime story.
- Blowing a kiss to the moon.
- Tickling of backs.
- Singing songs and lullabies.

Weekly rituals:
- Buying slap chips on the way home from church on Sundays.
- Having takeaways on Thursdays.
- Enjoying a games evening on Fridays.
- Cooking a family roast on Sundays.

Seasonal rituals:
- Enjoying a change-of-season dinner under the stars.
- Decorating the Christmas tree.
- Cooking and baking specific delicacies for certain celebrations.

Holiday rituals:
- Stopping at a certain place to eat en route to your annual holiday destination.
- Playing games in the car.
- Singing certain songs together.

Family celebration rituals:
What you do for family birthdays:
- Handing over presents in the big bed on birthday mornings.
- Decorating the doorway of the celebrant.
- Hanging balloons on their chair at the table.

Religious rituals:
- Following certain specific rituals dictated by the religion concerned, such as fasting over Jewish and Islamic holidays, or giving something up for Lent.

Coming-of-age/rites of passage rituals:
- Having a baby-naming, christening or bar mitzvah/bat mitzvah ceremony.
- Celebrating giving up the dummy.
- Being allowed to light candles (the gift of fire).
- Celebrating a coming-of-age.
- Holding a wedding ceremony.
- Marking a death in the family.

Both the Codrington and Bush families have created family rituals and consciously celebrate particular occasions. The Codringtons chose their children's third birthday as one important milestone. This is the occasion when they celebrate giving up the dummy. While doing so can be a traumatic experience for some children, the Codringtons have made it a really exciting event, as they happily celebrate leaving behind babyhood for becoming a little girl.

A few months before the child's third birthday, Graeme and Jane start building up to the momentous occasion by dropping hints in general conversation, such as 'Little girls don't need dummies; only babies do.' On the morning of the child's third birthday, the birthday girl takes her dummy and drops it into the dustbin. This ritual went down perfectly with Graeme's eldest daughter, Amy.

At the time of Hannah's third birthday, however, Graeme was going to be away. The Codringtons didn't want a glitch, so they were going to delay the ritual until Graeme's return. For a week or two before Hannah's birthday, they ignored the issue. But, on the morning of her birthday, Hannah decided to perform the ritual by herself, asking her mom if she could throw her dummy away. Because of the ritual involved, the Codrington girls remember giving up their dummies as a positive experience.

The Bush family celebrated their children's move into boyhood around their sixth or seventh birthday (depending on the child's level of maturity). Part of the celebration was to reinforce the fact that there are other loving and supportive adults in the child's life in addition to his parents, and that the child is loved and treasured for his special qualities and character traits (for who he is). As they are boys, the Bush sons could choose which significant men in their lives they wanted to share a special activity with.

Ryan's celebration took place in Knysna (his favourite place) when he was six and a half. He chose to go on the Outeniqua Choo-Tjoe and to visit the train museum with his grandpa. Then he went on the John Benn ferry through the Knysna Heads with his dad (an experience deliberately delayed for almost two years to coincide with his celebration).

> Ryan's godfather (an ex-Iron Man) did a mini-triathlon with him (a mini-run, -cycle and -paddle), then Ryan got to build and light his first official braai, and braaied (barbequed) a chicken for dinner. After the meal, those family members who were present took part in a 'wishing well' ceremony, telling Ryan why he was important to them and bestowing upon him a wish for his boyhood.
>
> Matthew's celebration took place in the African bush when he was seven. His choices were to play his first nine holes of golf with his grandpa, a mammoth cycle through the game reserve with his dad (the whole family was waiting at the top of the hill to celebrate this feat), and learning how to build and light a proper campfire with his uncle. Thereafter, the family all sat around the campfire under the stars and conducted Matthew's 'wishing well' ceremony.
>
> The next day, every member of the family – from the youngest (18 months) to the oldest (90) – painted his or her wish for Matthew onto fabric to make prayer flags, which blew in the wind for a month. These were then stitched together to form a quilt. Both boys' celebrations were wonderfully memorable moments of connection for everyone present, and the boys literally 'grew up' emotionally overnight. After receiving such strong support from loved ones throughout their celebrations, the boys were assured that they had a network that would catch and carry them on their journey into the future.

The examples above provide valuable storytelling and will form part of a child's lifelong memories. If no close family members can be present, then invite other significant adults with whom your child has a close affinity. Special rituals and celebrations fulfil many of a child's basic human and developmental needs, as well as the characteristics of a successful family brand. These rituals express the family's confidence in the child's ability to engage with life and to handle its challenges.

It's important to have rituals on a weekly, monthly, quarterly and annual basis; they should occur whenever appropriate. Don't wait for 'official' reasons to celebrate something – be creative and make up some just for fun. Kids love celebrations!

Anyone can build a family brand. You don't need any special qualifications. Even if you feel that your own childhood was less than satisfactory, or that you don't have a template for doing this, give it a try. The results will be so worthwhile! The things you value in life will be evident in the routines, rituals, celebrations and moments of togetherness that you create. It is an effective way to convey your values to your children and, at the same time, letting them know just how much you value them. Will your family and the values it stands for be your children's brand of choice as they grow older?

TOGETHER, APART, LETTING GO AND ADAPTING

> 'By the time your child embarks on his or her first school trip, you will know that change is just around the corner and your dependent 10-year-old is only a few years away from discovering their own independent life. They are just beginning to use their "wings" to fly out of the warm nest that was their entire world. Short hops away from the nest become longer flights. Don't think for a moment that your children will always want to be with you and need you. They won't, and if you aren't prepared for this fact, it will hit you like a ton of bricks.'
> Jill Shaw Ruddock, *The Second Half of Your Life*, 2011

As much as we want to hold our children close forever, and hope they are invested in our family values, the ultimate goal of parenting is to let our children go into the big wide world with confidence. We need to make ourselves redundant and let go of those kite strings little by little, encouraging their independence. There will still be times when we need to carry our children, or when we might need to catch them when they fall, or pick them up afterwards. But, eventually, we will need to let them go to navigate the world by themselves, on their own terms. This means that they will experience both the positive and negative consequences of their actions. As families, we also get to experience the upside and downside of change.

Nikki wrote this blog about change in 2014

It's a brand-new year in which we find ourselves in a totally new place as family. One child finished high school and is off to university, and our youngest has started at a new school; not only that, he is now a weekly boarder.

Nothing in our daily lives is as it was and we are all having to get used to lots of new things: new teachers, new facilities, new rules, new traffic patterns, driving in different directions and a totally new family routine. On some nights, my husband and I are alone at home for dinner, on others there are three of us, and on two nights of the week we are back to the original four. I no longer get up early to make school lunches or to do the school run (some of you may be green with envy, but I miss it). Wow, how things have changed!

My focus in the last few months of 2013 was on preparing myself to let go, as I knew what was coming. But no matter how much you prepare your head, your heart can only respond when the moment arrives. And, as with much of parenting, there are so many mixed emotions, just like the first and last days of preschool, primary or high school. Your heart could burst with pride, but at the same time you can feel so gutted and sore with the pain that comes with letting go, watching them fly solo, and the wrench of endings and new beginnings.

As we all move through the various stages and demands of being parents, we have to keep reinventing ourselves and adapting to new situations and circumstances. Right now, I am having to reinvent what it means to be a mom. Matthew phoned me from boarding school the other evening and said, 'Hi, Mom, we have a problem. I left my blazer at tennis practice,' to which I replied, 'We don't have a problem, *you* have a problem.' My, how things have changed.

So, whichever stage you find yourself at in your parenting journey, it is easier and far more enjoyable if you allow yourself to be:

- **adaptable** – things change constantly with children, and what you did today and how you did it may be very different tomorrow
- **flexible** – things don't always work out how you think they will, or happen as you think they ought to – be open-minded, as it will help you adapt more easily

- **responsible** – each moment of your life belongs to you, and you get to choose how to spend it, so make the best choices you possibly can and then move on to the next step, whether it be a big or small one. There is great wisdom in the saying, 'What's done is done, what's next is next,' in keeping you moving forward.

By the time my next blog comes along, we will all have settled into our new routines; all our ruffled feathers will be back in place again, and we will most probably be paddling along smoothly, as if we have been doing this for ages – until, of course, the next change, stage or bend in the road comes along, as it surely does if you have children.

As parents, your roles include being the:
- family brand manager
- chief experience officer
- guardian of hearts and minds
- conductor of the family symphony.

Children need their parents to show up and lead. There should never be a leadership vacuum. If we don't show up, step up and step out, they will step in, and that does not engender feelings of safety and security in our children. Drop your guilt – it's counterproductive. Be creative and transform guilt into love and connection. We hope we have shown you how to turn ordinary moments into extraordinary, memorable moments of connection and togetherness.

How we live our values, through our everyday actions, is of paramount importance in positioning ourselves as heroes in our children's lives, moment by moment. They are looking for an authentic relationship with us. They do not demand perfection, and we will make mistakes. Children want their parents to be genuine human beings who are prepared to step up to the plate, and are committed to lifelong learning, growing and connecting, together. You are their everyday hero.

Chapter 9

A call to action

'Ultimately, our children belong to the world. Their destiny is to leave us, to venture out into the world as adults and to create their own lives.'
John Kehoe and Nancy Fischer, *Mind Power for Children*, 2002

Our children will enter the workforce from 2030, and be in positions of leadership and power from around 2050, when the world will look and operate significantly differently from the world we live in today. Right now, they are living in a world of our creation and we are responsible for helping them navigate it. Our future, however, will quite literally be in their hands. This is why children need parental input and family support.

The number-one rule for parents today is to take personal responsibility for all the moves they make in the Age of Possibility. Don't fear it – run to it! In a connected, high-tech world, the only solution is to build bridges to connect with your children. And you must lead the connection process, ensuring that you and your children are the heroes in your family stories.

As parents today, we have to be wary of always reverting to our default setting, following the habits and norms we have lived by all our lives. We need to connect to our children consciously, not accidentally. We need to live by design and, indeed, by priority, now that we understand the importance of preparing our children for a world that does not yet exist.

This book is a call to parents to act wisely and courageously in the first 12 years of their children's lives (and beyond) to ensure that foundations are laid and connections made before they enter their teenage years and, eventually, adulthood. Keep your eye on the prize – the top of the triangle. Dig deep in the early years so that you and your children can enjoy the benefit of peace of mind and freedom of choice in a world that is going to change beyond our comprehension in the next few decades.

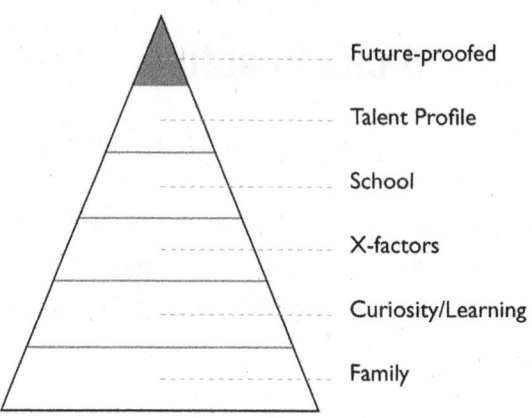

> 'This is our most important responsibility and challenge: to be, moment by moment, the very best we can be for ourselves because children are watching, becoming what they see. We cannot fail.'
> Michael Mendizza, *Magical Parent, Magical Child*, 2003

We know that this book contains a great deal of information and ideas, and we hope you will come back to them again and again along the way. To recap, here is a reminder of the steps you need to take as parents in the 21st century, culled from the various sections that comprise this book.

THE 10 STEPS FOR FUTURE-PROOFING YOUR CHILD

1. Understand the changing context: consider how the world has changed and contemplate the world of the future (Chapters 3 and 4).
2. Know yourself: develop your own Talent Profile (Chapter 7).
3. Know your children: help them to develop their own Talent Profile (Chapter 7).

4. Help your children to identify their own talent – the essence of who they are: help them to develop the X-factors for success (Chapter 5).
5. Understand your children's needs: understand your children's developmental and emotional needs now (Chapter 2).
6. Support their educational journey – support the schooling choices you make for your child (Chapter 6).
7. Build your family brand: create unique traditions and anchor them in your value system so that they can make their own value-based decisions and comparisons (Chapter 8).
8. Manage your time: make your limited face-to-face time count and manage the time you and your children spend on devices.
9. Future-proof yourself: develop the X-factors for success yourself, role-modelling them for your children (Chapter 5).
10. Do not panic, and make sure the process is a lot of fun!

There is an enormous benefit in taking up the challenge to future-proof your children for the world of work in the 2030s and beyond, which is that you will be future-proofing yourself at the same time. Take comfort from the particularly insightful and thought-provoking words of parenting expert Dan Allender:

> '[T]o be *great* parents, we must allow our children to shape our lives. We must not only guide and shape our children, but we must also go to them as students of life … Life doesn't unfold in a straight line, and our children aren't computer programs. Parenting is far from a scientific pursuit; it's messy and risky and a huge leap of faith.'
> Dan Allender, *How Children Raise Parents*, 2003

Parenting is one of the most challenging roles we will ever play in our lives; it is our biggest personal-development adventure. We will only see the real fruits of our labours at the end of a lifetime of investing in conversations, the right choices and connecting. We cannot merely squeeze our children into our diaries when it suits us. We need to choose to share time, space and pace with our children, on an ongoing basis.

Parenting is a process that takes place over an extended period of time. The choices we make as parents and the time we spend with our children are two of the most important factors in determining whether or not we are parenting wisely.

We believe that your child's future self will thank you for preparing him or her for a fast-changing path – for the world as it is and will become, and not as you would like it to be. If your wish for your children is happiness and success, then we urge you to change your parenting goal right now to something achievable and relevant for the future.

Raise your children to be resourceful and resilient so that they can adapt as the world changes and have the wherewithal to create their own version of happiness and success. We believe that this is doable, and we have provided you with the why, as well as some of the how. Although life doesn't unfold in a straight line – and we are both testimony to that with our real, human and imperfect lives, and there will always be twists and turns in the road – there are things you can confidently promise your child.

We wish you courage, a sense of adventure, and the gift of laughter and tears on your parenting journey. Bear in mind that you, your children and your family are unique, which means that you will always be a pioneer exploring new territory.

The world is as it is. Work with it. Learn from it. Master it. Enjoy the ride. You are the foundation builder of your child's future. Remember that the deeper and broader the foundations, the higher they will be able to climb. You are more important than you think.

POSTSCRIPT

A PROMISE TO MY CHILD

By Nikki Bush

I promise to feed you, clothe you and put a roof over your head,
Although this may vary in quality and quantity from time to time.
I promise to teach you to be resilient and resourceful,
So that you can succeed and thrive no matter what life may throw at you.

I can't promise you that you won't get hurt by life,
And that horrible things will never happen.
But, I do promise you that as long as I am alive,
I will love you and be there for you.

I promise to shower you with unconditional love and encouragement,
And to hold the space for you to become, well, YOU!
I promise to help you to discover your unique talents and gifts.
And I look forward to hearing the verse you will create and one day sing.

I promise that you will have good and bad moments,
But life may surprise you.
I promise that as you grow and gain perspective,
What might initially seem negative
May well be the best gift of all to help you to a better life.

I promise to keep growing and working on myself.
It's not your job to make me happy, it's mine.
You have helped me to discover more about me,
About parts of myself I have never seen or met before.

You create an invitation for me to dance with life,
And when you ask me to dance,

My answer is a resounding 'Yes!', and, 'Thank you!'
For the personal adventures you bring to me every, single day.

I promise you a place at my table, always,
Regardless of your choices.
When you were born, you were a precious gift from Life,
But you are also a gift to Life.

As your parent,
I promise to honour you and protect you,
And when the time is right, to let you go,
So that you can take flight and make a dent in the Universe.

You will forever be in my heart,
One that is so enriched by your being in the world.
I love you, my precious child.